A SHORT TEXTBOOK OF PSYCHIATRY

UNIVERSITY MEDICAL TEXTS

General Editor

SELWYN TAYLOR
D.M., M.Ch. (Oxon.), F.R.C.S.
Surgeon, Hammersmith Hospital,
Dean, Royal Post-Graduate Medical School

A Short Textbook of Medicine

J. C. HOUSTON
M.D., F.R.C.P.
Physician and Sub-Dean of the Medical School
Guy's Hospital, London

C. L. JOINER
M.D., M.R.C.P.
Physician, Guy's Hospital, London

J. R. TROUNCE
M.D., F.R.C.P.
Professor of Therapeutics, Guy's Hospital Medical School

Essentials of Chemical Pathology

D. N. BARON
M.D.
Professor of Chemical Pathology, Royal Free Hospital School of Medicine, London

A Short Textbook of Microbiology

D. C. TURK
D.M., M.R.C.P., M.C.Path.
Senior Lecturer in Bacteriology, University of Newcastle upon Tyne
and
I. A. PORTER
M.D., M.C.Path.
Consultant Bacteriologist to the Ayrshire Area Laboratory Service,
Formerly Senior Lecturer in Bacteriology, University of Newcastle upon Tyne

A Short Textbook of Gynaecology and Obstetrics

G. D. PINKER
M.B., F.R.C.S. (Ed.), F.R.C.O.G.
Consultant Gynaecological Surgeon and Obstetrician,
St. Mary's Hospital;
Gynaecological Surgeon, Bolingbroke Hospital
Examiner to the Universities of Cambridge, London, and R.C.O.G.

D. W. T. ROBERTS
M.Ch., F.R.C.S., F.R.C.O.G.
Consultant Obstetrician and Gynaecologist,
St. George's Hospital, London;
Gynaecological Surgeon, Samaritan Hospital;
Examiner to the Universities of Cambridge, London, and R.C.O.G.

A Short Textbook of Surgery

SELWYN TAYLOR
D.M., M.Ch., F.R.C.S.
Surgeon, Hammersmith Hospital,
Dean, Royal Postgraduate Medical School

L. T. COTTON
M.Ch., F.R.C.S.
Surgeon, King's College Hospital

J. G. MURRAY
Ch.M., F.R.C.S. (Ed.)
Professor of Surgery, King's College Hospital Medical School

A SHORT TEXTBOOK
OF
PSYCHIATRY

W. L. LINFORD REES
B.Sc., M.D., F.R.C.P., D.P.M.

Professor of Psychiatry
St. Bartholomew's Hospital
Medical College
University of London

THE ENGLISH UNIVERSITIES PRESS LTD
ST. PAUL'S HOUSE   WARWICK LANE
LONDON EC4

First printed 1967

PRINTED AND BOUND IN GREAT BRITAIN
FOR THE ENGLISH UNIVERSITIES PRESS LTD
BY HAZELL WATSON AND VINEY LTD, AYLESBURY, BUCKS

EDITOR'S FOREWORD

'Books must follow sciences, and not sciences books'

Francis Bacon

This entirely new short textbook of psychiatry will fill a gap in the library both of the medical student in training and the postgraduate with an interest in this field. It is also a most convenient work of reference for the general practitioner when he seeks guidance in the management of a particular disease. As a concise account of psychological medicine this book affords a splendid introduction to the subject for the newcomer. Since it is essential for all of us to have this kind of knowledge, no matter what particular branch of medicine we follow, this text should be universally welcomed. It would be impossible for any medical man to read this book through without deriving real practical help.

The author has his own method of tackling the subject and presents it cogently and lucidly. The general approach is an extremely good one and with the addition of a few references at the end of many of the chapters, the reader has the entrée to psychological medicine as a whole.

The aim of the University Medical Texts is to provide a series of textbooks giving excellent coverage of all aspects of modern medical practice. The books are produced at the lowest possible price so as to enable them to be owned by the majority of students. Medical textbooks rapidly become out of date and need replacing by up-to-date editions. These books are designed to be read and reread by students, carried about in the pocket for reference and used until they either fall to pieces or are replaced by a new edition. They are thus disposable textbooks.

This Short Textbook of Psychiatry is a valuable addition to the series of University Medical Texts and should prove one of the most popular.

Selwyn Taylor

Royal Postgraduate Medical School,
London W. 12.

PREFACE

Psychiatry is a rapidly expanding field of medical knowledge, and the social and medical importance of psychiatric illness is becoming increasingly recognised. Psychiatric disorders form a large part of the work of the general practitioner and, indeed, of all branches of medicine and surgery. The key person in psychiatric education is the medical student, and a number of important bodies have emphasised the need for more comprehensive undergraduate education in psychiatry. Among the earlier reports were those of the Royal College of Physicians and the Goodenough Committee, followed by the British Medical Students' Association, the Royal Medico-Psychological Association, the Royal College of General Practitioners and, quite recently, the General Medical Council. It has been recommended that in the pre-clinical period, instruction should be given in genetics, human growth and development, psychology and sociology, and that the teaching of psychiatry should be an integral part of the study of clinical medicine.

This book is primarily intended for medical students, but it will also be useful to students in other fields, such as social work, psychology, etc., where a knowledge of psychiatry is necessary. It is hoped that it may also be of value to newly-qualified doctors and to all practitioners, a knowledge of psychiatry (the subject is a generality as well as a speciality) being indispensable in all branches of medicine and surgery.

This volume differs from many other books on psychiatry in that psychology is given considerable emphasis, as are genetics and the social aspects of psychiatry—nowadays these subjects increasingly contribute to the knowledge and practice of psychiatry.

Psychosomatic medicine, child psychiatry and mental subnormality are also given prominence in view of their importance.

The approach in this book is practical and clinical, with emphasis on the thorough investigation of the patient, and the assessment of differential diagnosis in order to reach a diagnostic judgement on the basis of which planned management and treatment can take place.

The paramount importance of the interview and the doctor/patient relationship in all forms of treatment is emphasised throughout. The therapeutic approach is eclectic: the indications for psychotherapeutic techniques, the various pharmacotherapeutical and other physical methods of treatment, the place of social and occupational therapy, and rehabilitation are all discussed.

It is stressed that the student should use the book as a framework on which to build further knowledge obtained by extended reading for which selected references are given after each chapter.

W. L. Linford Rees

CONTENTS

S.T.P.—1*

CHAPTER ONE

DEFINITIONS AND SCOPE OF PSYCHIATRY

Psychiatry is the branch of medicine which deals with the recognition, treatment and prevention of mental abnormalities and disorders. It deals with illnesses which predominantly affect a person's mental life and behaviour, i.e. his feelings, his thinking, his behaviour and social relationships.

The field of psychiatry is diverse and extensive. There are special branches dealing with children (child psychiatry) and old age (psychogeriatrics). Forensic psychiatry deals with medico-legal aspects. Social psychiatry includes all environmental factors, including epidemiology.

Psychiatric ill health is of great social importance.

Nearly half of all the hospital beds in England and Wales are for mentally ill and mentally subnormal patients.

The most conservative surveys of general practice reveal that between 15 and 25 per cent of all patients seen by the general practitioner have a psychiatric illness or have important psychological features.

The prevalence of psychiatric illness as a cause of morbidity, loss of work and incapacity is revealed by Ministry of Pensions and National Insurance statistics (Vide Ch 17). Similarly, the extent to which psychiatric illness is responsible for illness and discharge from the Armed Forces and as a cause of breakdown in University and other students, further testify to its importance.

A **psychiatrist** is a physician who has been trained and has had experience in the diagnosis and treatment of psychiatric illness. Postgraduate training extends over 5–8 years, during which time higher qualifications in general medicine as well as specialist qualifications in psychiatry are usually obtained.

A **psychotherapist** is a person with special training in psychotherapy. A psychoanalyst is a psychotherapist who is trained in the method of Freud.

The term **Psychosomatic** means the influence of psychological factors in the production of physical disorders.

The term **Somatopsychic** refers to the effect of a physical disease or disability on the person's mental state and behaviour.

Psychology is concerned with the study of mental life and behaviour.

It stands in relationship to psychiatry in very much the same way as physiology does to general medicine.

A psychologist is not medically qualified and has a degree in psychology.

The clinical psychologist forms an integral part of the psychiatric team which comprises psychiatrist, psychologist, psychiatric social worker, nurses etc.

CHAPTER TWO

HISTORICAL DEVELOPMENT OF
MODERN PSYCHIATRY

Psychiatry has been described as the oldest art in medicine and the newest science.

It is the oldest art because mental disorders were among the first types of illness to be recognised. The oldest prescription in existence is from ancient Egyptian medicine and 'calls for the exhibition of green stone as a fumigation against hysteria'.

Ancient medicine, both Egyptian and Greek, considered all disease to be caused by evil spirits or demons and similar concepts continued in Europe with regard to mental disorders throughout the middle ages.

Hippocrates (460–377 BC) replaced demoniacal concepts of disease by a theory and practice of medicine based on observation and natural causes. Hippocrates regarded mental illnesses in much the same light as he did physical illnesses. He considered that mentally ill patients needed to be investigated to discover the causes of the illness in order that these should be dealt with as effectively as possible.

The theories of disease causation of Hippocrates and Galen regarded disease to be due to a disturbance in the body of the distribution of the four humours—black bile, yellow bile, blood and phlegm. We still pay reference to these humoural theories by the everyday use of the terms melancholia, sanguine, choleric and phlegmatic.

Despite the enlightened teachings of Hippocrates and Galen, beliefs that mental illnesses were due to possession by demons persisted throughout the middle ages and were responsible for cruelty to the mentally ill, who were flogged and ill-treated in order to drive out demons and evil spirits. Witch hunting occurred on a large scale in the fifteenth century and many supposed witches were put to death because they were believed to be possessed by evil spirits.

Two bright lights shone in the darkness of this period. One was a hospital which existed in the sixth century at Mount Cassino in Italy, which provided humane care for mentally ill patients and later other hospitals which, similarly, treated mentally ill patients with understanding and humane care were founded in Lyon in the 6th century and Paris in the 7th century.

DEVELOPMENT OF MODERN TRENDS IN PSYCHIATRIC CARE AND TREATMENT

It will be convenient to consider the development of modern trends is psychiatric care under the following headings:

(1) Hospital care, including social and legal aspects.

(2) The development of psychological methods of treatment.

(3) The development of the organic or biological approach to psychiatric illness.

(4) The development of drug treatment in psychiatry.

1. Hospital Care, Social and Legal Aspects of Psychiatric Care

One of the most important dates in the history of psychiatry is 1795, which marks the inauguration of the humane treatment of the mentally ill by *Pinel* in Paris.

Pinel gave patients increased liberty and provided them with work and activities in the hospital. Previously, they had been restrained and sometimes chained and were noisy, destructive and disturbed in behaviour but, when freed and given work to do, their behaviour dramatically improved and an air of tranquillity prevailed throughout the hospital.

This important social reform was continued by *Rush* in America and by *Connolly* and *Tuke* in England and these pioneers are the real founders of modern social psychiatry.

The work of *Tuke* in York and *Connolly* in Hanwell, Middlesex not only started the movement for more humane treatment for the mentally ill in this country but also influenced public opinion to regard mentally ill people as being ill and not criminals or possessed by devils, but that society had a duty to provide medical treatment as well as providing humane care.

A large number of mental hospitals were built during the nineteenth century. In 1890 the Lunacy Act was passed, which imposed on local authorities the duty of providing mental hospital accommodation. The Act made Certification and a Judicial Order a prerequisite for admission to public mental hospitals.

The effect of this was that persons with early or mild degrees of mental illness were excluded from treatment, as Certification was only invoked when the behaviour or the medical condition of the person made admission to hospital imperative.

The Maudsley Hospital, by a special Act of Parliament, was allowed to admit patients on a voluntary basis in the early nineteen-twenties. Subsequently, in 1930 the Mental Treatment Act enabled all mental hospitals to take voluntary patients.

This Act had far-reaching consequences; patients now sought admission at a much earlier stage of the illness, with the result that recovery and discharge rates improved. There was also a rapid development of out-patient clinic services to enable patients to be seen prior to admission and to be followed up after discharge.

The most striking change is social and legal provisions for psychiatric illness in this country is the Mental Health Act of 1959 which, in many ways, constituted a revolutionary change in psychiatric care.

The Act abolished Certification and also did away with the distinction, from the legal viewpoint, between mental and general hospitals. Patients can now be admitted informally to psychiatric hospitals, just as they can to general hospitals. Compulsory admission, when necessary for observation or treatment, is not a judicial procedure but based on medical recommendations. The Act lays much greater emphasis on the care of a patient in the community, with increased opportunities for treatment of psychiatric illnesses at out-patient clinics, day hospitals and in the patient's home.

The Ministry of Health, in its long term plans, proposes closing down many of the older mental hospitals and establishing large psychiatric units at general hospitals which will serve specific catchment areas.

2. The Development of Psychological Methods of Treatment

Paracelsus, in the fifteenth century, put forward the view that health and illness were controlled by astral bodies such as the stars and the moon. The term lunacy is a relic of these theories which alleged that mentally ill people are affected by the moon.

From this developed the concept of animal magnetism and *Mesmer* believed that ill health was due to a disturbance in the body of a fluid which was called animal magnetism.

Patients treated on the basis of the animal magnetism theory often went into a trance-like state, which was in fact identical with what we now know to be hypnosis. Hypnosis was later used by *Charcot* and others therapeutically. *Charcot* believed that hypnosis and suggestion were the keys to psychiatric treatment.

Freud started using hypnosis to treat psychiatric patients but later dispensed with it, as he found it was unnecessary and often created undesirable dependence on the part of the patient. He replaced it by his method of free association. This became the foundation of psychoanalysis, which proved to have far-reaching influences on thinking and attitudes as well as providing a method of treatment for certain psychiatric disorders and laid the basis of modern dynamic psychiatry.

3. The Organic or Biological Approach

The organic or biological trend paid due attention to physical factors in mental illness and initiated somatic treatment methods, starting in the eighteenth century with *Morgagni* who held the view that mental illness was an organic disease. This concept was refined by various other neuropsychiatrists, laying the foundation for a biological, constitutional and organic type of psychiatry.

This led to a number of important treatments; in 1917 *Wagner von Jauregg* introduced malarial therapy for general paresis and, later, *Klaesi* introduced prolonged narcosis therapy, *Sakel* introduced insulin coma therapy and *Meduna* cardiazol convulsive therapy. *Moniz* introduced prefrontal lobotomy in 1936 and in 1938 *Cerletti* and *Bini* introduced electroconvulsive therapy.

4. Development of Drug Treatment

Herbal remedies and concoctions were used for the treatment of mental disorder by Hippocrates and were described by *Burton* in his Anatomy of Melancholy. Chloral hydrate was introduced into medicine in 1869 and *Fisher* synthesised the first barbiturate in 1903.

The drug treatment of mental illness has developed with remarkable rapidity during the past decade or so. New drugs with potent actions on the higher functions of the central nervous system (Psychotropic Drugs) have been discovered, which have transformed psychiatric treatment.

The field of study of these drugs is termed Psychopharmacology, which is one of the most rapidly developing areas of psychiatry (Vide Ch 32).

Conclusions

The history of progress in medicine generally during the past two hundred years shows that the pattern of progress develops from clinical descriptions of symptoms and signs of the disease, description of morbid anatomy and the possibility of treatment and prevention, depending on the discovery of the relevant causal factors and the extent to which these could be modified by medical intervention.

This mode of progress has also applied to psychiatry but also advances involve social, administrative and legal aspects culminating in the Mental Health Act of 1959 and the plans for transforming community and hospital care for the mentally ill and mentally subnormal.

FURTHER READING

A History of Medical Psychology by G. Zilboorg & G. W. Henry. Norton & Co., New York.

The Historical Development of British Psychiatry by D. Leigh. Pergamon Press, London (1961).

Three Hundred Years of Psychiatry 1535–1860 by R. Hunter & I. MacAlpine.

PART I
PSYCHOLOGY

CHAPTER THREE

'MILIEU INTERIEUR'

'LA CONDITION DE LA VIE LIBRE EST LA CONDITION DU MILIEU INTERIEUR'

Every organism has two environments, namely an external environment to which it must adjust and an internal environment (milieu interieur) which for health, growth and well-being must be maintained relatively constant within narrow limits.

Claude Bernard propounded his now famous dictum that 'the condition for a free life is the condition of the internal environment'.

Any variation in the internal environment, beyond certain permissible narrow ranges, causes a disturbance of well-being and abnormality of functioning in the organism and invariably the first functions to suffer with any change in the internal environment are the highest functions of the central nervous system.

Cannon introduced the term Homeostasis to refer to the maintenance of a steady state within the organism.

The internal environment refers to the body fluids which bathe the cells of the organism. It is a product of the organism and controlled by it and is the medium for the transfer of oxygen, foodstuffs and waste products.

Homeostasis involves:

(1) Obtaining from the external environment oxygen, food and water.

(2) Eliminating waste products.

(3) Maintaining temperature and the manifold physicochemical properties of the internal environment relatively constant.

(4) Appropriate periods of activity, rest and sleep.

MECHANISMS INVOLVED IN ACHIEVING HOMEOSTASIS

Homeostasis is achieved by:

(1) Regulatory mechanisms occurring within the body.

(2) Alterations in behaviour of the organisms as a whole.

Internal Regulatory Mechanisms

These vary in complexity, the simplest being:

(1) Chemical buffer systems. These are automatic changes which

serve to control slight variations in chemical composition; e.g. in acidity or alkalinity of the internal environment the addition of acid or alkali to body fluids results in conversion to an inert form so that the pH remains constant.

(2) At the cellular level homeostasis is achieved by enzymatic balance; e.g. an excess of substrate will stimulate the production of the enzyme, whereas an excess of enzyme will result in a decrease in enzyme production. This is a feed-back mechanism which serves to control enzyme balance.

(3) Mechanisms of storage and release; e.g. for the maintenance of constancy of blood sugar level the control of the rate of the absorption of the intestines and the rate of excretion from the kidney are controlled by endocrine mechanisms and regulated to maintain the level of blood glucose constant.

For emergencies, such as dangerous hypoglycaemia, other mechanisms come into operation; e.g. glycogen in the liver is converted to sugar, tissue proteins are broken down into sugar and utilization of sugar by tissues is lowered by a decrease in insulin secretion.

Hypoglycaemia causes a release of adrenaline which causes a rapid breakdown of tissue glycogen to sugar. It also stimulates the release of ACTH from the anterior pituitary which stimulates the release of cortisol from the adrenal cortex which causes the breakdown of protein to sugar.

In view of the fundamental importance of maintaining the blood sugar level for survival and well-being, it is desirable not to have to rely on a single mechanism but on several mechanisms which subserve the same objective.

(4) *Neuroendocrine and Neurovegetative Control.*

The autonomic nervous system plays an important role in internal mechanisms involved in homeostasis.

The sympathetic part of the autonomic nervous system, by release of adrenaline, serves to mobilise the organism for activity to be able to deal with threats. The parasympathetic nervous system, on the other hand, is concerned with restitution, repair and procreation.

The central nervous system and the autonomic nervous system form a functional unit which is integrated to subserve the functional unity of the individual. The central nervous system also governs the organism's behaviour.

The central nervous system through the cerebral cortex, the limbic system, the reticular system and the hypothalamus also influences neuroendocrine mechanisms in a variety of ways including the pituitary. The anterior lobe of the pituitary secretes trophic hormones which stimulate the thyroid, adrenal cortex, sex glands, etc. These glands in turn produce hormones which inhibit the activity of the anterior lobe of the pituitary, thus constituting a self-regulating mechanism.

Chapter 9 describes how the autonomic nervous system and the adrenal gland play a role in dealing with the effects of stress and maintaining homeostasis.

Some Effects of Changes in the Internal Environment

(1) *Acidity and Alkalinity.* A slight shift towards acidity of the blood results in drowsiness or, if greater, leads to coma and possibly death. A shift towards greater alkalinity causes tetany, twitchings and fits.

(2) *Oxygen.* In conditions which cause a fall in oxygen level in the blood the brain is the first to suffer. The cells of the grey matter of the cortex will die if deprived of oxygen for more than five minutes, whereas the cells of the medulla oblongata can survive up to thirty minutes' deprivation of oxygen. The oxygen needs of the brain as a whole are great and it has been estimated that during a state of bodily rest one quarter of the oxygen needs of the body are utilized by the brain.

J. B. S. Haldane, during an experiment, stayed in a chamber in which the concentration of oxygen was gradually reduced. Haldane wished to determine the onset of colour changes in his face and lips and had a hand mirror with him for the purpose. After being in the chamber for some time he picked up the mirror and kept peering at the back instead of the mirrored surface, not realizing the absurdity of his action. This is a striking illustration of how lack of oxygen can impair judgment without the individual realizing it. With further reduction in oxygen pressure an impairment of recent memory and a tendency to impulsive and irrational behaviour develops.

Exposure to high oxygen pressure will give rise to oxygen poisoning shown by faintness, fall in blood pressure and convulsions.

The body will only function properly if its oxygen content is kept within narrow limits.

(3) *Water.* Hydration is a state of excessive water content of the body, as found in congestive heart failure and certain forms of nephritis or in any process causing retention of sodium.

Hydration may be deliberately produced by giving a person large quantities of water to drink and at the same time administering pitressin, an antidiuretic. Hydration causes general malaise and can cause convulsions. The latter occurs more readily in epileptic subjects. Administering water and pitressin as described above is a diagnostic test for epilepsy.

Dehydration resulting from any cause also causes malaise and, if continued, death.

(4) *Blood Sugar.* With a progressive fall in blood sugar level, as will happen after a large dose of insulin, a series of changes in function and behaviour can be observed. These changes have been studied in detail during the treatment of schizophrenia by insulin coma treatment and

the treatment of certain neuroses by modified insulin (subcoma) treatment.

With slight falls in blood sugar the subject feels weaker and relaxed. As hypoglycaemia deepens he becomes confused and later his response to stimuli diminishes and he becomes soporose. Eventually consciousness is lost and purposive responses cease. If the level of blood sugar continues to fall, we can observe a progressive loss of function starting with the higher levels, viz. the cerebral cortex, then the basal ganglia, then the midbrain and, finally, the medulla. Medullary function maintains the vital functions of breathing and circulation and further increase in hypoglycaemia will cause loss of medullary function resulting in death.

Sugar is of supreme importance in the body economy as the brain can use oxygen and function in its presence and, if deprived of sugar, it ceases to function.

Homeostasis by Behaviour of the Organism as a Whole

For example, when the body is deprived of food the level of sugar in the blood is prevented from falling by mobilising reserves, e.g. conversion of liver glycogen to sugar. This permits the continuation of normal functioning of cells, tissues and organs.

Further lack of food will also induce feelings of hunger which cause the organism to seek food to satisfy it.

Interesting animal experiments have been carried out which indicate that the behaviour of an animal may be determined by homeostatic needs. Rats in which the adrenal cortex was removed differed from intact rats, in that they tended to seek salty foods for which they developed a special appetite. This change of appetite and behaviour enabled the sodium needs of the rat to be maintained and the rats did not die.

If no salty food was provided, death ensued. If adrenal cortex is implanted in adrenalectomized rats, their appetite for salt diminishes and returns to normal.

In animals with parathyroid glands removed there is excess urinary calcium loss and blood calcium. Such animals develop an increased appetite for calcium.

Similarly, animals with posterior lobe of the pituitary removed pass large quantities of urine. These animals develop an appetite for water and drink large quantities to maintain water content of the body normal. If such animals are deprived of water, they die much more quickly than those with an intact posterior pituitary lobe.

A further interesting experiment consisted in allowing rats freedom to select from 15 purified substances—fat, protein, carbohydrate. These rats grew as well as those given a carefully balanced diet.

A study carried out on children revealed that when they were given free access to a variety of natural foods, they chose a well balanced diet resulting in normal growth and development. This finding may surprise many people and it seems that faulty parental guidance and the effect of advertisement may be responsible for faulty dietary choice.

Thus, appetite and behaviour develop according to the physiological needs and to maintain homeostasis. There seems, therefore, to be some scientific support for the old saying 'a little of what you fancy does you good'.

Conclusions

Nature has provided the human being with a variety of mechanisms and processes which serve to keep the internal environment relatively constant, and that the behaviour of the organism may be determined by homeostatic needs. Man's ascent on the evolutionary scale was dependent on acquiring efficient homeostatic mechanisms. With any change that occurs in the composition of the internal environment the first to suffer is the brain, and the recent advances in knowledge give the strongest support to Claude Bernard's dictum that proper and healthy functioning is dependent on the constancy of the internal environment.

Disease in the final analysis is a disturbance of homeostasis.

FURTHER READING

An Introduction to the Study of Experimental Medicine by C. Bernard. Mac-Millan & Co., New York (1865).
Bodily Changes in Pain, Hunger, Fear and Rage by W. B. Cannon. Branford Co., New York (1953).

CHAPTER FOUR

BASIC NEEDS

THE ROLE OF INNATE AND ENVIRONMENTAL INFLUENCES

An instinct is an innate disposition to perform a certain pattern of action without previous training. It refers to comparatively complex patterns of behaviour which are largely innate, present in all members of the species and aroused by perception of certain objects or stimuli.

Instincts in clear cut form are not seen in the human and, when instincts are in operation, they are often largely masked by learning and cultural influences. Instincts can be seen most clearly in lower animals, particularly in insects.

The term drive is preferred, by many, to the word instinct but has a wider connotation as it covers all the various forms of impulsion to activity. The term drive does not necessarily imply innateness; it is the resultant of the processes of heredity, maturation and environment.

A drive is a state of disequilibrium of the organism, set up from within or from without, which profoundly influences or directs the course of response and leading or tend to lead as shown in the diagram below to a state of equilibrium.

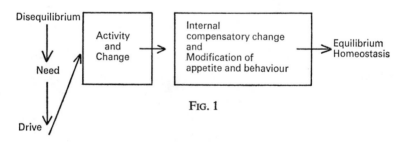

Fig. 1

The following are the primary drives:
(1) Hunger and food-seeking.
(2) Thirst and water-seeking.
(3) Maintenance of body temperature.
(4) Eliminative functions of micturition and defaecation.
(5) Rest after prolonged exertion.
(6) Activity after prolonged rest.
(7) Sex and parental activities.

CONTRIBUTIONS FROM ETHOLOGY

The study of the nature of instinctive behaviour in the human has not proved fruitful and, in recent years, considerable knowledge regarding the nature of innate patterns of behaviour has emerged from the field of Ethology.

The term Ethology is derived from the Greek ethos, meaning custom or habit, and is a new field of knowledge and enquiry based on the behaviour of animals studied with scientific rigour. The development of this field is associated mainly with the names of *K. Lorenz* and *N. Tinbergen.*

Observations of behaviour are made in the field rather than under laboratory conditions and ethology is concerned with their systematic observation and interpretation.

Innate behaviour has figured prominently in the studies of ethologists, who favour the view that an instinct is not a complex reflex system bet is a hierarchy of directed activities motivated from within and susceptible to priming and release at different levels by appropriate stimuli.

An instinct is a hierarchically organised nervous mechanism, which is susceptible to certain priming, releasing and directing impulses of internal as well as external origin, and which responds to these impulses by co-ordinated movements that contribute to the maintenance of the individual and the species.

The term hierarchic organisation means that each part of the behaviour pattern is mediated by a discrete structure and that, in normal behaviour, these fragments are integrated into patterns by other mechanisms which co-ordinate the activities of various structures. For example, the consummatory thrusts of the act of coitus are mediated by the sacral segment of the spinal cord, yet the entire body is involved in coitus.

Priming impulses are clearly distinguished from releasing impulses. Priming impulses, by their effects, build up a potential to act which is triggered off by the releasing impulses. Among the priming influences are:

(1) Endocrines, which facilitate certain patterns of behaviour.

(2) Tissue needs.

(3) Intrinsic activities of the central nervous system.

Instinctive activity is set into action by specific stimuli which are referred to as *sign stimuli*. Animals, despite the complex pattern of stimuli available at a particular time respond only the the sign stimulus. This specific response is probably genetically determined.

The male stickleback will fight another male stickleback intruding into his territory. Detailed experiments using different models resembling sticklebacks revealed that the sign stimulus has the red belly of the other male stickleback.

The sign stimulus acts upon an *innate releasing mechanism* (I.R.M.). A special type of innate releasing mechanism is imprinting. *Imprinting* is a process observed among some birds and fish whereby the young acquire the image which will subsequently come to serve as a releaser of filial or sexual behaviour, as a result only of confrontation soon after hatching.

Imprinting is a mechanism involving both the immediate response to the first sign stimulus experienced and a rapid or immediate learning of such a response. Lorenz became 'imprinted' to a newly hatched gosling by presenting himself as the first available large moving object and allowing the gosling to follow him.

Ethological studies have thrown interesting light on mechanisms which may be relevant in human behaviour, particularly the development of abnormal or disorganised behaviour.

BEHAVIOUR IN CONFLICT SITUATIONS

Sometimes animals are in situations in which conflicting tendencies occur. For example, the territorial song bird will attack a male of the same species within its territory and, when the latter is off the territory, it flees. When the boundary of the territory is reached, the tendency to attack and the tendency to flee become similar in degree and then the bird may show alternating attack and escape behaviour, i.e. *ambivalent behaviour*.

In the presence of two conflicting drives, either to attack or to escape, or when confronted with two contrasting sign stimuli or when instinctive drives are frustrated or thwarted, the animal may show a number of forms of *derived activities*, e.g.:

(1) A bird when feeding will stop feeding when it sees a flying predator and immediately flees to cover. This may become an established pattern by a process of avoidance conditioning.

Masserman, in his experiments on experimental neurosis in cats, found that they would not feed in the situation in which they had been frightened, even though they were on the point of starvation.

(2) Intention movements appropriate to only one of the conflicting drives. For example, a bird might repeatedly carry out a fraction of the movements involved in attack and this fractionation of behaviour may become a fixed pattern of behaviour by learning.

For example, elephants in close confinement show an unhappy rocking, which is derived from intention movements of locomotion.

(3) *Compromise behaviour:* the animal shows aspects of two types of behaviour which, in themselves, are incompatible but nevertheless share some components:

(a) There may be *alternation* between attack and flight.

(b) The animal may show *ambivalent posturing*, showing some aspects of attack and some aspects of retreat.

(4) *Redirection activities:* for example, the female black-headed gull elicits both sexual and aggressive behaviour from her mate who may redirect his aggressive behaviour on to a passer-by.

(5) *Displacement activities:* this is when an animal, whilst showing behaviour belonging to one function or group of activities, suddenly shifts to behaviour more usually characteristic of a quite different context, e.g. fighting starlings may suddenly start to preen their feathers in the middle of a fight.

Displacement activity occurs when the animal is subjected to conflicting tendencies or when the animal is thwarted and the excess drive then sparks over into the displacement activity.

SEXUAL INVERSION

This is another example of apparently irrelevant behaviour but can be understood in terms of priorities. Behaviour of lower priority appears when patterns of high priority are temporarily impossible.

Inversion of sexual behaviour in birds can be understood on the assumption that sexual arousal in either sex involves an increased tendency to show both male and female patterns, although the male pattern is normally of a higher priority in males and vice versa. If the behaviour of the characteristic type is thwarted, the other may be shown.

REFLEXES

Instincts have been compared with reflexes and at one time were regarded as a chain of reflexes. There are, however, important differences between reflexes and instincts. A reflex may be defined as a response of a muscle or gland to a stimulus applied to a sense organ and traversing the path of a reflex arc.

Thus the contraction of the pupil to light is a reflex contraction of the muscle of the iris, brought about by the light stimulus traversing the reflex arc consisting of nerves travelling down the optic nerve and relaying in the midbrain to motor nerves which cause contraction of the pupil.

TABLE I

Reflex	Instinct
Reaction of part of the organism.	Reaction of whole organism.
The operation of a reflex is not conscious.	The operation of an instinct involves consciousness (e.g. perception of the object and emotional accompaniment).
The response is immediate.	The response can be postponed.
The response has absolute priority.	The response can be varied and modified.

INSTINCTIVE BEHAVIOUR IN THE HUMAN BEING

Instincts, by definition, have certain characteristic features:

(1) They are present in all members of the species.

(2) Relative perfection (i.e. biological adequate) at the first performance.

(3) Although they can be modified and postponed, there is relative invariability.

(4) They are adaptive and subserve the needs of the individual or race.

In human beings the importance of instincts is not at all clear.

McDougall described 18 instincts which were varied, ranging from such actions as breathing, coughing and excretion, which are usually classified as reflexes, to such forms of behaviour as flight, curiosity, pugnacity, self-abasement and self-assertion, parental care, reproduction, acquisition, construction and so on. According to McDougall, these instincts were associated with specific emotions, e.g. flight associated with fear, repression with disgust, pugnacity and aggression with anger etc. Considerable controversy has taken place regarding the validity of McDougall's description of instincts.

ENVIRONMENTAL INFLUENCES

In the above list it is difficult to pick out what is innate and what may be determined by learning, social or cultural factors.

Thus, Margaret Meade found that even such fundamental drives as maternal and sex behaviour may be largely culturally determined. In a study of three tribes in New Guinea of similar racial composition considerable variation occurred.

In one tribe, which was peaceful and docile, there was a minimum of distinction between men and women. Boys and girls play the same games which are co-operative and gentle. The father takes as much interest in the upbringing of the children as the mother and both parents give plenty of love and attention to the children.

In another tribe there are also similarities in temperament of the sexes, but both men and women are aggressive and violent. Children are given little affection and are resented and generally rejected.

In the third tribe the women are dominant, aggressive and do the important work. The men do the domestic tasks and are more submissive and do all the gossiping.

This shows the extent that temperamental characteristics can be determined by the cultural and social factors.

Again, with regard to aggressive behaviour, it is known that many factors may be responsible; for example, certain parental attitudes may foster aggressive reactions in children. Certain relationships with the father may produce, in later life, aggressive attitudes to authority. In some unstable individuals, aggressive behaviour can be related to changes in the electrical activity of the brain which may be brought out by hypoglycaemia, overbreathing or hydration. Cultural patterns may also foster aggressive behaviour.

FURTHER READING

A Study of Instinct by N. Tinbergen. Clarendon Press, London (1951).
King Solomon's Ring by K. Lorenz. Methuen, London (1952).
Male and Female by M. Meade. Morrow, New York (1949).

CHAPTER FIVE

DEVELOPMENT DURING INFANCY AND CHILDHOOD

THE NEEDS OF INFANTS

Infancy is the period extending from birth until the end of the second year.

Before birth, the infant is completely dependent on the mother for all its needs, e.g. food, oxygen and warmth.

The newborn child, despite its physical separation from the mother and the establishment of independent respiratory and circulatory and functioning, remains dependent on the mother for important physiological and psychological needs.

The newborn child has the basic need to maintain homeostasis in order to permit growth and development.

Homeostasis is achieved inter alia by obtaining oxygen, food and water and by eliminating waste products. Other basic needs are periods of sleep, rest and activity and to receive appropriate sensory stimulation.

Oxygen

The birth cry is a reflex and serves to bring into action the infant's automatic adjustment to post-natal respiration. During the first few months of life, prolonged crying may be due to lack of oxygen and the principle of letting a baby cry it out does not apply at this early age. It will be seen later that mothering and sucking activity have an important bearing on the proper establishment of breathing functions.

Feeding

The second basic need of the infant is intake of food. The process of feeding in early infancy is sucking and it is only in recent years that proper recognition has been given to the physiological and psychological importance of sucking.

Sucking, which is usually regarded as an automatic and readymade function, is not always found in adequately functioning form in a newly born child.

In addition to its primary purpose of feeding, sucking has other functions which are important in development:

(1) Sucking brings a better blood supply to the face, thus aiding the development of facial structures.

(2) Sucking makes breathing deeper and more regular.

(3) The process of sucking is associated with various kinds of sensory stimulation:

    (a) Touch sensations from the mouth.

    (b) Touch and pressure sensations from the body surface.

    (c) Proprioceptive impulses from muscles and joints.

    (d) Auditory and visual stimuli from the mother.

All these stimuli impinge on the child's consciousness during sucking activity and form the very beginnings of consciousness.

(4) Sucking is a source of pleasure to the infant. The mouth is one of the early erogenous (pleasure-producing) zones in the body. Oral pleasures continue into adult life, hence the popularity of smoking and kissing.

Studies of a group of babies allowed unrestricted sucking revealed that in this group breathing was deeper and more regular, digestion, gastro-intestinal and eliminative functions were better and the infants were more relaxed and contented. Infants who, on the other hand, had restriction or frustration of sucking activity tended to show two distinctive types of reaction. One group was restless, tense and crying a great deal and the other tended to be inert, atonic and rather stuporous, with a high incidence of gastro-intestinal disturbances. Babies allowed complete freedom regarding sucking, only rarely exceeded two to five hours a day in sucking activity and were usually free from thumb sucking later. Sucking activity spontaneously wanes during the fourth month when oral activity is supplemented by biting and vocalisation.

It may be concluded that adequate sucking activity is a very important need in the first few months of life.

Sensory Stimulation

It is not sufficiently realised that an adequate amount of sensory stimulation is essential for normal healthy development of the child. The degree of stimulation, however, must not be excessive, as this may give rise to apathy, inanition and lack of emotional and general development. The process of mothering provides the type and degree of sensory stimulation needed by the infant. Mothering really consists of the sum total of the various acts relating to which a normal mother consistently shows her love for the child and, thus, instinctively, stimulates its emotional development. Inadequate mothering can have serious effects on the child. Ribble found that in a group of babies that had not received adequate mothering, two main kinds of response tended to develop:

(1) A negativistic response.

(2) An aggressive type of behaviour.

The negativistic reaction consisted in restlessness, resistiveness and hyperextension of the trunk. Other infants showed another reaction to inadequate mothering, the skin becoming paler and losing its normal turgor, breathing becoming irregular and gastro-intestinal disturbances occurring. Vomiting and diarrhoea give rise to dehydration.

The treatment of this condition consists in giving saline to restore body fluids, bodily massage to provide sensory stimulation. The infant's first satisfaction, that obtained by sucking, is derived from his mother, and the instant attachment to the mother grows as satisfaction is obtained by sensory stimulation and soothing sounds of the mother's voice. The importance of sensory stimulation in invoking responses of the emotions is strikingly shown in the case of the 'Wolf child'. The child, which had apparently been abandoned in the wilds of India, was reared by wolves. When found by a missionary, the child walked on all fours, emitted unintelligible sounds and showed no social responses. The first sign of affection occurred when the missionary's wife began to massage the child.

Kinesthetic stimulation is also required by infants, and the old methods of rocking a child in a mother's arms or cradle supplies this need. It has been found that the children receiving inadequate mothering tend to develop head rolling and body rolling which, as it were, tend to make up for the lack of rocking. Thus, mothering provides an adequate source of sensory sensations of the right kind and degree, and it helps functional integration and emotional and general development.

Eliminative Functions

In the exercises of the eliminative functions of urination and defaecation, the infant is no respecter of time or person. Nowadays there is a tendency to start the child's toilet training very early, even during the first few months of life. The tenth month is early enough to start toilet training, and any attempt to start before this is merely the establishment of a conditioned response, and often breaks down at the end of the first year. Toilet training should not be started before the infant can sit up securely and not before he is able to give some sign of his urge to defaecate. Furthermore, toilet training should not be started before he has a strong positive and emotional attachment to someone. Toilet training, in effect, constitutes a frustration of natural impulses and it is important that it should be carried out without emotional tension. Often mothers are so concerned with cleanliness and regularity of bowel action that toilet training may be enforced too early or too harshly. It must be remembered that training must be based on love and security, and the less anxiety and tension focused on eliminative functions the better it will be for the child and the more normal and regular will his elimination functions be.

THE EFFECTS OF LOSS OF MATERNAL CARE

Dependency is a central feature of infancy. During the first months of life the mother needs to suffer infant's needs as an individual and not merely act as provider of food and comfort. All feelings of security in fact are all vested in his mother. The child of 18 months to 2 years is fiercely possessive, selfish and utterly intolerant of frustration. When a child of 18–24 months of age who has previously had a normal relationship with his mother and has not been separated from her for more than a few hours, is brought up in an impersonal environment, he usually progresses through three phases of emotional responses—protest, despair and denial.

Protest

Lasts for a few hours to 8 days. He is anxious that he has lost his mother and is confused by the unfamiliar surroundings. He will cry loudly, shake his cot and throw himself about and look urgently towards any sight and sound which might be his missing mother.

Despair

He may cry monotonously and intermittently. He is withdrawn and apathetic. He is quiet but in a state of mourning. This is often mistakenly taken to indicate reduced distress.

Denial

If a substitute mother is available he reacts with a denial for the need of mothering by his own mother. The second type is denial of all need for mothering. He becomes more and more self-centred, transferring his desires and feelings from people on to material things such as sweets, toys and food. These are dependable satisfactions.

These reactions can be avoided or minimised by extended visiting and allowing mothers to help in the care of their children.

Summary of General Principles

We may now formulate certain psychological rules on the care of upbringing in infancy:

(i) The baby should have a long and uninterrupted period of consistent and adequate mothering. If the mother is not available, it should preferably be given by one person.

(ii) Freedom of sucking activity is a necessity during the first few months of life.

(iii) Child's stage of development should determine the age of weaning and toilet training.

    (a) Weaning should be initiated gradually when the child supplements sucking by biting and vocalisation and then is able to grasp and carry things to its mouth.

(b) Toilet training should not be started before the infant can sit up alone and can indicate his needs.

(iv) The infant must be given time to learn and accept one thing at a time as he progresses from infancy to childhood.

(v) One must provide consistent and healthy emotional satisfaction.

(vi) Consistent security lays the foundation for the transformation of the energies of the primitive impulses into activity to satisfy the child and acceptable to others and achieve better emotional, intellectual, social and ethical development.

FORMS OF BEHAVIOUR DURING INFANCY AND CHILDHOOD

The behaviour of the infant falls into four groups of activity: (1) Motor behaviour (2) Speech (3) Emotions (4) Social.

Motor Behaviour

The following are useful guides:
1 month—should attempt to lift head when held on the shoulder.
2 months—can hold head erect for few moments.
4 months—can hold head steady when carried.
6 months—sits up momentarily without support.
9 months—can sit without support.
1 year—can walk with help; can lower itself from standing position.
15 months—standing and walking.
18 months—climbs stairs and gets on to chair.
2 years—run and build a pile of 6 blocks.
2½ years—build 7–8 blocks and go down stairs alone.

Linguistic and Speech Behaviour

2 months—attends to speaking voice.
6 months—syllables.
9 months—'Da-da'.
1 year—knows about two words.
15 months—four words.
18 months—six words; can point to eyes, nose.
2 years—can name objects.

Emotional Behaviour

Emotional reactions are shown early by satisfaction or frustration of instinctive drives.

In the first few months emotional disturbance is shown by increased muscular tension. Oxygen want may be the first stimulus to produce anxiety but later hunger is the most frequent cause.

The infant's awareness to the outside world develops from the 3rd–6th month and specific reactions to the mother begin to appear.

Six months—obtaining pleasure from defaecation. Bowel control achieved about 18 months; this coincides with greater play activities. The great value of play in canalizing instinctive energies is not sufficiently realised.

Social Behaviour

Although the infant is mainly biological and governed by bodily needs, for instance, care and protection, he has to participate in social interaction to obtain satisfaction of these needs. The infant is not born into a vacuum but into a world in which persons, customs and other environmental influences are brought to bear on the infant at a very early age.

The first social influence is that of the mother who, if she did not provide for nourishment, care and protection, the infant would not survive. This dependence of the infant on the mother for its primary needs essential for survival is the basis on which love, sympathy and co-operation are built.

In the early months of infancy there is no appreciation of what is self and non-self. The idea of self is only gradually built up and it is only during the second year and later that the child has a clear knowledge of himself as an entity. This is probably first noticed when the child finds that certain things, e.g. his limbs, can be moved when he wishes, whereas objects in the environment do not respond in this way.

DEVELOPMENT DURING CHILDHOOD

The period of childhood extends from infancy until puberty.

All schools of psychological thought agree that the period of infancy and childhood are of paramount importance in determining and patterning future character development and behaviour.

The human being, compared with other animals, has a long period of dependency. Many actions which are spontaneous in animals have to be acquired gradually in the human, e.g. walking. The child has to learn a variety of performances which in adult life become habitual, e.g. dressing, personal care and hygiene, talking, control of desires and emotions in a socially acceptable way.

During growth and development the child has to adjust and adapt himself to the needs of the environment. The adjustments required become increasingly complex and he has gradually to learn a greater degree of independence.

There are two main sets of factors determining behaviour and personality:

(1) The individual with inborn and learned needs which demand satisfaction.

(2) The environment, both physical and social-cultural (i.e. persons, groups and traditions), to which the individual must adapt.

Three phases of social development can be described in infancy and childhood:
(1) Elementary
(2) Domestic
(3) Community

Elementary Socialization

The period of elementary socialization extends from birth until 18 months to 2 years.

During this stage, the infant is governed by physiological needs and urges. The satisfaction of these needs is provided by the mother.

During the first two years, growth and development are proceeding which permit of greater degrees of adaptation. The infant develops a greater physiological integration and is developing his sensory capacities of sight, hearing and perception in general. Motor skill and co-ordination improve. The period is characterized by marked dependency on the mother for psychological and physiological needs which are inextricably intermixed.

Domestic Socialization

The family is the unit of society. The new born infant is a result of inherited qualities and pre-natal growth, and it is upon this that society in the form of mother, father and other persons begin to influence its patterns of life and behaviour.

As we have seen, the primary needs of the child for nutrition and bodily care and protection are satisfied by the mother. Later the child is trained to exercise control over the eliminative functions, and over sleeping and eating. The modification of primary needs to meet the requirements of the family is the first process in training.

The satisfaction of physiological needs gives rise to a pleasurable state. The child tends to seek stimuli which are pleasurable and to avoid those unpleasant or painful. This pleasure seeking (hedonistic) tendency has to be modified and controlled to meet the needs of other people. The child has from an early age to conform to conditions and rules laid down for him by older and more experienced persons. The child demands satisfaction of his needs but has to find means which are acceptable to others. This, in fact, is the process of education and training.

Security

One of the most important needs for satisfactory development in children is a feeling of emotional security.

The child must feel safe and secure in his relationships, firstly with his mother and later with father and other members of the family. A feeling of security develops from interaction between the child and his parents or others participating in his upbringing. A feeling of security will depend on:

(1) Love and affection
(2) Approval
(3) Consistency in relationships

Love and Affection

Love and affection to the child is as important for his development as food and other bodily needs. This fundamental truth has only been sufficiently stressed in comparatively recent times. The child deprived of love is stinted in his personality development. Affection must be genuine and direct and not given in the form of tokens such as presents.

Approval

Everyone likes to feel that he or she is acceptable and approved by others. It is important for the child to feel that he is liked as a person not so much for what he does or achieves but for what he is.

Consistency

Consistency in all matters and relationships helps the child to form a stable attitude to life and enables him to develop standards and rules of behaviour which help him in reaching decisions and appropriate behaviour.

Consistency is important in:

(1) Love and affection
(2) Approval
(3) Training
(4) Praise, reward and punishment

Consistency in love and affection is important for feelings of security. If the mother lavishes affection one day and the next day has a different attitude because she may be feeling off colour, it does not give the child an opportunity for forming stable attitudes or habits. In the case of praise and punishment, consistency is of the utmost importance. It is important for the child to know why he is being punished and that it is because of the act itself and not because he himself is rejected. If punishment is given because the parent is in a bad mood or suffering from a hangover the child becomes bewildered and is prevented from establishing stable rules of conduct and behaviour.

For proper and healthy personality development the child must be loved, accepted and approved by the parents in a consistent manner. Certain parent-child attitudes have undesirable effects on the child and militate against his normal personality development. Examples are attitudes of rejection and overprotection.

Rejection

Parents have attitudes of rejection to a child which may vary in degree and also in the way in which they are manifested. A parent may have this attitude to a child for the following reasons:

(i) The child may be unwanted. The parents may have enough children and rejection is on economic or selfish grounds.

The child may be unwanted for other reasons:

(ii) Some parents are unwilling to accept responsibility of rearing a child because it might interfere with their freedom and their pleasure.

(iii) Sometimes the child may be wanted for a special motive e.g. to cement an unhappy marriage. If the advent of the child fails to achieve this it may then on this account be rejected.

(iv) Fear that the child might inherit some undesirable mental or physical condition.

(v) Because the child is a product of an unhappy marriage.

A parental attitude of rejection may show itself directly by neglect or excessive punishment. The parents may not be aware of their underlying attitude of rejection but show it by refusing to give the child affection or by demanding high standards of behaviour and achievement. This perfectionistic attitude accepts him only if he is perfect, giving him affection and approval only when he achieves the high standards set in behaviour, industry and obedience. Affection is only given when he reaches the high standards set for him, and not for the person he is.

Another manifestation of rejection is over-protection. Here the parents overcompensate for a feeling of rejection by oversolicitude and by doing so, try to expiate their guilt.

Over-protection

Over-protection may be due to other causes in addition to rejection:

(i) It may be a manifestation of the mother's temperament. She may be over-anxious and have an apprehensive and anxious attitude to life in general. She seeks out potential dangers. She sees dangers lurking round every corner from which she feels she must protect her child. She fears germs and may give excessive medicines, may clothe him excessively, etc.

(ii) If the parents have previously lost children through illness or accident, they may fear that something may happen to the child and for this reason over-protect him because he has now become very precious. Only children may be over-protected for similar reasons.

(iii) The parent may be suffering from her own emotional problem which makes her anxious; this results in over-anxiety for the child and consequently over-protection.

The over-protected child is usually timid and apprehensive and usually more childish than his years. His development has been hindered by 'smother love' instead of aided by mother love.

DEVELOPMENT OF SPEECH, LANGUAGE AND THINKING

Speech has three main functions, (1) Representation, i.e. to convey meaning, (2) Expression of the individual's needs, desires and ideas and (3) Appeal, that is to attempt to control other people's behaviour.

The birth cry is the first use of the respiratory mechanisms involved in speech and is of physiological rather than psychological importance.

The earliest vocalisations are reflex and have no meaning.

The infant responds to the sound of the voice between 2–3 months. During and after the third month cooing and babbling occur and the child expresses pleasure in this way. After the 6th month the child will imitate sounds and echo-babbling increasingly develops. By the end of the first year the infant knows 2 or 3 words such as mama, dada and bye bye.

The above may be regarded as a preliminary period to speech and the first period of speech development is between 12–18 months. The first words are really sentences of one word; the child saying 'ball' may mean 'give the ball to me'. At this stage there is no understanding of grammar.

From 18–24 months the infant gradually becomes aware of the object of speech, i.e. that everything has a name. His will to master it increases and he asks questions about the names of things and his vocabulary shows a sudden increase. He first learns nouns, then verbs and lastly adjectives and adverbs.

From 2–2½ years he learns the finer shades of ideas by modifying words and his vocabulary is now between 300–400 words.

After the age of 2½, the vocabulary rapidly grows and he has about 900 words at 3 years, 1,500 words at 4 years, 2,000 at 5 and 2,500 at 6 years.

Speech development falls into the following stages:

(1) Preliminary—during the first year.

(2) True speech, from 1–5 years, in which words as symbols of objects, acts, situations, qualities and relations are learned in a manner more or less acceptable to the particular society or group to which the child belongs.

Development of Thinking

Words therefore become linked with objects, relations, qualities etc. and are, in fact, symbols for them.

Meaning has two features:

(1) Denotation, i.e. the properties and qualities of the object perceived or conceived in time and space.

(2) Connotation, i.e. the suggested and implied ideas and feelings attached to a word.

The following are the stages in thought development in children:

(1) *Physiognomic or Syncretic stage*, in which the child gives animate or human physiognomic qualities to inanimate objects. If he falls on the floor, he may kick the floor for coming up to meet him; if he jams his finger in the door, he may say the door has bitten him. He may play with a broom-stick and refer to it as a horse.

Thinking at this level is asocial and is used merely to express the child's needs. It is egocentric and unreal.

(2) *Concrete thinking* is realistic and literal. Each object or situation is regarded by its individual qualities. It is the main mode of thinking up until the age of 7 years. Thinking may remain at this level in mental defectives or may revert to this level in patients with organic brain disease.

The word chair to a child of six years will usually mean a particular chair he is familiar with and will not conjure up an idea of a class of objects with certain common features which would bring them into the generic meaning of the word chair.

In concrete thinking things may be regarded as the same because of some common feature; thus, if Daddy has a blue car, the child will refer to all blue cars as Daddy's because they have the same colour.

An individual who is only able to think at this level will not be able to see the deeper meanings of proverbs, e.g. if asked what 'a new broom sweeps clean' means, he is likely to tell you that a new broom will sweep cleaner than an old one.

(3) *Conceptual or Abstract thinking* gradually develops after the age of 7 years and is characteristic of the educated adult.

Conceptual thinking is an active process which involves the voluntary assumption of a mental set and the ability to shift from one aspect of the situation to another and making a choice. Various aspects of the situation have to be kept in mind and the whole has to be split up into parts and common qualities abstracted. It involves active intellectual exercise and involves planning ahead intentionally and thinking symbolically.

A concept represents a reorganisation of various aspects of perceptual experience, in which some element or feature with a verbal level comes to stand for the whole experience.

It involves finding both similarities and differences in the larger field of concrete experiences with specific objects or persons. Thus, a child comes into contact with chairs, tables, sideboards, etc. and eventually will be able to classify such objects under the term furniture. The word green will come to stand for a variety of shades of the colour. Similarly, honesty, justice, etc. will come to mean general attributes of everyday conduct.

Conceptual thinking is the highest level of thinking and it enables us to use concepts (ideas) instead of concrete situations and may allow us to form conclusions without resort to direct experience or trial.

The development of new knowledge depends on certain processes. Firstly we experience certain things, e.g. colour or odour and then we tend to perceive various relations, that one red is like another or one odour more pleasant than another. Having noticed relationships between things, the knowledge of an object and a relationship can give rise to a new idea.

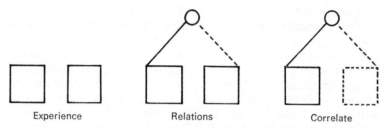

Experience   Relations   Correlate

The development of a new idea.

The continuous lines denote occurrence and dotted lines tendency.

The operation of these processes can yield entirely new ideas by the eduction of correlates.

Sometimes new ideas are elaborated subconsciously. We may have been grappling with a problem for a long time and we 'sleep on it' and it may happen that when we wake up in the morning the solution appears; we may even wake up at night with the answer we have been seeking.

Thus, subconsciously a sorting out of the relationships has been occurring, resulting in the discovery of the solution. This process is referred to as Subconscious Elaboration.

Helmholtz, the famous physicist, when confronted with a problem used to read as much as he could about the various aspects of it and he used to find that, although deliberate effort would not produce the answer, the answer would come into his mind during moments of relaxation, e.g. whilst in the bath or going along a country walk.

Darwin used to keep a series of envelopes in his pocket to jot down the various ideas that used to come into his mind at odd times.

The perception of relations and the education of correlates is a high level of thinking and obeys the laws of Logic.

FURTHER READING

Determinants of Human Behaviour by H. F. Harlow (Ed. B. M. Foss). Methuen, London (1961).

Maternal Care and Mental Health by Bowlby. World Health Monograph Series No. 2.

CHAPTER SIX

INTELLIGENCE AND ABILITY

Intelligence has been variously defined as all-round general ability, the capacity to benefit from experience, the ability to see relationships and to utilise such knowledge in future thought and action.

It is difficult to obtain a definition which will cover the manifold aspects of intelligence. It is generally agreed that general intelligence is the innate potentiality of the individual which determines how educable he is in any direction. A person's innate intelligence determines the maximum level that he can achieve, although other factors will influence what is actually achieved. It is necessary to distinguish between ability and capacity; ability refers to achievement and capacity to potential.

For many years there has been considerable controversy regarding the essential components of intelligence.

Spearman carried out a wide variety of tests of ability in a random sample of the population. The tests included performance ability; verbal and non-verbal intellectual ability. The results in all the tests were intercorrelated; then, by means of the statistical procedure of factorial analysis, it was found that there was a general factor which influenced all tests. This was called the general factor of intelligence or 'g'.

In addition to general intelligence there are specific factors such as verbal ability, numerical ability, spatial ability, perceptive ability, inductive reasoning, ability to remember etc. These are relatively independent but not fully so.

General intelligence can be measured, at least fairly efficiently if not with complete accuracy, by standardised tests such as those devised by *Burt, Thompson, Raven* and others.

The scores obtained on such tests in samples of the normal population reveal that it is distributed along the normal frequency (Gaussian) curve. This means that there will only be a comparatively small number of people with the very highest ranges of intelligence, a larger proportion above the average and below the average and there will be a small proportion with very low intelligence. At the lower end of the I.Q. distribution curve there is a small hump in the frequency curve which represents those persons suffering from special types of mental subnormality.

Although the actual success achieved by a person will depend on other aspects of personality, particularly industry, persistence and will power, in general, it is possible to relate intelligence level to vocational categories as follows:

Highest professional and administrative	I.Q.	150+	(0.1% of adults)
Lower professional and technical	I.Q.	130–150	(3%)
Clerical and highly skilled	I.Q.	115–130	(12%)
Skilled and ordinary commercial	I.Q.	100–115	(26%)
Semi-skilled and poorest commercial	I.Q.	85–100	(33%)
Unskilled and coarse manual labour	I.Q.	70– 85	(19%)
Casual labour	I.Q.	50– 70	(7%)
Institutional mentally subnormal patients	I.Q.	50 and less	(0.2%)

During the growth of the individual child intelligence becomes progressively more and more specialised, more and more comprehensive and differentiates into a hierarchy of cognitive abilities—sensory, perceptual, associative and relational. The basic quality common to all these is referred to as intelligence.

Binet (1857–1911) held the view that intellectual backwardness was not a result of lack of education but of some basic handicap arising from defect of or damage to the central nervous system. Binet considered that intelligence in the normal person and the capacity to acquire knowledge was dependent not on education but mainly on some inherited endowment.

In 1904 he was requested by the authorities of Paris to devise a method of identifying, at the earliest possible stage, children who were unlikely to be able to cope with normal schooling.

Binet was anxious to differentiate between ability and capacity and he applied to all age groups a large variety of tests, which were believed to involve intelligent behaviour and to be independent of what had been taught. From the results he was able to devise an age scale. The test scores, which related to performance of the normal population, provided a measure of the individual's mental age.

The intelligence quotient (I.Q.) is the ratio formed by dividing mental age by chronological age and multiplying the result by 100 as follows:

$$I.Q. = \frac{\text{Mental age}}{\text{Chronological age}} \times 100$$

INTELLIGENCE—HOW MUCH INNATE AND HOW MUCH ACQUIRED?

Orphans and foster children who are not brought up by their own parents, nevertheless continue to show some correlation in intelligence with their true parents. Also, many intelligent individuals come from a poor background and, on the other hand, professional parents sometimes have a very dull child whose educational and vocational achievements remain low, despite the best upbringing and intellectural stimulation that they can provide. These differences between child and parents are to be expected on a genetic basis and cannot be accounted for by the influence of environmental factors.

Studies on identical twins reared apart and non-identical twins reared together show very clearly that both intelligence and tests of educational attainment are affected by heredity and environment but the relative effects of the factors are markedly different. Intelligence test scores depend very heavily on heredity and attainment test scores more heavily on environment.

In the case of children, it is important to have suitable environmental stimulation in order that intellectual capacity may develop to its maximum. Similarly, thinking processes also need stimulation and exercise provided by the home and school environment.

Hebb makes the useful distinction between what he calls Intelligence A and Intelligence B. Intelligence A is the innate potentiality which we can never observe or measure since from birth there is no interaction with environmental stimulation. Intelligence B is the intelligence we actually observe and measure. It is the all-round capacity to comprehend, to learn new habits and skills, to grasp relations and to build-up and use abstract concepts.

According to *Burt*, 80 per cent of intelligence is determined by genetic factors and only 20 per cent by environmental differences.

In addition to the genetic contribution to intelligence, environmental factors are important in order to enable the person's innate capacity to develop to the optimum. A person's intellectual capacity is built up gradually as a result of his interaction with the environment.

The intelligence we measure is, therefore, a product of the innate potentiality and its interaction with environmental influences.

MEASUREMENT OF INTELLIGENCE BY TESTS

Intelligence tests may be classified in various ways, e.g. group tests, individual tests, paper and pencil tests, oral tests; verbal and non-verbal tests, perceptual tests and performance tests.

The following are the tests in common use:

Verbal

(1) *Binet type of test* consisting of questions arranged in mental ages corresponding to the ages of children who could pass them. The test has been restandardised by Burt, Terman and Stanford. The results of the test are expressed as mental age from which one can easily calculate the Intelligence Quotient (I.Q.).

$$\text{I.Q.} = \frac{\text{Mental age}}{\text{Chronological age}} \times 100$$

The disadvantages of the Binet scale are, that it is not very satisfactory for adults, both on account of the fact that the questions appear childish to the adult and also because of the small number of items for the higher mental age groups. Furthermore, the tests are heavily loaded with tests of educational achievement.

(2) *Spearman's Approach.* Spearman declared in 1904 that all branches of intellectual activity have in common one fundamental function or group of functions, whereas the remaining or specific elements seem in every case to be different from that in all the others. The common factor he called 'g' and the specific factor 's', specific for each test.

The following are the kinds of tests used to measure 'g' analogies: inferences, classifications, synonyms and antonyms.

(3) *Weschler-Bellvue Scale* has been standardised for adults in America and consists of:
   1. Information test.
   2. Comprehension test.
   3. Picture arrangement test.
   4. Digit span test.
   5. Arithmetic test.
   6. Picture completion test.

(4) *Raven's Mill Hill* vocabulary test, used as a verbal complement to the non-verbal perceptual Raven's matrices test.

(5) *Kent Oral* consists of a short battery of tests and can be given to both adults and children.

Non-Verbal Tests

(1) *Sleight's non-verbal intelligence test* for ages 6–10 years. The series of ten tests consist of pictures and drawings for substitution, classification or series continuation.

(2) *Raven's Progressive Matrices* consists of 5 sets of 12 designs of matrices. The tests are progressively more difficult, both in the series of matrices comprising a set and in the series of sets. The matrix contains a missing piece and the testee has to select from a number of designs underneath the correct one, so that the analogy between the designs is completed. The analogy may be similarity, opposition or addition.

Performance Tests

The following are some performance tests of intelligence in common use:

(1) *Koh's Blocks.* The test consists of 16 coloured inch cubes. All the cubes are printed in the same way—white, yellow, blue, red; red and white diagonally divided and yellow and blue diagonally divided. The subject has to construct designs with the blocks, according to given

patterns of increasing difficulty. The result is usually expressed as M.A. (Mental Age) and I.Q.

(2) *Knox Cube Test* consists of five 1-inch cubes painted black. Four of the cubes are placed in front of the subject about 2 inches apart. The 5th is used by the examiner and subject for tapping. The examiner taps out a pattern of movements or taps with his cube on the four placed cubes, then hands the cube to the subject who has to repeat the movement or pattern. 12 patterns of increasing complexity are used.

(3) *Domino Test.* This, like the previous test, is a test of memory span like the memory span for digits.

(4) *Size and Weight Test* consists in arranging in order of size, five cubes, five others being used for demonstration purposes, and arranging five blocks of wood in order of weight and five brass weights being used for demonstration.

(5) *Manikin and Profile Test* consists in noting ability to rebuild Manikin or reconstruct profile of face from component pieces.

(6) *Form Boards* are of various types and consist in fitting pieces correctly into spaces of a board. Examples—Pintner's, Seguin, Goddard, Minnesota.

(7) *Cube Construction Test* consists in reconstructing a cube from a number of component pieces.

(8) *Picture Completion Tests*, e.g. Healy's are self-explanatory.

(9) *Carl Hollow Square Test* consists in fitting pieces of wood of varying sizes, shapes and bevelled into a hollow square space in a block of wood. The pieces are arranged in a series of increasing difficulty and the results are scored on the time taken and the number of trials to achieve success.

(10) *Maze Tests*—Porteus and others.

Advantages of Performance Tests

(1) Can be used on illiterates, foreigners, deaf mutes and those with speech difficulties.

(2) Measures ability to deal with concrete problems and practical usefulness in addition to 'g'.

(3) Less determined by education than verbal tests.

Disadvantages

(1) Usually take a long time to do.

(2) The norms of many are inadequately standardised.

Assessing a New Intelligence Test

The assessment of the value of a new intelligence test is made by applying certain criteria, e.g.:

(1) *Reliability.* This term refers to the constancy of results given by a group at different times. Obviously if the same group gave divergent

results on different occasions, some other factor would be influencing the results in addition to the trait one wishes to measure. The reliability is calculated by correlating the results of the test given to the same group at different times. The degree of correlation indicates the retest reliability.

(2) *Validity*. The term validity refers to the degree to which a test measures what it sets out to measure.

Validity may be determined by:

(1) *External criteria*, e.g. correlating the results of the test on a sample, with gradings made by teachers or others on the same sample.

(2) *Internal criteria*. If one applies various intelligence tests to a group of people and calculates the intercorrelations between the tests, one will be able to ascertain how closely they agree with each other, as it is assumed that there must be a common factor.

In the above experiment one would expect to find significant correlations, as the tests are all supposed to measure intelligence. Spearman found that a general factor of 'g', as it is called, is present which accounts for the correlation between the tests. The presence of such a factor can be elicited by the statistical technique of factorial analysis, which will also tell us how much each test correlates with this general factor 'g' or, in other words, how much the test is saturated with 'g'.

This gives us a method of determining validity. If the test is devised to measure general intelligence, its validity is indicated by its saturation with 'g'.

(3) *Norms and Standardisation*. Norms for the general population should be available and expressed in terms of Mean, Standard Deviation or Percentile Ranks, and the norms should also be standardised for age and sex.

(4) *Objectivity*. The less subjective interpretation required for a test, the more reliable and valid it is likely to be. The scoring of the test should be objective, so that results by different markers will be comparable.

(5) *Practicability*. The test should be easily given and scored and the results graded without difficulty.

(6) *The Items*. The number of items in the test should be large enough to allow a sufficient range of variation.

(7) The test results should not be greatly influenced by knowledge and education as opposed to native intelligence.

FURTHER READING

See page 47.

CHAPTER SEVEN

LEARNING AND REMEMBERING

Learning is probably the most important field of psychology. Most of our behaviour is learned. In fact, all the behaviour which characterises the civilised person and that which distinguishes a particular person as a member of a race, a religion or a social group is learned.

It should also be noted that man learns reactions of guilt feelings, fear and anxiety and many symptoms found in psychiatric illness.

Essentially, learning is the modification of behaviour by experience as a result of interaction of the individual with his environment.

Instincts and reflexes are unlearned forms of response to stimuli.

The learning process may be described as establishing new connections between sensory organs and effector organs.

The form that learning takes varies in complexity from simple conditioning reflex responses, as when children learn to avoid fire, to very complex acts and processes whereby a scientist constructs a theory.

All forms of learning, from the simplest to the most complex, have important common factors—viz. drive, response and reinforcement.

Drives

The term *drive* refers to the force which impels the subject to act or respond. Any stimulus which impels action is a drive. The intensity of the drive usually increases according to the strength of the stimulus.

Primary Drives

Primary drives are stimuli fundamentally important in determining motivation. Examples are pain, thirst, hunger, fatigue, cold and sexual stimuli.

The strength of primary drives, as a rule, increases with deprivation.

Secondary Drives

Social-cultural influences provide secondary (learned) drives. These are based on unlearned drives and are important in human behaviour, in processes of social adjustment and also in achievement.

Cues denote stimuli which determine when the response to a drive actually takes place; for example, when the motorist applies his brakes on seeing the traffic lights change to amber and red.

A cue can be any stimulus which is sufficiently distinctive.

Response

A response to a drive must occur before it can be learned. Some responses do not become learned, whereas others do.

The factors which determine whether or not a response is learned are:

(1) Frequency of occurrence of response.

(2) Whether a reward is associated with response.

Among the various possible responses to a drive and cue, the particular response rewarded is the one most likely to be learned.

If the correct response is achieved the first time and rewarded, learning is greatly facilitated and automatically takes place.

Trial and Error Learning

Animal studies have thrown light on the various types of learning. The method usually employed is to place the animal (dog, cat, rat, etc.) in a maze, puzzle box or some other obstacle between the animal and the satisfaction of some need, e.g. hunger. When a dog, for example, is placed in a cage with food outside, he first of all makes various attempts to get out and eventually might touch the latch which opens the door of the cage. If the experiment is repeated over and over again, the successful action is reached earlier, until eventually the correct action is carried out without errors.

This is an example of trial and error learning. It is learning by parts of a whole until the successful response becomes stamped in by practice. The golfer learns the proper stance, the correct way of holding the club and the follow through, etc. Many of the preliminary efforts are in the nature of trial and error but, in the human being, observation of someone else carrying out the skilled movement and training in the various actions greatly shortens the period of learning, as compared with trial and error methods alone. The golfer practises the strokes and actions until they all become co-ordinated and the drive sends the ball with the desired force in the desired direction.

Conditioned Responses

One of the simplest forms of learning is by the establishment of conditioned reactions.

We owe much of the knowledge of conditioned reflexes to the Russian Physiologist, Pavlov. Pavlov made intensive use of the reflex secretion of saliva in dogs for his studies on conditioned reflexes.

The secretion of saliva in response to eating food is an innate reflex, is therefore unlearned and is present in all members of the species. Pavlov found that if a bell was rung at the same time as the dog was given food to eat and, if this was repeated over and over again, eventually the ringing of the bell alone produced a secretion of saliva. In other words, a new reflex has been established by the conditions of the experiment. This new reflex of salivary secretion in response to the ringing of a bell produced by the experiment is called a conditioned reflex.

The establishment of conditioned reflexes is one of the simplest and earliest forms of learning. The process of conditioning may be illustrated as follows:

Unconditioned stimulus → Unconditioned response
(Eating food)   → Secretion of saliva

Unconditioned stimulus
and   → Secretion of saliva
Conditioned stimulus
(sound of bell)

Conditioned stimulus   → Conditioned response
alone

Sound of bell   → Secretion of saliva

The watering of our mouths when we are hungry in response to the smell of food or the sight of a well-laden table is a typical example of a conditioned response. Another example is the baby's sucking movements of the lips when he sees the feeding bottle.

Some conditioned responses are negative, such as a child who avoids fire after being burned.

Conditioning makes us seek pleasurable activities or objects and avoid unpleasant activities or situations. Habits to Pavlov were a series of conditioned reflexes, the arousing of one reflex serving to stimulate the next. Although some simple habits may be conditioned reflexes, many habits are more complex and not based on reflexes.

Conditioning is probably most important in the early years of life. Some phobias (fears of certain objects, things or situations) may be the result of conditioning; for example, a fear of being in enclosed spaces may have arisen from a frightening experience in early life of being locked up in a cupboard as a punishment for some misdemeanour.

Verbal Learning

Verbal learning refers to learning in which language predominates. Learning to speak is based on attempts to imitate and also on trial and error activity. Verbal skills are to some extent motor as the mechanism of articulate speech is involved and motor skills in man may also have verbal components.

Configuration in Learning

We know from personal experience that all learning is not achieved by trial and error. For example, in solving a mechanical puzzle we make a number of trials without success and then suddenly the solution becomes apparent and the successful action is carried out forthwith. This becomes possible when insight into the solution of the puzzle occurs; i.e. when the parts and the problem are seen as a whole. When we learn a melody we learn it as a whole and it may be recalled entirely even after only a few bars are played. The melody is retained even if all the notes are changed, as happens when it is played in a different key. In other words, we appreciate the parts as having a certain relationship to each other, i.e. belonging to either.

In an experiment in which an animal was placed before two open boxes illuminated by lights of different brightness, one being twice as bright as the other, it was trained to go into the more brightly lit box. Later the brightness was changed but the ratio of brightness was maintained. The animal continued to go to the brighter box indicating that the animal reacts to the total situation, in particular the relationships between the stimuli rather than the stimulus itself.

An experiment by Kohler which has now become classical, was that of a chimpanzee named Sultan who was put in a cage outside which food was placed beyond his reach. Two sticks were placed in front of Sultan; neither stick was long enough to reach the food by itself but they were so constructed that they could be fitted into each other like the pieces of a fishing rod. Sultan tried reaching the banana with his hand, then with each stick separately without success. He then played with the sticks inside the cage and quite suddenly found that they fitted each other. He then immediately, without further trial and error, used the conjoined sticks to bring in the banana.

This method of learning is learning by insight. Insight appears when the various aspects of the situation are seen as a whole, each part having a definite relationship to the other.

In other words, he had learned the appropriate action to reach his goal. The correct action being the last one carried out before the next trial would be more likely to be remembered as it was the most recent.

This is the Law of Recency. Another thing which tends to make the correct action learned is that it was the one achieving the desired effect, i.e. getting out of the cage and obtaining the food. This is expressed in the Law of Effect, which states that an action resulting in reward is the more readily learned than an action not resulting in reward and, associated with discomfort or punishment, will tend not to be repeated.

Motivation in Learning

We have noted that rewards influence learning. In animals, drives arising from basic physiological needs relating to food and sex, etc. are the strongest motives in learning. The strength of motivation will depend on the state of the organism and, in general, the stronger the motivation the more efficient the learning.

Factors influencing Learning

A study of the factors influencing learning is of great practical as well as theoretical interest:

(1) Exercise
(2) Effect
(3) Reward
(4) Incentive

Exercise

The Law of Exercise is pithily expressed in the saying 'practice makes perfect'. The more often we repeat an action or a response to a situation or stimulus, the more firmly and strongly will such an action or response be established. This applies to conditioned reflexes which require a certain number of repetitions before the conditioned reflex becomes established.

All learning activities, e.g. from multiplication tables to serving effectively in tennis, depend on practice. Genius has been said to be 90 per cent perspiration and 10 per cent inspiration.

Rewards are better than punishment but a combination of both are better than either alone.

Competition stimulates learning providing it is not extreme, when it may interfere with it.

Whole versus Part Learning

The question whether it is better to learn material in parts or as a whole is a matter which is continually put forward. Children tend to learn better by part, whereas adults and more intelligent children learn better by whole. If the material is long it may be necessary to break it down in order to learn it. The important thing is that we should learn as large an amount as can be grasped at one time.

Distribution of Learning

It is found that learning is more effective if distributed over a period. Thus, learning to serve in tennis would be less effective if done three times during a day than if the same time were spread over three successive days.

It has been found that learning new material tends to inhibit material learned previously; this effect is called retro-active inhibition and is one of the disadvantages of cramming.

Over-Learning

In order to achieve skills and knowledge which will be retained and made available most efficiently, it is desirable to practice for a longer period than is necessary to learn the action. This is called over-learning and it is found that over-learned material is retained and remembered for the longest time.

Over-learning is clearly seen in the learning of multiplication tables by children. Soldiers in training also have to over-learn various things so that they will be able to carry them out in unfavourable circumstances.

MEMORY

Memory involves three processes:
(1) Registration
(2) Retention
(3) Recall

Registration

Registration is the imprinting of an experience in the mind. Registration will be influenced by the factors governing perception. The more lucid the perception, the better the registration. It will, therefore, be affected by attention and we have noted that the most clearly perceived objects are those in the focus of attention. Concentration and focussing our attention on the task to be learned will greatly influence the quality of registration or impression.

Attention may be interfered with by fatigue, anxiety and pre-occupation. Concentration of attention will also be influenced by interest, motives, mental set, etc. Interest and motive will determine how concentration will be applied and how long sustained. Mental set and attitude will determine what things in particular are registered.

Students often complain that they cannot concentrate. It is usually found that the difficulty in concentration is due to lack of interest or preoccupation with some personal worries. When the worry regarding the problem is resolved, the student is able to study quite easily and concentrate well because these worries no longer distract attention.

Similarly, people in love often have difficulty in concentrating because their minds tend to wander to the beloved person more than the particular work in hand.

Retention

There are marked differences between shorter memory and long term memory. Shorter memory, involving seconds or minutes, is much more easily disturbed during the period immediately following learning. The nature of the memory trace remains unknown.

Recently it has been suggested that storage of information may involve changes in the structure of D.N.A. molecules within the neurones. However, it is also assumed that storage involves either changes in synaptical resistance or the creation of reverberating activity within neural loops.

Memory is more readily disturbed within a few seconds of learning and is more difficult to disturb after more than an hour has elapsed.

Persons show considerable differences in their power of retention. Some people are able to retain almost everything—their minds are like sealing wax on which impressions make a permanent and clear imprint —whereas in others the mind reacts like jelly which, when touched, wobbles but is left with no permanent impression.

Intimately related to retention is the opposite process of forgetting. One of the best studies on the processes of forgetting was carried out by Ebbinghanns. He learned a list of nonsense syllables until he could repeat them correctly. Then he tried to repeat them at intervals of time. It was found that 50 per cent was lost by the first hour, 66 per cent by twenty-four hours and 80 per cent by the end of a month.

Relearning, however, was achieved much more quickly. The reason nonsense syllables were chosen for the study was because they had no association with anything else, enabling the process of retention and forgetting to be studied more simply. Nevertheless, it was soon found that people even with nonsense syllables tried to form association, e.g. some people saw associations between the syllables wed and nag.

In normal life, however, we learn meaningful material and it has been shown that we retain material that is well understood much better than poorly understood facts. In order to improve our ability to retain learned material, we must try to form as many bonds of association as possible. Many schemes for memory training depend on the principle of developing as many associations as possible with material that is being learned.

Retention, of course, will also depend a great deal on how effectively registration is carried out. If the person concentrates well and is interested in the task, retention will be improved. Similarly, practice, repetition and recitation will improve retention.

Recall

The process of recall, or remembering an experience, is quite an active process and is far from being like a photographic reproduction of the experience. The experiments of Bartlett have shown that we tend to remember the main outlines as a frame of reference and that we fill in details and often distort things in the process. In forming the frame of reference, people will tend to select different things from their own experience and, in recalling it, will distort it. For example, the parlour game in which people form a ring and something is whispered into the next person's ear and the message has to be passed from one person to the next all round a circle. The message coming out at the other end is usually totally different from the one going in. The message is continually changed as it is passed on from one person to the other. There is a story of a message sent from the front line—'The General is going to advance, please send re-inforcements'. By the time it got to headquarters it read 'The General is going to a dance, please send three and four pence'.

When people are asked to remember stories at intervals, they also tend to distort the material in various ways such as:

(1) Rationalisation
(2) Conventionalisation
(3) Omissions
(4) Displacements

Rationalisation is the tendency to make the material understandable, reasonable or meaningful. Conventionalisation is the tendency to bring the material within usual or commonplace limits. Omissions are frequently made and material is frequently displaced.

The distortion of material in this way has an important bearing on the validity of the testimony of witnesses in Courts of Law and explains why even well intentioned and sincere witnesses are sometimes quite inaccurate and misleading, even though they do not realise it. This is also why it is desirable for policemen or other people reporting on accidents or events to observe accurately and to commit to paper their observations without delay. The longer the delay, the more likely is distortion to occur.

This also has an important bearing on the writing of medical and other notes. Clinical observations should be recorded immediately and not entered later, when the processes described above may lead to distortion of the material so as to make it fit into some preconceived idea.

Other factors operate also in remembering—thus, we tend to remember pleasant experiences easily, whereas unpleasant or painful experiences tend to be forgotten. This is why, when we look back on our lives, they often appear much more rosy than they actually were.

People often forget to do things that they do not really want to do— this explains the high frequency with which people forget their dentist's appointments, forget to pay back debts or to return borrowed books.

HOW TO IMPROVE EFFICIENCY IN STUDY AND LEARNING

Some of the most important factors in study and learning are Interest, Motivation and Incentive. Motivation refers to a drive from within, whereas incentive refers to the external stimulus.

There is probably an optimum level of anxiety to promote learning. Too much anxiety impairs performance, whereas the person who 'never has a care in the world' is probably operating below his best level.

Planning of Work

The most difficult part of any task is the beginning. One has to overcome inertia to make a start and, in all forms of work, a warming up period is necessary to get accustomed to the task and reach optimum output. Interruptions tend to cause loss of efficiency because the warming up process has to be repeated.

It is important to tackle work when one is fresh and to tackle it with vigour. It is better to work for suitable periods—say one hour to two hours—with intensity and then to take a break before starting again. Attempts to work hour after hour throughout the day or night leads to boredom and fatigue.

Interest, once it develops, tends to continue on its own momentum; this is an example of the operation of the law of autonomous functions. Fatigue can, to some extent, be relieved by changing the task but eventually, general fatigue develops to an extent that change no longer gives relief. It is important to have adequate sleep and periods of recreation in order to maintain alertness and freshness.

Efficiency in the Initial Act of Learning

It is important to work with intensity and concentration so that registration is clear and accurate. Attention and concentration determine the success of registration. Interest, motivations and incentives will stimulate application to work, acuity of attention and concentration and, also, the amount of effort put into the task.

Improvement after the Initial Act of Learning

Revision shortly after learning a particular task is a good thing followed by revision at intervals. Recall, Repetition and Recitation are the keynotes for consolidating what is learned.

A student should develop as many associations as possible with the learned material, both by discussion with fellow students and by further reading. It is desirable to learn in meaningful wholes and as much as one can at a time. It is also desirable to have a basic book to serve as a frame of reference, to which further material and additional associations can be made by reading, discussion and experience.

One of the best ways of imprinting learned material is by committing it to writing. Bacon said ... *'Reading maketh a full man, talking a ready man and writing an exact man'*.

Cramming has disadvantages as it does not give the opportunity to develop adequate associations and it may inhibit recall of material previously learned by the process of retro-active inhibition.

Plan of Work

In planning one's work it is necessary to allow sufficient time for learning and revision. It is essential that the newly learned material has a chance to become linked up with the knowledge one already possesses.

It is also important to give learned material time to be assimilated, as there is evidence that mental activity proceeds below the level of consciousness. Scientists and others have often found that, having been perplexed by a problem for long periods without success by conscious deliberation, they have reached the answer during periods of relaxation —for example, when lying in the bath or going for a walk in the country. This process is termed subconscious elaboration of ideas.

FURTHER READING

Handbook of Tests by C. Burt. Staples Press, London (1949).
Know Your Own I.Q. by H. J. Eysenck. Harmondsworth: Penguin (1962).
Memory Facts and Fallacies by I. M. Hunter. Harmondsworth: Pelican (1958).
Methods of Learning and Techniques of Teaching by J. R. Ellis (Ed.). (1962).
Textbook of Psychology by D. O. Hebb. W. B. Saunders, Philadelphia.
The Structure of Human Abilities by P. E. Vernon. Methuen, London (1950).
Uses and Abuses of Psychology by H. J. Eysenck. Pelican, London (1953).

CHAPTER EIGHT

PERSONALITY

The term personality is frequently used to refer to certain qualities possessed by some people which influence or impress others. This notion of personality is incomplete and superficial.

In psychology the term personality has a wider meaning and refers to the sum total of a person's psychological and physical characteristics which make him a unique person. The term embraces his behavioural tendencies, his intellectual qualities and his emotional disposition.

Character

The term character refers to an evaluation of personality according to some standard whether moral, ethical, religious, social, etc. In describing the person as good, dishonest or wicked we are describing his character.

Temperament

The term temperament refers to the emotional aspects of personality, namely the person's enduring emotional disposition. For example, a person may be anxious, pessimistic or cheerful in temperament.

Two fundamental concepts have operated in the description of personality in the past, namely concepts of types and concepts of traits. A trait of personality is defined as the observed constellation of individual action tendencies. A type may be defined as a group of correlated traits.

Throughout the ages man has tended to classify his fellow beings into types. In the time of Hippocrates and Galen four temperaments were described corresponding to the four humours—blood, black bile, yellow bile and phlegm—and we still use terms derived from this concept, e.g. sanguine, phlegmatic, etc.

Very many classifications of personality type have been proposed in modern times, e.g. Introvert and Extrovert type of Jung and the Schizothymic and Cyclothymic type of Kretschmer.

Whichever typological classification is used, we find no evidence of separate and disparate personality types. Instead there is a continuous gradation from one extreme to its antithesis at the other extreme distributed along the normal frequency curve. For example, with regard to introversion and extroversion the majority of persons are midway between the two extreme types.

As Pope succinctly put it . . . 'Virtuous and vicious all men must be, few in the extreme but all in a degree'.

DETERMINANTS OF PERSONALITY

Personality is the product of the interaction of genetic constitutional (intrinsic) factors and the environmental (extrinsic) factors.

Among the *intrinsic* factors are:

(1) Genotype.
(2) Genotypic milieu.
(3) Constitution comprising physical, physiological and biochemical aspects.
(4) Endocrine influences.
(5) Growth and maturation processes.

Extrinsic factors include:

(1) Parental and family influences.
(2) Social cultural factors.
(3) Life experiences.
(4) Physical or mental handicaps, reaction to illness.

Genetic Factors

Genetic studies in animals and the human have shown that certain emotional and autonomic characteristics are inherited.

The closer similarity in personality between siblings than between unrelated persons and the high correlation found in identical twins in personality attributes testify the importance of heredity. Furthermore, identical twins who have been brought up apart still show a close similarity in personality even when brought up by parent figures of markedly different personality.

The distribution of most measurable personality traits is along the normal frequency curve and this indicates a polygenic mode of inheritance.

Constitution

Constitution denotes the sum total of an individual's morphological, physiological and psychological characteristics determined mainly by heredity.

Physical Constitution

That there is a relationship between mental and moral qualities and physical attributes has been held from ancient times.

Various types of physique are held to be correlated with personality. In Shakespeare we find *'let me have men about me that are fat, sleek headed men and such as sleep at nights'*.

An old proverb says *'Fat and Merry, Lean and Sad'*.

Kretschmer (1921) described the following types of body build:

(1) Asthenic of Leptosomatic characterised by being narrow in relation to length with narrow, shallow thorax with narrow subcostal angle. The limbs are long and the neck slender with a prominent *Adam's apple*. The very marked asthenic person tends to disappear when he turns sideways.

Pyknic type is characterised by large body cavities, relatively short limbs and large subcostal angle with rounded head and short, fat neck.

Athletic type has wide shoulders and narrow hips with well developed bones and muscles.

The leptosomatic and athletic types tend to be associated with shyness, seclusiveness and self-centredness.

The pyknic build is associated with an outgoing, frank, sociable and extraverted personality with a tendency for recurrent changes in mood, varying from depression to elation.

In recent times a number of newer techniques for classifying physique have become available. *Sheldon* in the U.S.A., from a series of standardised photographs, concluded that there were three main components determining the variations in physique which he termed Endomorphy, Mesomorphy and Ectomorphy as he believed that they consisted of structures derived from the three primary germinal layers. Each of these components was rated on a 7-point scale; a person rated as a 711 would be an extreme endomorph and would preponderate in breadth and circumferential measurements compared with length, whereas a 117 would be an extreme ectomorph, would preponderate in length compared with breadth. This system has been criticised because the available data enables the correlations to be explained in terms of two factors instead of three.

The method of factorial analysis has proved fruitful in the study of physique. This consists in taking a random sample of physical measurements, intercorrelating them and then carrying out an analysis to elicit the factors responsible for the correlations. Two factors are usually extracted; (1) A general factor of body size and (2) a factor of physical type, with persons at one extreme being narrow and preponderating in length and at the other extreme broad and of relatively short length.

The distribution of these types, according to the author, using the *Rees-Eysenck* index derived from the results of factorial analysis, was along the normal frequency distribution curve using as arbitrary points of demarcation one standard deviation above and below the mean, three ranges of physique designated the Leptomorph, the Mesomorph and the Eurymorph.

The correlations which have been reported between various physical types, personality and various diseases are given in the following Table.

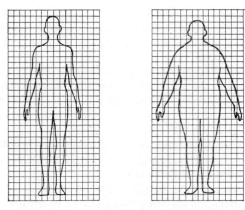

FIG. 2 Some correlates of physical type.

	Author	Linear	Lateral
Typology	Hippocrates	habitus phthisicus	habitus apoplecticus
	Beneke	habitus scrofulous-phthisical	rachito-carcinomatous
	Italian School	microsplanchnic	macrosplanchnic
	Kretschmer	leptosomatic	pyknic
	Rees and		
	Eysenck	leptomorph	eurymorph
	Sheldon	ectomorph	endomorph
Personality		introvert	extravert
characteristics		schizothymic	cyclothymic (syntonic)
		inhibition, anxiety and depressive tendencies	sociability and cheerful emotions
		Form reactions in tests	Colour reactions
		more persevering	less persevering
		quicker tempo	slower tempo
		autonomic instability	greater autonomic stability
Neurosis		anxiety and reactive depression	hysteria
Psychosis		schizophrenia	manic depressive psychosis
Physical disease		duodenal ulcer	gall bladder disease in women
		cardiac neurosis (effort syndrome)	coronary disease
		pulmonary tuberculosis	arterial disease

ENDOCRINE GLANDS

The role of endocrine glands in determining personality has been a subject of much interesting speculation and research. Certain facts are clear. For example, over-action of the thyroid gland makes the person over-active, restless, tense and anxious; personal tempo is increased, there is a general alertness and a quick response to stimuli.

When the thyroid functions inadequately we get the apathy and inertia found in myxoedema, the person is slow and lacking in energy and inactive and he finds everything too much trouble. His skin is dry and his hair tends to fall out. Over-secretion of the cortex of the adrenal gland tends to produce masculinising effects. Women tend to grow beards and to have a husky voice.

Male hormones produced by the adrenal cortex and the testes are responsible for the external secondary sexual characteristics and some of the masculine traits of personality.

It is interesting to note that birds, when living in a group, have a certain peck order. The highest pecks all those below it and so on. If a bird low in the peck order scale is given male sex hormone, it soon gets on top of the scale and pecks other birds who previously pecked *it*.

Similarly, female sex hormones influence mood and interests. When the oestrogen level in the blood is high the women tend to be more active and restless, whereas high progesterone level is associated with a calmer and more receptive attitude.

We may conclude by saying that, whereas endocrine glands can have an important influence on our mental life, emotions and behaviour, the main effects of hormones become apparent when marked deviations from the normal occur. Providing there is a constancy in the internal environment with regard to hormones, endocrines cannot be regarded as one of the more important determinants of personality.

ENVIRONMENTAL FACTORS

In the factors determining personality we can include:
(1) Family influences and early experiences.
(2) School and community influences.
(3) Social and cultural forces.
(4) Personal experiences.
(5) Illnesses, accidents and disabilities.

Family Influences.

We have already seen how important the mother and other members of the family are in determining the child's behaviour reactions.

It is commonly said that the first five years of life are the most important in moulding future personality and character. Normally, personality development in children requires:
(1) Adequate affection and love.
(2) Security.
(3) Consistency in relationships.
(4) Proper balance between stimulus and outlet.

If the family unit is happy and stable and the child is accepted, loved and brought up with consistency, he will have favourable conditions for his personality development and his future adjustment to society will be helped.

Over-protection tends to give rise to timidity and delay in emotional development. Rejection produces a variety of reactions from apathy to resentment and aggression.

Maladjustment and delinquency are sometimes traceable to faulty homes and parental attitude. Similarly, attitude to brothers and sisters, jealousy and undue rivalry can influence the personality of the child.

School and community influences, by education and interpersonal influences influenced the development of character.

Personal Experiences

Experiences in early life can play an important role in determining personality. If the child is deprived of its mother or a satisfactory substitute at an early age, or has not the advantage of a stable family background, he will be at a great disadvantage in personality growth and development.

The reaction of the child to illness to disability may be important. If the child has had to spend any period in bed or in hospital during his childhood and if managed at this time, he may develop an invalid attitude which may affect his adjustment in life and predispose to breakdown under stress.

Reaction to disability

The person's reaction to a disability varies; some reactions are favourable, others are not orbutary.

A person can react to a disability such as paralysis of one or more limbs in the following possible ways:

(1) He can accept the disability and try to compensate for his deficiencies in a way which helps his happiness and adjustment. This method is the most satisfactory.

(2) He may use his disability to avoid taking his proper role in life and to avoid responsibility. He succumbs to the disability and uses it as an excuse for his shortcomings or failures.

(3) He may over-compensate for his disability in an undesirable way such as becoming unduly aggressive, competitive or hostile, or by becoming spiteful and trying to elevate himself by running other people down. He may become sly, spiteful and jealous and become morbid in his personality in this way.

Social-cultural influences play a very important part in determining the characteristics of a race or nation and, to a lesser extent, individual personality differences. The importance of cultural influences in determining personality is strongly borne out by the studies of Ruth Benedict and Margaret Meade.

ASSESSMENT OF PERSONALITY

Personality can be assessed by:
(1) Subjective Methods.
(2) Objective Methods.

Subjective Methods include interview by one person or by a panel, as in Officer Selection procedure in the Forces.

Objective Methods utilise various tests such as:

(1) Questionnaires containing items relating to various aspects of temperament and personality. These are easily applied but are not always reliable or valid.

(2) Projection Tests.

An example of a projection test is the ink blot test of Rorschach. This consists of a series of black ink blots, some of which are also coloured. The ink blots are a plastic medium which the individual alters according to his personality pattern. People react differently to the shape, colour, details, shading etc. Extensive research has now enabled a detailed personality assessment to be made from the person's response.

The Thematic Apperception Test consists of a series of pictures with persons and objects in ambiguous situations. The person is asked to describe how he thinks the situation in the picture was reached, i.e. what events led up to the situation in the picture and what he thinks will be the outcome.

The Rorschach Test is valuable for giving the basic personality pattern and the T.A.T. the mind superficial, motivational and adjustment aspects of personality.

Some Clinical Personality Types

The following are varieties of personality type or traits which are important in clinical practice. They are not mutually exclusive as one person may show a number of traits, e.g. timidity, sensitivity and anxiety often go together.

General Instability

Difficulties in adjustment at school, at home, at work, in marriage, with frequent succession of jobs and a tendency to impulsive behaviour without due regard to the consequences, are all manifestations of emotional immaturity and will be considered in more detail later when we deal with Psychopathic Personality.

Timid Personality

This person shows subnormal assertiveness, is aware of feelings of anger or hostility but has difficulty in verbalising these, even to the physician. This type of person, when he is assertive, experiences anxiety or guilt feelings and subsequently withdraws to his habitual pattern or for a time becomes excessively ingratiating, submissive, apologetic etc.

Sensitive Personality

A tendency to take offence, even when none is intended, being easily hurt and tending to brood over hurts or insults.

Anxious Personality

This person is always worrying unduly, even about trivial matters; he meets troubles half way and anticipates apprehensively problems and difficulties that lie ahead. He crosses his bridges before meeting them; he is tense, apprehensive fearful regarding himself and everything else and constantly in need of reassurance.

Obsessional Personality

This can vary in degree. Obsessional traits consist in meticulousness, over-conscientiousness, attention to detail, a resentment if plans are interfered with. They are tidy, orderly, cannot stand anything out of place, are painstaking, persistent, rigid in habits.

Hysterical Personality

This person craves attention, always wants to be in the limelight, tends to exaggerate, will manipulate people and situations in order to get the attention and affection they crave for. They are excessively demanding and dominating, their emotions tend to be superficial and they are, in general unreliable.

Schizothymic (Introverted) Personality

A schizothymic person is shy, reserved, has difficulty in making social contacts and in communicating with others. He prefers to be solitary when in trouble, tends to be awkward, tense and rather inhibited.

Cyclothymic (Extraverted) Personality

These are outgoing persons, express themselves freely, make social contacts easily, are warm, friendly. In the cyclothymic person, mood swings varying from mild depression to elation are common but sometimes their mood is equable; this is referred to as the syntonic personality.

S.T.P.—3

Clinical Description of Personality

In describing a patient's personality, he should be described as a living person; his attitudes, conduct and general demeanour and, when significant, his attitude towards the life situation and his illness. It should give into account his aspirations, goals and whether these are realistic, his drive and energy, special skills; his affective disposition, his interpersonal relationships, his attitude towards others, whether he is excessively dependent or tends to deny dependent needs, becoming emotionally detached, or whether he is actively aggressive and immature. His attitude to himself, what degree there is of self-absorption or egocentricity; what his views are of himself, the basis of his self-esteem and confidence and the specific areas of failure of self-esteem; his goals and actual achievements, to what degree do they coincide, to what degree is there a discrepancy. His capacity for rapport, his interests.

FURTHER READING

Handbook of Abnormal Psychology by H. J. Eysenck. Pitman, London (1960).

CHAPTER NINE

EMOTIONS AND STRESS

DEFINITION

Emotions (Affects) are more or less intense feelings with the following components:
  (1) Affective (feeling) aspect.
  (2) Cognitive (knowing) aspect.
  (3) Behavioural changes.
  (4) Bodily concomitants.
    (a) Facial expression, posture and mobility.
    (b) Changes in neurohumoral functions and autonomic activity.

Watson, from his studies of infants, concluded that there were only three innate emotional reactions—fear, rage and love. Fear could be aroused by loud sounds or sudden removal of support, rage by hampering the infant's movements and love by gentle stroking or rocking.

Babies were found to have no inborn fear of snakes, rats etc. and only developed fears of these objects by learning (conditioning). One of the babies studied by Watson played with a rat without fear; subsequently a loud noise was made when he was playing with the rat and the child showed the natural fear reaction to the noise. After the loud sound had been repeated a number of times in the presence of the rat the baby developed a fear reaction to the rat itself. The child subsequently showed fear reaction, not only to rats but to all furry objects.

Watson maintained that all emotions were derived by conditioning from the three primary emotions of love, fear and anger.

PHYSICAL ASPECTS OF EMOTIONS

It would indeed be difficult to imagine emotions without their physical accompaniments.

A theory that emotions were the conscious appreciation of body changes was put forward in 1886 by William James in America and shortly afterwards by Lange, a Danish psychologist.

Common sense tells us that when in danger we feel afraid and then run, or we feel angry and then strike our opponent. This sequence is wrong, according to the James-Lange theory, who considered the proper sequence is that we run away and feel afraid, anger follows physical action.

The James-Lange theory is not accepted nowadays and there is convincing evidence against it:

(1) The physical concomitants of widely different emotional states are often similar.

(2) There is not sufficient range or diversity of physical change to account for the variety of emotional experiences.

(3) Sherrington was able to show that in dogs on which autonomic connections between head and body were severed, and also when the spinal cord in the neck region was divided so that all forms of sensation between somatic tissues and viscera were cut off from the head region, all emotional reactions were manifest as in intact dogs.

(4) The example of a patient with a cervical injury which resulted in completely cutting off sensations from the body, in fact felt all emotions as he used to previously.

Emotions, therefore, are not dependent on peripheral stimuli and in fact can be experienced in the absence of such stimuli.

Emotions are always the reactions of the total organism.

STRESS

The term stress in medicine and biology today is used in a number of different ways. It may refer to external forces or conditions experienced by the organism, or to the reaction of the organism to these. When applied to external forces the term stress is similar to its use in physics and applies to an external stimulus or force which is strain-producing, or potentially strain-producing, to the person to whom it is applied. Anything may be considered a stress if it threatens the biological integrity of the organism, whether directly by its physical or chemical properties or indirectly because of its symbolic meaning.

Selye uses the term 'a state of stress' to denote a specific syndrome occurring in the body in response to certain agents to which he refers as stressors.

In medicine and psychiatry the term stress is usually used to denote various psychosocial situations which can produce disorganisation of behaviour, including physical and mental illnesses.

A convenient definition of stress is any stimulus or change in the external or internal environment which disturbs homeostasis which, under certain conditions, can result in illness.

Adaptability and resistance to the effects of stressful stimuli are fundamental prerequisites for life and survival.

Stresses cannot be considered in isolation. We need to know what stimuli or situations are potentially stressful and we need to know the effect produced by such stresses on the organism and, finally, the pathways and mechanisms mediating the organism's response to stresses.

PATHWAYS MEDIATING THE REACTIONS OF THE ORGANISM'S RESPONSES TO EMOTIONAL CHANGES AND VARIOUS STRESSES

Three principal systems are involved:
(1) The Autonomic Nervous System.
(2) The Neuro-endocrine System.
(3) The Neuromuscular System.

The autonomic nervous system and the neuro-endocrine system are concerned with maintaining the relative constancy of the internal environment of the body (homeostasis) whereas the neuromuscular system is concerned with the organism's external reactions to the external environment, including behaviour in its many facets. The co-ordination of these three systems to various stresses and emotional changes is complex and illustrates the psychosomatic unity of the organism, and these reactions are of vital importance to adaptation and survival.

The Autonomic Nervous System

The autonomic nervous system has two main divisions, the sympathetic and the parasympathetic, and both these divisions are controlled by higher centres at various levels in the brain.

The sympathetic nervous system arises from the thoracic and first three lumbar segments of the spinal cord, whereas the parasympathetic arises in its cranial part from the cranial nerves 3, 7, 9 and 10 and in its sacral part from the 2nd and 3rd sacral nerves.

The sympathetic and parasympathetic nervous systems are anatomically and physiologically distinct. The sympathetic nervous system is principally concerned with the mobilisation of the organism's resources to deal with emergencies or threats. Most of the functions of the sympathetic nervous system deal with increasing alertness, reactivity and increasing the efficiency of the organism to deal with a threat by action, whether it be by fight or flight. The parasympathetic nervous system, on the other hand, is concerned with repair and restitution; whereas the sympathetic nervous system tends to discharge and function en masse, as it were, the parasympathetic has a more discrete function supplying certain organs, glands, tissues and functions.

It is very important to remember that in certain emotional states both sympathetic and parasympathetic manifestations may appear, particularly when they serve the needs of the organism for survival; for example, during marked fear the bladder and bowel may be emptied, along with generalised sympathetic over-activity. This gets rid of unnecessary weight, thus increasing efficiency of activity to deal with emergencies.

With regard to effect on functions of individual organs and tissues, the sympathetic and parasympathetic tend to have antagonistic actions as shown in the Table below.

When we consider the role of emotions in the aetiology of various physical illnesses, both sympathetic and parasympathetic nervous systems will be seen to play an important role.

Neuro-endocrine Mechanisms

Adaptability and the development of resistance to the effects of stresses and noxic stimuli are prerequisites for life and survival. Such adaptation may involve specific defence reactions as exemplified by the development of specific antibodies to allergens, the mechanisms involved in adaptation to cold or to life at high altitudes and the hypertrophy of muscles which are subjected to prolonged heavy work.

Adaptation may be non-specific as described by *Selye* in the form of a general adaptation syndrome.

THE GENERAL ADAPTATION SYNDROME

Selye of Montreal described a syndrome of adaptation to non-specific stresses which he referred to as the General Adaptation Syndrome (G.A.S. for short). G.A.S. has three stages: (1) The alarm reaction with two component phases of shock and countershock, (2) the stage of resistance and (3) the stage of exhaustion.

Alarm Reaction

The phase of shock is mediated by neural mechanisms involving the sympathetic nervous system stimulating the medulla of the adrenal gland. Similarly, higher centres stimulate the anterior and posterior lobes of the pituitary, which increase production of ACTH from the anterior lobe of the pituitary and a hormone controlling water balance from the posterior pituitary.

The phase of shock is followed by the phase of countershock in which the various changes occurring in shock are reversed.

Stage of Resistance

This is characterised by hypertrophy of the adrenal cortex, increased parasympathetic activity, increased secretion of glucocorticoids from the adrenal cortex and increased secretory activity of the thyroid, Islets of Langerhans and, in general, increased protein anabolism.

Stage of Exhaustion

When exposure to the stressor is sufficiently prolonged and severe, the adaptation which has been developed is no longer maintained and this leads to the changes which comprise the stage of exhaustion.

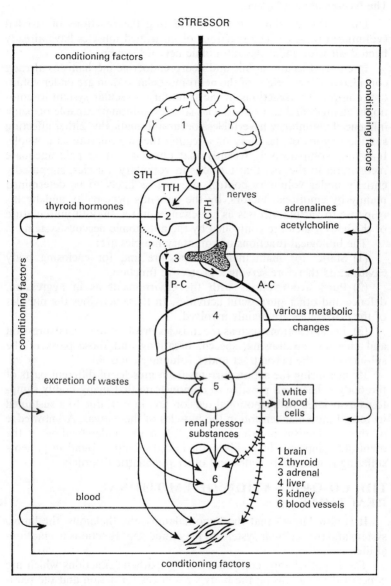

FIG. 3 Mechanisms of the General Adaptation Syndrome (G.A.S.)

The Neuromuscular System

Under this heading we are considering the reactions of striated (voluntary) muscles. The reactions of unstriated muscles have already been dealt with under the autonomic nervous system.

In contrast to autonomic and neuro-endocrine mechanisms already considered, the reactions of the neuromuscular system are under voluntary control. The reactions in the voluntary muscular system to emotional changes and to psychosocial stresses, although capable of being influenced voluntarily nevertheless occur automatically, either affecting specific regions of the body or affecting the musculature as a whole. It is only comparatively recently that physicians have paid adequate recognition to the fact that tensions in voluntary muscles, supposedly entirely under voluntary control, are just as likely to be determined mainly by emotional factors, by the patient's personality and by his response to various stresses as are changes in the smooth musculature of the body which are controlled by the autonomic nervous system.

The biological functions of voluntary muscles are:

(1) Static, for maintanance of posture and for enclosing body cavities and therefore serving a protective function.

(2) Purposive relations with the environment as in aggression, defence and other purposeful activities. In these activities the muscles of the extremities are mainly involved.

(3) Local reactions such as the muscles involved in facial expression and chewing, swallowing, speech, breathing and those parts of the sphincters of the pelvic tract under voluntary control.

By measuring the action currents from muscles of different parts of the body it has been possible to demonstrate that many bodily symptoms associated with emotional tension are, in fact, due to a sustained increased muscular tension in the muscles of these areas. A knowledge of this mechanism is extremely helpful in the understanding of the manifold symptoms of bodily pains and disabilities found in patients suffering from anxiety states and other psychiatric disorders.

THE CO-ORDINATION OF EMOTIONAL REACTIONS

It is now known that the hypothalamus, the thalamus, the limbic system and the reticular system all play important functions in emotional life.

The hypothalamus controls both sympathetic functions which are concerned in mobilising the body's resources for action and the parasympathetic which is concerned with restitution and repair.

In the limbic system the amygdala complex is concerned with food intake, i.e. the preservation of the body, and the septal area with sexual and reproductive activities, i.e. the preservation of the species.

The reticular system integrates sensory modalities and is concerned with wakefulness.

All these structures are interconnected in the form of reverberating circuits.

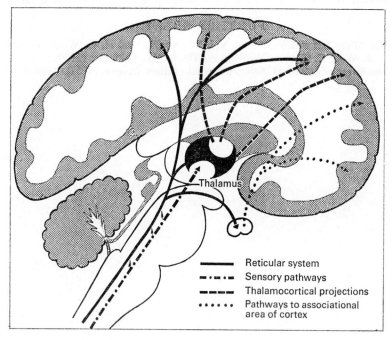

FIG. 4

The famous circuit described by Papez is as follows:

Hippocampus → Hypothalamus
↑　　　　　　　↓
Cortex ← Thalamus

This circuit is concerned with reactions related to emotions attaining awareness.

The reticular system is connected to some of these structures as follows:

Reticular system → Hypothalamus
↓
Amygdala and Septal area

By means of these circuits the functions of self-preservation and species-preservation can enlist the hypothalamus in support of their functions. Similarly, these circuits linking the reticular system, hypothalamus, hippocampus, thalamus and cortex serve to mobilise the body resources in times of danger and stress.

Many of the patent psychotropic drugs used in treating various mental illnesses exert their main actions on these important structures.

FURTHER READING

Life Stress and Bodily Disease, Vol. XXIX; (Editors) H. G. Wolff, Stewart E. Wolf, C. C. Hare. Williams & Wilkins Co., Baltimore (1950).
The Stress of Life by H. Selye. Longmans Green, London (1957).

CHAPTER TEN

SLEEP AND DREAMING

Sleep is essential for health and for mental and physical well-being. Our knowledge of its nature is scanty not even why it is necessary for us to spend at least one third of our lives asleep.

Throughout the animal kingdom there are periodic sleep-wakefulness periods. During development the sleep-wakefulness relationship changes, and in the adult more wakefulness is possible during the 24 hours which approximates a fourfold increase on that of early childhood. The newborn child has two hours sleep for an hour of wakefulness, whereas the adult has half an hour's sleep for the same period.

Changes during the Period immediately before Sleeping

Some persons slip into sleep with great ease and rapidity, others more gradually and some experience unusual sensations. Jerking movements are common at the point of falling off to sleep and many people experience hypnagogic phenomena, such as fleeting visual hallucinations or voices or changes in body image or feelings of floating in space.

Changes during Sleep

The most obvious change during sleep is generalised inertia and muscular relaxation. Not all muscles, however, relax; the eyeball exhibits rapid movements during dreams and at intervals limbs are moved and many changes of posture occur during the night. Sleepers usually change their position 25 to 40 times during the night, irrespective of the depth or shallowness of sleep. Blood flow through muscles is decreased but blood flow through the skin is increased. The skin is flushed and the sweat glands function freely. It is for these reasons that the body tends to lose heat quickly during sleep. Heart rate and blood pressure falls, breathing is slower, deeper and more regular. Relaxation of the jaw and throat muscles is responsible for snoring.

Levels of Depth of Sleep

Depth of sleep can be monitored by recordings of the electro-encephalogram, eye movements, blood pressure, heartbeat etc. Recent work has shown that there are three to five distinct stages from the onset of sleep to very deep sleep. Dreaming occurs in the shallow levels of sleep.

The following stages usually take place: When one is falling asleep, thoughts become inconsequential, reveries or visual images pass through the mind. This is followed then by a more rapid passage into deep sleep reaching the deepest level of sleep for the entire night. This deep sleep period lasts half an hour. Then there is a gradual lightening of sleep, reaching the lightest stage of sleep about 70 minutes after falling asleep. It is during this stage of light sleep that the first dreaming spell occurs and lasts about 10 minutes. This is followed by a deeper phase of sleep but not quite so deep as the first. This is followed during the third hour of sleep by a lighter phase with a second and more protracted spell of dreaming. The third spell of dreaming occurs in the fifth or sixth hour of sleep and lasts for 25 minutes. In the seventh hour there is another spell of light sleep and dreaming for another hour or so.

Recordings of eyeball movements have been found to be a reliable indicator of active dreaming. During sleep the eyes usually make slow movements, the eyeball being directed upwards and inwards, but from time to time bursts of rapid eye movements occur (R.E.Ms.) side to side or up and down movements which may last 20 minutes or more. If the person is woken during a spell of rapid eye movements (R.E.Ms.)and a tape recorder description made of whether he has been dreaming or not, it reveals that on the large majority of occasions the rapid eye movements, coincide with dreams.

Most people probably have a series of dreams throughout the night separated by deeper, dreamless sleep; this applies even to those who firmly assert that they never dream.

Sleep Deprivation

During recent years studies have been carried out on the mental and behavioural effects of depriving a person from sleeping. A critical period of sleep deprivation is 100 to 120 hours, after which a characteristic abnormal mental state develops. This is preceded by a prodromal phase which develops during the first 4 or 5 days without sleep and is characterised by a progressive increase in drowsiness and by brief lapses of awareness (these are micro-sleeps which last only a few seconds).

There is an increasing tendency to stare; auditory sensations increase as the prodromal phase continues, with feelings of pressure bands on the head, tingling feelings in the skin, noises in the ears, a decrease in vigilance, a growing sense of fatigue, drowsiness and disinterest.

On the fifth night a 'psychotic' syndrome develops with gross disturbances of reality, testing which may persist for varying periods of time. Hallucinatory experiences become more prolonged and vivid, the person's facial expression is elongated and immobile, brows are furrowed and he has a great effort to keep his eyes open. There is intermittent clouding of consciousness and disorientation for time, then place and person. Paranoid ideas are common.

By night the picture resembles a delirious state. During the daytime the picture somewhat resembles paranoid schizophrenia.

When the person eventually sleeps he is usually likely to sleep for 12 to 15 hours and during this period dreaming occurs frequently and quickly, as if the person is catching up not only with his sleep but also his dreams.

Recent work in fact has demonstrated that a certain amount of dreaming each night is a necessity for health. When persons were prevented from dreaming by being deliberately awakened at the commencement of their R.E.M. periods, it was found that there was a marked increase in percentage dream-time on subsequent recovery nights of undisturbed sleep. It was also found that such dream-deprived subjects became unhappy and ill at ease.

Content and Meaning of Dreams

Freud was able to demonstrate that dreams had a manifest content which were derived from events of the preceding day or from the person's life which were not very revealing, but that there was also a latent content which can be revealed by getting the dreamer to free-associate to the manifest content of the dream.

A number of processes occur in dreams which are collectively referred to as a dream-work. For example, condensation is common, e.g. parts of a number of people may be all condensed into one person.

Displacement is another mechanism; important or serious happenings may be made to appear trivial and vice versa.

Ideas are usually presented in a concrete form and usually in images, and often in the term of symbols. For example, dreaming about missing the bus may stand for letting an opportunity pass by.

There are some symbols which tend to be universal; for example, sharp, pointed objects like daggers, swords, steeples usually denote male sexuality, whereas caves, tunnels, jewel boxes refer to the female.

At the point of waking dreams tend to be distorted in order to be made meaningful or worked up into a story; this is the process of secondary elaboration. If one intends analysing dreams it is important that the patient should have pencil and paper ready to jot down the dream as early as possible to avoid the distorting effect of secondary elaboration and to avoid the very rapid forgetting of dreams.

Dissociation of Sleep

Sometimes various components of activity may be dissociated from sleep such as:

(1) *Somnambulism*, in which the body is awake and the mind is asleep.

(2) *Sleep paralysis*, where the mind is awake and the body is asleep.

(3) *Sleep terror:* usually a child wakes up in a state of marked terror with amnesia for the experience afterwards.

(4) *Hypnagogic and hypnapompic phenomena.* Various perceptual disturbances can occur at the point of going off to sleep and are referred to as hypnagogic, and if they occur at the point of waking up they are referred to as hypnopompic. The phenomena include disturbances in body image, visual hallucinations and auditory hallucinations. Illusions are quite common just as people drop off to sleep.

FURTHER READING

Sleep by Ian Oswald. Penguin, Harmondsworth (1966).

CHAPTER ELEVEN

PERCEPTION

Perception is the process whereby a meaning is given to a sensation produced by sensory stimulation.

Perceiving involves both the awareness and the recognition of meaningful sensory stimuli. It is an active process whereby present experience is related to past experience and given a meaning.

Perception involves a two way process of organism-environment interaction. This interaction is an active process throughout life and it is believed that perceptual mechanisms are slowly established by initial learning in childhood but that, later, the established mechanism permits more rapid learning in new situations.

Properties of the Stimuli

Perception depends on sensory data, both from the environment and from within the body. An interesting example is provided of the role of internal stimuli when a person wears an inverting prism; everything appears upside down at first but, after a period of about 8 days, the world becomes normally oriented.

The process of perception is often a response to change in the environment. For example, at the surface of the earth there is a pressure of 15lbs. in each square inch of our bodies and yet we feel nothing; but if 15lbs. *more* pressure were applied to one square inch we would perceive it acutely.

Perceiving is selective. At any given moment hundreds of stimuli are impinging on our sense organs; the organism has to select the particular one to which he will attend.

OBJECTIVE FACTORS IN PERCEPTION

The sense organs and the brain together organise a number of stimuli into a larger unit to which the organism may respond in a simple fashion.

The grouping together of stimuli by the brain is based on a number of principles:

(1) *Similarity*

	A		B

```
          A                       B
    .  o  .  o  .  o        .  .  .  .  .  .
    .  o  .  o  .  o        o  o  o  o  o  o
    .  o  .  o  .  o        .  .  .  .  .  .
    .  o  .  o  .  o        o  o  o  o  o  o
    .  o  .  o  .  o        .  .  .  .  .  .
    .  o  .  o  .  o        o  o  o  o  o  o
```

In A we perceive the dots and circles running vertically and in B horizontally. This is because stimuli which are similar tend to be grouped together.

(2) *Proximity*. In the following series;　　00　　　　　　　0 we see the near circles as a pair.

(3) *Closure*

The following 8 lines (A) appear as separate units with little tendency to be grouped:

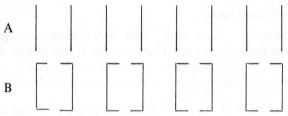

If a short line is added to the ends of the lines as in B, we now see them as 4 pairs of incomplete squares.

(4) *Symmetry*

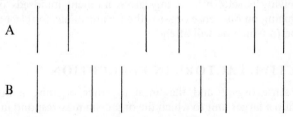

In A proximity makes us group the lines into pairs. In B the end lines are paired, not because of proximity but because of symmetry.

The mind likes to group stimuli into wholes—a tendency seen by the principle of closure.

(5) *Good continuation*

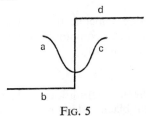

FIG. 5

Fig. 5 is seen as a curved line and a line with two right angle bends, although proximity would tend to link a with b, or c with d.

This principle was made use of in camouflage of factories, aeroplanes etc. during the war. The 'good continuity' of the outline was broken up in the camouflaging process by wavy lines and coloured patches, thus tending to make the object merge with the surrounding land when seen from the air.

Thus, we tend to perceive any change and we select stimuli which tend to be grouped into a simple pattern or unit.

SUBJECTIVE FACTORS IN PERCEPTION

The actual object, thing or stimuli perceived is influenced by the attention of the subject. Attention will be attracted by the intensity of the stimulus, e.g. a very loud noise, the nature, location, colour, movement, repetition or unusualness of the stimulating conditions.

Subjective factors influencing attention and perception include:

(1) Needs.
(2) Interest.
(3) Desires.
(4) Attitude and mental set.
(5) Mood.

Need

When we are hungry we will pay particular attention to things related to food.

Interests

We all do not necessarily see or perceive the same things. Thus, if a geologist, artist and botanist went for a walk together and were asked to describe the walk after, the respective accounts would probably differ considerably and to such an extent that one might think they had been on different walks. The geologist would describe the conformation of the land, the type of rocks seen etc., the botanist would pay particular attention to the plants, trees and flowers seen, whereas the artist would notice features of beauty or artistic interest.

Mental Set

When we are meeting someone from a train and as we scan the crowds along the platform, we commonly mistake people in the distance for the person we are waiting for.

Mood

Our moods also influence our outlook and perception. When we are sad things tend to appear black and unpromising and when we are happy the same things take on a different and more pleasing appearance.

There is much truth in the old saying 'we see things not as they are but as we are'.

ANOMALIES OF PERCEPTION

Illusions

An illusion is a misinterpretation of a stimulus. There are four types of illusion:

(1) *Optical Illusions*. Experienced by everyone, irrespective of emotional state. These include the Muller–Lyer and Danzio illusions, as seen from the diagrams, where one of the lines is longer due to the position of the neighbouring lines. In the Muller–Lyer illusion the diverging end lines make the line look longer and in the Danzio illusion the converging lines are typical perspective lines, giving a depth effect and setting the scaling for size accordingly.

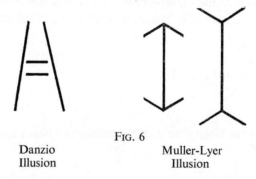

Fig. 6

Danzio   Muller-Lyer
Illusion   Illusion

(2) *Illusions due to lack of attention and concentration*. We have noted that many subjective factors can influence what is perceived.

In reading we quickly scan the written word and, if not sufficiently attentive, we may make a mistake. We overlook misprints and interpret the meaning according to the general context.

Some illusions in Delirium. Subdelirium and Dementia are of this type. The way in which a person recalls the experience may also distort the reported perception.

(3) *Emotionally determined Illusions.* Whilst walking home in the countryside in the dark, many people have experienced the misinterpretation of shadows, trees and other objects as human figures or animals.

In depressive states with feelings of guilt and the conviction that punishment is rightly coming, various stimuli may be misinterpreted as the police coming for them.

Illusions of this kind are usually fleeting and understood in terms of the prevailing mood at the time.

(4) *Pareidolia.* This form of illusion arises from ill-formed stimuli such as the flames in the fire, clouds in the sky, patterns on curtains, patchy walls etc.

Emotions do not come into this type and the person knows it is not real but a product of imaginatory activity.

Hallucinations

Hallucinations are the experiencing of a perception with more or less sensory vividness in the absence of the relevant stimulus. They are false perceptions which are not distortions of real perceptions and may occur along with normal perceptions.

Hallucinations vary in complexity, from simple sounds or flashes of light to complex and highly differentiated perceptions.

They may occur in a setting of clear consciousness as in schizophrenia or in clouded consciousness as in delirium and confusional states.

Observer Error

Clinical skill depends on the ability to perceive similarities between members of the same class and differences from members of a different class. In the wards we must perceive features indicative of a particular illness and how it significantly differs from the normal and even from other persons with the same illness.

These similarities and differences are perceived via the sense organs. We have noted the variety of factors which can influence what is perceived. Even carrying out straightforward readings such as that of a burette are found to be influenced by expectations. The observer unwittingly moved his head up or down to get the preferred result, whether this was derived from a previous estimation or from knowledge of the expected result.

Similarly, in reading X-rays a wide variation was found, even among highly qualified physicians.

Errors will be minimised by:

(1) Knowledge of what there is to see.

In detecting signs of disease a knowledge of what is to be found will make its discovery more likely.

(2) Concentration and alertness will facilitate accurate perception.

(3) Avoid prejudging the case, as we may overlook features which do not fit in and only perceive those which support our preconceived idea of the disorder.

(4) Improved methods of records and measurement will also minimise the likelihood of error.

The physician should be familiar with all these above factors which influence accuracy of perception if he is to improve and perfect his clinical skill.

BODY IMAGE

The body image, or body schema, is the plastic tridimensional perception of the body at the fringe of consciousness.

The image we have of our body is not provided in ready-made form but is gradually built up during childhood.

By the age of 9 months the child is able to distinguish himself from the environment but it is not until the age of 2 years that he learns to appreciate himself as a unit.

The body image is gradually built up out of various perceptive elements, viz. proprioceptive, vestibular, visual, superficial and deep sensibility.

The orifices of the body are the first clearly demarcated limits of the body image.

Play is an important factor in helping to form the body image. It is unlikely that the body image is fully developed until the age of 8 years.

The three cardinal factors which contribute to the formation of the body image are visual factors, tactile impulses and proprioceptive stimuli. All are usually important but none is essential; a blind person will have his own type of body image. which will be determined by tactile and proprioceptive impulses.

In patients who have lost a limb, all three factors are excluded, i.e. there is no limb to be seen and the proprioceptive and tactile stimuli no longer ascend from the periphery yet, despite this, a phantom sensation of the limb persists, thus keeping the integrity of the body image.

Pathological Changes of the Body Image

Any type of pain or discomfort is liable to cause the affected part to loom largely in the body schema. Patients suffering from Buerger's disease complained that the affected leg felt bigger and heavier compared with the good one.

Some patients, after anaesthesia or during toxic infective states or at the point of going off to sleep, experience disturbances of the body image various parts appearing larger, smaller or otherwise changed in size or shape.

Sometimes the body image may be projected outwards, the so called somatic doubling. The projected body image may be similar or different in size and characteristics from the person's normal body image. This can occur during narcosis or in states of fatigue, with hypnosis and in states of intoxication.

Disturbances in body image can also occur in neurological disorders, particularly lesions of the parietal lobe, especially the left side. One such disorder characterised by finger agnosia, acalculia and agraphia is known as Gerstman's syndrome.

An allied condition to somatic doubling is when the patient has the mental impression, but does not have an actual hallucination of body, that he is not alone. This occurs in states of exhaustion, hunger, thirst or loneliness; it has been described by antarctic explorers, ship-wrecked sailors and by climbers marooned on the Alps, and is known as the Capgras syndrome.

Vestibular disturbances can also affect the body image and produce distortions of part of the body image or may cause somatic doubling.

Disturbances of the body image also occur with states of sensory deprivation and with drugs such as Sernyl, which produce effects similar to sensory deprivation, and with hallucinogenic drugs such as Mescaline–Lysergic acid.

The Effects of Prolonged Sensory and Perceptual Deprivation

The Central Nervous System is not only bombarded by stimuli from visual, auditory, tactile and kinaesthetic and other sense modalities. Great interest has been devoted in recent years to the study of the effects of reduction in environmental stimulation. Professor Hebb was the first to investigate the matter thoroughly, as he wished to understand the mechanisms underlying brain-washing and the lapses of attention which occur under monotonous environmental conditions. The results of his researches were startling. The subjects who were paid to do nothing except to lie in a cubicle and wear translucent goggles became hallucinated, deluded and had distortions of the body image; they became disturbed and emotional.

There are two main forms of reduction of sensory and environmental stimulation:

(1) *Sensory deprivation*, in which the sensory input from the outside world is as low as possible, using dark, soundproof rooms and keeping the subject by himself and lying quietly. Ear plugs or ear muffs are used and communication between subject and experimenter is minimal.

(2) *Perceptual deprivation* attempts to reduce the patterning and organisation of sensory import while maintaining the level of input nearly normal.

In perceptual deprivation the subject lies in a cot in a cubicle with translucent goggles, which permit diffuse light to enter the eyes but eliminate all pattern vision. A masking sound (white noise) is piped into both ears. White noise is produced by mixing together tones with frequencies from the whole range of audibility, in equal amounts.

The Effects of Sensory Deprivation

(1) *Affective changes include* panic, fear and anxiety, depression and irritability.

(2) *Changes in perception:* the room appears to alter in size and contour. Pronounced negative 'after' images occur.

(3) *Changes in perceptual motor skills*, a significant decline in rotary perceptibility and also gross motor skill, e.g. a rail-walking test was adversely affected, especially after 72 hours of sensory deprivation.

(4) *Time* was usually over-estimated by half an hour to three hours.

(5) *Changes in level of consciousness.* In all the lengthy periods of deprivation, subjects passed varying periods in sleep.

(6) *Level of attention.* Inability to concentrate was frequent.

(7) *Cognitive efficiency.* Abstract thinking, distortion of thinking, concentration was diminished or lost with lack of clarity in thinking, difficulty in organising thoughts.

(8) *Disturbance of body image.*

(9) *Imagery*, auditory phenomena like voices, visual, day-dreams to hallucinatory experiences, kinaesthetic tacta, gestatory and olfactory images.

(10) Some experimenters found *sensitivity feelings* of a rather paranoid character.

(11) *Somatic complaints*, complaints of weakness etc.

These effects sometimes last for over 24 hours after the completion of the experiment. Gross visual disturbance usually disappear quickly.

The reticular activating system, situated at the cross roads of input and output systems, is able to sample and monitor all such activities. If the reticular system is deprived of its sensory input, it meets an unfamiliar situation. It is believed that this change accounts for the manifestations of sensory deprivation. This adaptive capacity of the normal brain depends on sensory input to maintain its reality-adapted activity.

Interference with input allows function to continue but it tends to become increasingly out of phase. It is interesting that Sernyl, a drug which interferes with sensory input if given under conditions of sensory deprivation, did not result in its somatic and psychological sequelae.

FURTHER READING

A Textbook of Psychology by D. O. Hebb. W. B. Saunders, London (1958).

CHAPTER TWELVE

SCHOOLS OF PSYCHOPATHOLOGY

Psychoanalysis and Related Schools

The historical development of psychological methods of treatment up to the discoveries of *Freud* was briefly outlined in Chapter One.

Sigmund Freud, born in 1856, studied physiology after qualifying as a doctor and later devoted his attention to neurology. In 1885 *Freud* went to Paris to work under *Charcot*, who had impressed him greatly with the use of hypnosis as a method of treating hysteria.

Freud, however, found hypnotic suggestion, by itself, to be of limited value. In collaboration with *Joseph Breuer* who, incidentally, had also started his career as a physiologist, he developed a method of treating patients in which they were allowed to talk out their emotional difficulties during hypnosis.

Under hypnosis the patient was able to remember past experiences more clearly and to release emotions associated with forgotten experiences. *Breuer* and *Freud* were impressed by the curative effect of talking out difficulties and referred to the process as mental catharsis. The term abreaction was used to denote the liberation of emotion whilst talking about emotional problems and experiences.

Both *Breuer* and *Freud* found that, during treatment by these methods, some female patients appeared to fall in love with them. This alarmed *Breuer* but *Freud* soon realised that it was not his own personality that was attractive but merely that he was serving as a substitute for the original person they loved. The love was transferred to the physician and this process was referred to as 'transference' which *Freud* dealt with by maintaining an impersonal attitude and, in fact, utilised the transference reaction in the resolution of problems and promoting recovery.

Freud discontinued hypnosis and instead instructed patients to relax in a reclining position and to talk freely about their problems. This method was referred to as free association and patients were encouraged to tell everything that came into their minds, even if it appeared embarrassing, ridiculous, irrelevant or unimportant.

In order to facilitate and expedite progress achieved by free association, *Freud* also used interpretation of the patient's dreams, again using free association. He found that there were many suppressed desires and complexes and that these were often of a sexual nature. Sex desires when in conflict with the requirements of society were repressed.

Freud found that exploring deeper and further back into the patient's history was more effective in treating his patients. Many patients re-called emotional shocks in childhood, often of a sexual nature and related sexual assaults by relatives. *Freud* realised that many of these accounts were fantasy rather than fact.

The main pillars of Freudian doctrine are:

(1) The role of the unconscious.

(2) The libido theory of psychosexual development.

(3) Psychic determination and goal-motivated behaviour.

STRUCTURE OF THE MIND

(1) *The id.* The term id is the term applied to basic drives, instinctive drives such as those concerned with survival, sex and aggression. The id demands immediate satisfaction and is ruled by the pleasure-pain principle and is illogical. It is non-verbal and does not enter conscious-ness.

(2) *The ego* is conscious and attempts to be the mediator between the drives derived from the id and the outer world. It is influenced by the super-ego.

(3) *The super-ego* arises out of the ego by a process of learning from experience to deal with the needs of society. It is mainly unconscious. The super-ego is composed of the conscience, the ego ideal and is derived from primitive conditioning.

The ego is concerned with reality testing, discrimination, integration, adaptation, learning, consciousness, reason, intellect, memory, judg-ment and will power.

Libido Theory and Psychosexual Development

The term libido is used to describe sexual drives in the widest sense and includes pleasurable sensations relating to bodily functions.

The libido can be attached to a variety of objects and undergoes development through different phases.

Freud described the following stages of psychosexual development:

(1) *Auto-erotic:* that is pleasurable sexual feelings resulting from stimulation of the body, subdivided into the oral phase which starts at birth and continues for about 18 months. It is divided into a receptive phase and later a sadistic phase when the child acquires teeth and be-comes more aggressive.

(2) *The anal phase* develops during the first year and continues until approximately 3 years.

(3) *Genital erotism.*

(4) *Alloerotic.*

1. The Oedipus situation in boys where the libido is directed towards the mother; the father is seen as a rival and hostile thoughts are develop-ed towards him.

In girls the corresponding situation is referred to as the Electra complex.

(5) *The latency period* is said to exist between the ages of 7 and 12 years. During this time the oedipus situation is resolved and a stronger super-ego is developed as a result.

In adolescence sex interest is re-awakened, with interest sometimes in the same sex followed or accompanied by heterosexual drives.

The libido may, therefore, be directed to the body and if it consists in stimulation of the body per se it is called auto-erotism.

Narcissism means a love of self. Narcissism can only occur when a concept of self and non-self has developed, that is after the first year. Narcissism may find expression in auto-erotic practices but can exist without this.

Libido may be relatively fixated at various stages of psychosexual development; the oral stage, the anal stage, the oedipus situation and so on. There may be a regression or a return to an earlier level of psychosexual development. It may be repressed; this occurs when there is a conflict between expression of the libido and socialised standards of conscious.

In Freudian doctrine repression is persistent and all important. It is dynamic and incessant in action and, if released, would result in chaos.

Sublimation is the expression of the libido in some cognate activity which is socially approved.

Psychodynamic Processes and Mental Mechanisms

Repression is one of the most important concepts in Freudian doctrine.

Repression involves two processes: (1) Relegation into the unconscious of memories and experiences which are unacceptable, (2) the control of basic impulses such as sex drives, aggression, greed, wishes to run away and so on.

Repression enables an individual to defend himself against unwelcome impulses or the anxiety arising from the arousal of these impulses. The voluntary control of impulses is referred to as suppression.

The following mechanisms may operate as a result of repression:

Reaction Formation

Reaction formation is the tendency to exaggerate the converse or the opposite of a repressed impulse. Aggressive feelings or hostility may be compensated for in behaviour consisting of excessive solicitousness.

Displacement and Substitution

Repression of punished impulses may be maintained by displacement, in which some substitute gratification is accepted.

In the development of obsessional symptoms, sex drives may be dealt with by displacement into washing activities acting as a purification.

Projection

Projection is the process whereby some attribute of the self or some quality or property of the self is attributed to the environment. It is a common mental mechanism as well as an important pathological process. It is well known that what is perceived is, in part, a function of the motivational structure of the personality. This forms the basis of projective tests.

In experiments it has been found that the frequency with which food is mentioned in speculations about the missing parts of incomplete pictures correlates positively with the degree of hunger.

As a psychopathological mechanism, projection may be a defence mechanism against anxiety and it has been found experimentally that individuals who possess more than an average amount of a particular trait tend to attribute that trait to others, providing that insight is lacking. People with a strong tendency to dishonesty will suspect others of being dishonest.

Various symptoms of schizophrenia and other mental disorders may be produced by the projection of dissociated complexes; for example, hallucinations, delusions of persecution and grandeur.

Rationalisation

This is an attempt to make understandable and logical, feelings or actions or attitudes which are emotionally influenced and irrational.

ANALYTICAL PSYCHOLOGY

Carl *Jung* of Zurich, born in 1875, was originally a follower of *Freud* but later developed his own school of psychotherapy and psychopathology.

In treatment, *Jung* also used the technique of free association and dream analysis but started with the study of the patient's present problem and sought to discover the elements of weakness in his manner of dealing with it. Jungian analysis gives the patient an understanding of his present state as well as of his infantile past.

The concept of libido to *Jung* is of a general life force. It is the total vital energy seeking the goal of growth as well as of activity and reproduction.

Jung, if anything, makes more of the concept of the unconscious; he distinguishes between the personal unconscious and the collective or racial unconscious. The personal unconscious is formed partly by repression from the conscious and other material that has been acquired unconsciously. The collective unconscious or racial unconscious is inherited and consists of instincts and primordial ideas or archetypes. The instincts are primitive ways of acting and the archetypes are primitive ways of thinking.

Dream interpretation to *Freud* is carried out in terms of causality and determinism but, to *Jung*, dreams are symbolised accounts of what has happened but also provide symbolic guidance for the present and the future.

INDIVIDUAL PSYCHOLOGY

Alfred *Adler*, born in Vienna in 1870, also broke away from *Freud* because of disagreement over the importance of infantile sexuality and the validity of the libido theory of *Freud*.

Adler placed much greater emphasis on the ego as against the libido and placed more emphasis on the influence of the social environment and, as each person was unique in his psychology, he termed his school that of individual psychology.

The following are some of *Adler's* concepts:

(1) Inferiority feelings are fundamental in the development of neurosis.

(2) The study and analysis of the individual patient is designed to discover his pattern of life, or Life style as *Adler* calls it and in particular the goal of superiority which he has set himself and which he still follows in some form or another.

Adler emphasised that individuals tended to cope with inferiority feelings by elaborating compensatory attitudes and patterns of behaviour. He laid great emphasis on the will to power, characterised by strivings for power, dominance and superiority.

FURTHER READING

A Short History of Psychotherapy by N. Walker. Routledge & Kegan Paul, London.

Current Approaches to Psychoanalysis by P. H. Hoch, J. Zubin (Ed.). Grune and Stratton Inc., New York and London (1960).

General Psychopathology by K. Jaspers, translated by J. Hoenig and M. W. Hamilton, Manchester University Press (1963).

CHAPTER THIRTEEN

GROWTH and MATURITY

ADOLESCENCE

Adolescence is the period of transition from puberty to adult life. Roughly speaking, it extends from 13 years to 21 years in girls and from 15 years to 21 years in boys. Adolescence is a period of profound changes in physical, psychological and social spheres.

The individual has to adjust to manifold changes. In the majority of people the period is passed through uneventfully, but in others it may be a period of instability and adjustment difficulties.

Physical Changes

During the early years of adolescence growth becomes greatly accelerated. This adolescent growth spurt results in increase in height and weight.

Growth occurs at varying rates in different parts of the body. Growth of the long hairs of the extremities is marked. In boys the chest becomes deeper and broader and in girls the figure becomes more rounded, the hips broaden and the breasts increase in size. Concurrently with skeletal growth, bodily muscularity increases in size and strength.

Puberty is the period in which the individual becomes capable of fulfilling reproductive functions. In girls it is marked by the appearance of the menses, the age of which shows considerable individual variation with an average of about 14·5 years.

Girls, in the average, reach puberty 1½–2 years ahead of boys.

Glandular changes occur and most of the endocrine glands increase in size and, in particular, the ovaries and testes.

Thus the accelerated general growth and differential growth rates, the complex glandular changes, the maturation of reproductive organs and functions and the development of secondary sexual characteristics make the adolescent period a period of marked physical change.

Psychological Changes

Intellectual. Intellectual growth proceeds steadily during childhood and in the majority of people maximum mental capacity is reached by middle adolescence. In individuals of low intelligence the maximum capacity may have been reached earlier and in some individuals of superior mental capacity intelligence may continue to grow throughout the adolescent period.

Following the achievement of maximum intellectual level, further mental enrichment occurs by the acquisition of knowledge, study and experience.

Interests grow and spread over wider spheres including vocational, recreational, intellectual and social.

Emotional Changes

The physiological changes at puberty result in reinforcement of heterosexual drives and of strivings for independence and personal responsibility. The physiological changes stimulate sex drives and the adolescent normally develops greater interest in the opposite sex. Frequent associations occur and falling in and out of love is common in adolescence. These experiences help the individual to decide on the sort of person he really likes.

During adolescence the individual has to wean himself from the family and acquire a greater degree of independence and responsibility. This may evoke in some individuals feelings of insecurity and anxiety

Parents may not like the emotional changes that may accompany the striving for independence.

Previously the individual might have been docile and co-operative and may now become resistant, irritable and disobedient.

The chief characteristics of the normal adolescent are hope, ambition, being affectionate and desire for social contact. He tends to feel anger, disappointment and other emotions more acutely. In some individuals serious maladjustment may develop during adolescence such as delinquency, neurosis, psychosis, marked emotional instability etc. The tendency to maladjustment will be determined by the individual's constitution and personality, his upbringing, the nature of parental influences and the unfavourable environmental influences he has had to contend with in the past and in the present.

During adolescence the individual gains a keener appreciation of the needs of society, develops standards in moral, ethical and religious matters and, in short, develops his philosophy of life.

MATURITY

Maturity refers to the full development of the individual's capacities and potentialities. This is, of necessity, a relative matter as we have to take into account the great range of individual variations in what may be termed maturity of personality in its manifold aspects. Furthermore, the concept and definition of maturity has to be related to social and cultural standards.

Physical and physiological maturity are the easiest to define.

Physical maturity is reached when skeletal and bodily growth reaches its maximum. Similarly, physiological maturity can be readily defined.

Emotional maturity, on the other hand, is a more complex matter requiring a more detailed assessment.

A person may show mature behaviour in certain situations, e.g. at work and may show emotional instability in his home and marital life.

The concept of emotional maturity denotes a stable, satisfactory adjustment to life in its various spheres. Such adjustment is achieved when the individual is able to control his selfish interests to meet the needs of society and other people.

The main processes involved in the achievement of emotional maturity are:

(1) The achievement of independence and self-reliance.

(2) The diversion of biological urges and emotional outlets into social accepted outlets.

(3) The person must have a clear appreciation of reality and, whilst having imagination, should not distort reality unduly by phantasy or fanciful thinking.

(4) The individual has to achieve a balance between giving and receiving.

(5) Must be relatively free from undue egoism and excessive competitiveness.

(6) Aggression and hostility must be controlled. Only the strong can be gentle and hostility is a sign of weakness.

(7) Goals must be reasonable and within the person's opportunities and capacities.

(8) The individual should have reasonable appreciation of his assets and handicaps, in work, play and leisure.

(9) He must show flexibility and adaptability to meet the demands of new situations.

(10) Pleasure needs of the moment must be considered and fulfilled in relation to future needs.

(11) The development of conscience should be to guide and to further development. Excessive conscience training in childhood will give rise to anxious and inhibited adults. Inadequate training in this respect will give rise to impulsive and childish behaviour.

Thus, the achievement of emotional maturity involves overcoming the dependency and egocentricity of childhood and controlling desires and impulses to meet the needs and wishes of other people with the aim of increasing personal and social good.

Ideally, the mature person should:

(1) Be independent and self-reliant with little need to return to childish attitudes or patterns of behaviour.

(2) Have his desires and interests reasonably controlled to meet other people's needs and wishes.

He should be able to give as well as receive.

(3) He should be co-operative and live and let live.

(4) He should have minimum hostility and aggression to himself or others but this should be fully available for defence and constructive activity when needed.

(5) He should be in relative harmony with his conscience.

(6) He should have a realisation of his assets and handicaps and their relevance or influence on work, play and rest.

(7) He should have good habits of work, sleep, eating and leisure.

(8) His goals must be reasonable and within his capabilities.

(9) His grasp of reality should be clear and, whilst having imagination, it should be checked by reality.

(10) His personal needs should be acceptable and modifiable in relationship to reasonable ethical ideas.

(11) Moods must be amenable to control.

(12) His behaviour should be relatively predictable.

INVOLUTION AND SENESCENCE

Later in adult life there occurs a gradual falling off of various capacities, e.g. visual activity, learning and reasoning. The gradual loss of physical and mental capacity becomes more marked during the fifth decade and after.

The period of decrease in various physical and mental capacities is referred to as the Involutional Period. Roughly speaking, it extends from 45–60 in women and 50–65 in men.

Following this period and merging with it is the period of Senescence, which is characterised by an increased impairment in mental and physical capacity a narrowing of interests and increasing rigidity in personality and outlook.

The term senility refers to a pathological state in which the above processes become very marked and new changes supervene which interfere with the person's happiness, behaviour and adjustment.

Senescence, therefore, is the normal process of growing old and the term senility refers to the abnormal mental states which sometimes supervene towards the close of life.

The study of the cause and medical treatment of ill health associated with old age is called Geriatrics. The study of the processes of ageing in health and disease is called Gerontology, from which geriatrics derives its knowledge and guidance. Gerontology is to Geriatrics what physiology and pathology is to medicine.

Senility occurs when impairment of physical and mental capacity becomes excessive and when initiative, the ability to form well considered opinions and sustained effort fail and social maladjustment results.

Patients become less concerned with external events, become increasingly egotistical and their emotional life becomes impoverished.

Memory, which is the keystone of mental life, becomes impaired—especially memory for recent events—whereas memories of the past which are well established can be recalled vividly. The past, therefore, for the elderly patient is often more realistic, important and significant than the present. The failure in remembering recent events causes failure of appreciation of current events which may cause the elderly person to be suspicious of his surroundings.

Previous emotional conflicts which were successfully kept under control during adult life may now appear.

The elderly person tends to be anxious, depressed, to have anxious forebodings for the future and is restless, particularly at night.

The tendency for senescence to develop into senility will depend on a number of factors. It will partly depend on heredity and constitution as senility has a familial tendency. The person's physical health will also have a bearing, such as the degree of arteriosclerosis and kidney function etc., which may reduce the ability of the elderly person to adjust to stressful situations. The person's way of life and his personality and previous level of adjustment will also affect his ability to maintain a satisfactory adjustment during senescence.

Retirement

The individual's reaction to and method of dealing with retirement has an important bearing on mental health. If the individual feels that he is finished and is incapable of further useful work or activity then he will tend to become morose, apathetic or depressed. If he feels that he is now superfluous and unimportant this will exaggerate feelings of inadequacy and inferiority. If he now enters into a scale of relative inactivity in place of his regular routine of work and leisure, he will lack adequate outlets for his constructive and creative urges.

Reaction to retirement in the above ways will tend to lead to inefficiency and maladjustment. The person should therefore continue to engage in work, hobbies and activities which will continue to give a good outlet for his creative energies and to give him feelings of confidence and the satisfaction of achievement. He should maintain and broaden his interests, take an active part in current affairs and express his opinions on them in discussions with his friends. He should, by taking a greater interest in others, try to counteract any tendencies to increasing egocentricity.

Medical and Nursing Care of the Elderly Patient

A knowledge of the psychological and physical changes in old age will greatly help in the understanding and treatment of elderly patients. Due allowance for the patient's handicaps must be made. The elderly person has a special need for affection and attention but requires to be treated as an adult. Patience and a sense of humour is important. The elderly patient must not be expected to remember instructions as well as younger people. All efforts should be made to increase the person's confidence and self-esteem. He should not be expected to do things beyond his capacity. He should be encouraged to talk and to describe events about his younger days. Interest in current things should be fostered. He should be allowed to do simple tasks and persuaded to complete them even if they may be slow and clumsy.

The keynote of nursing and medical care from the psychological point of view is to make due allowance for handicaps, being patient, encouraging, good humoured and treating the person as an interesting adult, doing everything possible to encourage confidence and self-esteem and trying to maintain and widen the patient's interests.

COMPARISON OF PHASES OF HUMAN DEVELOPMENT

Physiological and Physical Aspects

Childhood	Maturity	Senescence	Senility
Anabolism.	Anabolism = Catabolism.	Catabolism.	Catabolism.
Organs developing.	Fully developed.	Organs lose in efficiency.	Pathological degenerative changes.
Homeostasis—unstable at first.	Homeostasis stabilised	Homeostasis within narrow limits.	Homeostasis impaired.
Physiological Integration becoming more perfect.	Integrations well established.	Integrations less secure.	Loss of Integration.
Increase of physical capacity.	Full development of physical powers.	Decline of physical powers.	Decline with pathological changes.
Increase of mental capacity.	Mental capacity maintained or slowly rises.	Increasing decline in mental capacity.	Pathological loss of mental capacity.
Increasing development of independence.	Independent.	Increasing dependence.	
Flexibility.	Flexibility diminishing.	Rigidity increases.	Rigidity.
Interests increasing.	Interests continue.	Interests diminish.	Interests limited.

FURTHER READING

Emotional Maturity by L. M. Saul. J. B. Lippincott Co., Philadelphia (1960).

PART II
PSYCHIATRY

CHAPTER FOURTEEN

PSYCHIATRIC EXAMINATION

Psychiatric examination comprises:
(1) History-taking.
(2) Examination of physical state and any special investigations which are indicated.
(3) Examination of the patient's mental state.

HISTORY-TAKING

The taking of the patient's history is of fundamental importance, both for investigation and for treatment.

The history, when completed, should give a picture of the patient's development and adjustment during his life. It should contain relevant information on possible genetic and family influences on his personality and his illness. It should portray his development from childhood to adult life. It should provide evidence of adjustment to school, work, marriage, society together with a record of his physical and mental health and previous personality.

Before discussing fuller details of history-taking, we should consider more fully the interview itself.

THE INTERVIEW

The psychiatric interview is of paramount importance as it is the basis of all treatment and investigation. The psychiatrist, in his conduct of the interview, can demonstrate the art of psychiatry at its best. Interviews can be fact-finding, therapeutic or both. In either type the interview enables rapport to be developed between the patient and the doctor.

The setting of the interview room is important. The patient should not be made to feel inferior or small by the presence of a huge desk from which he is separated from the physician by a long expanse of desk.

The physician must allow adequate time for the interview and have freedom from interruption. Both physician and patient should be comfortable and relaxed.

Patients are usually anxious and frightened when coming for a psychiatric interview and they must be put at their ease. If necessary the physician should get up from his chair, go to meet the patient and a handshake is usually very helpful in welcoming and reassuring the patient.

The physician places the chair comfortably for the patient and then himself sits down. He should adopt a listening attitude and should avoid interrupting the patient, at least in the early stages.

The interviewer must not only feel interest but should make it clearly manifest to the patient and be friendly and accepting in manner. Note-taking is generally better left till afterwards as it often puts the patient off and may interfere with the establishment of a good doctor-patient relationship.

The physician must never give the impression that he is in a hurry. He must be flexible in taking the history and in carrying out the interview. It is necessary to have a scheme in mind in order to ensure that important aspects are not overlooked but the course the interview takes will largely depend on what emerges initially and subsequently the physician should let things come gently and naturally.

Questions which can be answered 'yes' or 'no' should be avoided. Questions containing a lead must not, of course, be given. The wider the question the better, as this will give the patient a chance to reply as he wishes, will not restrict or impede him in so doing and will give the best opportunity of obtaining relevant and important data.

The interview is a two-way process and the physician must convey his interest by nodding the head and by making remarks such as 'surely', 'naturally', 'of course', 'I see' etc. A friendly attitude and demeanour are much more important than the particular words chosen. If there are silences, the physician should show greater interest; leaning forward, repeating the last word or phrase and urging the patient to carry on will often overcome the silence. Emotional expression should be encouraged. The interview should be channelled towards topics of relevance and importance; such topics can be encouraged by increasing one's interest and uttering suitable remarks. Unimportant or irrelevant topics can be discouraged by showing less interest.

Careful note should be made of the patient's facial expression, change of colour, halting evasion of a topic, sudden silences, increased rapidity of speech, pleading or laughing. Points made by the patient should be emphasised to let him know that you understand his feeling. Repeat the patient's statement or reformulate what he has said in order to reinforce the understanding and rapport.

GENERAL RULES FOR INTERVIEWS

(1) Make no promises. Questions can be countered with other questions for further information.

(2) Reassurance must only be given after careful enquiry and investigation. Interpretation is very dangerous unless done appropriately at the right time.

(3) Don't take sides with the patient.

(4) Don't egg the patient on to action.

(5) Don't give advice.

Historical Anamnesis

Having ascertained the patient's complaints or difficulties or, if he has no complaints, enquire the reason for his referral. Following this it is usually convenient to start with the history of the present illness.

In recording this, facts should be included rather than technical terms. It is important that the present mental state and the history should not be mixed up.

Whilst the history is being taken, the patient's behaviour, his reactions should be observed and should later be recorded under 'general behaviour.'

It is also important that objective and subjective data should not be mixed up. It is undesirable to make the greater part of the record a mere transcript of what the patient has said. The examiner's observations, summaries and conclusions should be recorded as well.

Family History

One usually starts with parents, enquiring if they are alive and, if so, are they in good health; if not, what is wrong or, if dead, what they died from.

It is important to assess the social position and general efficiency of the family, as well as the occurrence of familial diseases and, also, a note made of the home atmosphere, particularly any significant happenings among parents and siblings during the patient's early years and the patient's relationship to parents, siblings and others.

It is always wise to obtain a history from a second person as well as the patient, as important additional information may be acquired, and, in any event, any discrepancies may be valuable in the assessment and understanding of the patient.

Personal History

Ascertain the date and place of birth, whether the birth was normal or prolonged, instrumental or premature, the mother's health during pregnancy and after birth, whether the patient was breast or bottle fed, brought up by the mother or, if someone else, the reasons for this.

Infancy and Childhood

The age at which the patient passed the milestone of development such as teething, talking, walking, achievement of bowel and bladder control. Note general health and any nervous traits in infancy and childhood.

Note the occurrence of neurotic traits in childhood such as night terrors, somnambulism, tantrums, enuresis, nail-biting, stammering, fear states, school phobia, model child, chorea, convulsions etc.

School

Age of starting and finishing, standard reached, attitude to teachers, attitude to school work and success achieved, attitude to school mates, whether he played games, mixed well, was bullied, able to stand up for himself or not.

Work

Age when started work and the jobs held, listed in chronological order with dates, reasons for change; (poor work record with unduly frequent changes of employment is often an indicator of personality instability).

Menstrual Functions

Age of menarche, reaction to menarche. Regularity and duration of menses, length of cycle, amount of loss, dysmenorrhoea, premenstrual tension, date of last period, climacteric symptoms.

Sexual Inclinations and Practice

How sexual inclination was gained and received, whether prudery, worries about masturbation, homosexuality, heterosexual experiences apart from marriage.

Marital History

Time marriage partner known before marriage and engagement, compatibility. Sex relations—whether satisfactory or not, contraceptive measures used. Any financial, domestic or temperamental difficulties.

Children

Give chronological list of children, miscarriages, with ages, names etc.

Personal Habits

Amount of alcohol, tobacco, drugs taken recently and previously.

Medical History

Details of illnesses, operations and accidents, in chronological order.

Previous Mental Health

History of any previous psychiatric illnesses, whether medical attention sought and treatment given by G.P., as an out-patient or in-patient, duration and description of such illnesses.

Personality

Describe the personality before the onset of the present illness and aim to present a picture of an individual and not a type, give illustrative anecdotes and detailed statements rather than relying on a series of adjectives.

CONDITION ON EXAMINATION

General Appearance and Behaviour

When taking the history, a great deal of information about the patient's appearance and behaviour will already have been obtained.

The first thing to observe is whether the patient looks ill, whether he looks his age or looks much older or younger. Note his general posture and facial expression. The tense, anxious patient sits on the edge of the chair, jumps at sudden noises. The depressed patient lacks muscular tone, has a dejected posture.

Is he in touch with the situation? does he behave appropriately to it? does he respond to the requirements of the examination? Does he show any oddities or eccentricities in speech, dress or manner?

Motor activity may be diminished the patient being slow in his movements and slow in his replies. Marked reduction of activity, with the patient showing no spontaneous activity and little response to stimuli is termed *Stupor*.

Over-activity may be the manifestion of general pressure of activity found in the hypomanic patient, in which there is general psychomotor activity, restlessness, circumstantiality in speech, or it may be in the form of the agitated movements found in agitated melancholia, the patient continually fidgeting, picking his clothes, wringing his hands and walking to and fro.

Are there tics, mannerisms or stereotyped movements? Is the activity abrupt, fitful, erratic or constant?

In catatonic schizophrenics the following phenomena may be found: *Automatic obedience*, *Echolalia* (repetition by the patient of what is said to him), *Echopraxia* (imitation of actions). *Waxy flexibility* with maintenance of postures even in uncomfortable positions. *Negativism* in which the patient doing the opposite of what is required or resisting attempts to help him, e.g. if when you offer to shake hands with him he moves his hand away, when you withdraw your hand his hand will come forward.)

Finally, a note should be made of his eating and sleeping habits, whether he is clean and how he spends his time.

Form of Talk

Observe whether he says a great deal or is uncommunicative or retarded in speech, whether he talks spontaneously or only in answer

S.T.P.—4*

to questions, whether he is hesitant, slow, fast, discursive, disconnected; sudden silences, changes of topic, going off at a tangent; whether he uses rhymes, puns or strange words.

Perseveration in speech is found in organic mental states; the patient, when asked to do a certain thing, will continue doing this action even though he is asked to do other things. This is a case of momentum and inertia carrying on and interfering with following events.

Mood

The patient's mood will already have been reflected in his general behaviour, in speech and manner. He should be asked 'how do you feel in yourself? what are your spirits like? what is your mood'? Note the constancy of mood, whether it changes rapidly or whether it is constant, the factors which change the mood and, also, whether the patient's behaviour, facial expression agree with what he says about his mood.

Mental Content

Enquire about the patient's attitude to himself, to the people around him and to the various things in his environment; does he feel a special reference is made to him, does he feel that people shun him or admire him, does he tend to depreciate himself regarding his past behaviour, morals, possessions and health or, conversely, is he expansive and grandiose about his possessions and personal abilities? Enquire about the predominant thoughts or preoccupations that the patient has; in depressive states these are characteristically painful and unhappy, full of regrets, dwelling on the past, the present or the future in a hopeless and gloomy way.

Disorders of Perception

It will be necessary to know whether the patient has auditory, visual, olfactory, gustatory, tactile or other hallucinations. It is usually convenient to broach this by asking the patient if he ever hears noises later communications and then definitely voices. It is important to note at what time the hallucinations occur, whether by night or by day, their complexity, their vividness and how received by the patient. If they occur when falling asleep, it is usually of little significance. In severely depressed patients, they report that there are unusual sensations, lack of sensations or lack of organs.

Consciousness (Sensorium)

It is important to note whether the patient is alert, dull, self-absorbed confused or delirious. Try to discover his grasp of the environment and his judgment. Enquire into his orientation in time, with regard to place and to persons.

Compulsive Phenomena

Does he get any recurrent thoughts which distress him, which are unwanted and which he finds difficult to dismiss? Does he feel them to be a part of his own mind or to come from without? Does he regard them as inappropriate or irrational? Are they related to his emotional state, e.g. a state of depression or anxiety? Does he tend to repeat actions with compulsions and a tendency to resist such as touching things, washing his hands unduly frequently?

Orientation

General orientation can be assessed by questions such as 'Where are you now'? 'What is the name of this place'? 'Where is it situated'? 'What day of the week is it today'? 'What month are we in'? 'What day of the month is it'? 'What is the year'?

If he is in hospital one can ascertain his orientation in the ward, such as 'Show me the nearest lavatory', 'Where is the bathroom'? 'Where is the main entrance'? 'Are there any other ways out'? 'Where is the television'? 'Where is the nurses' office'? etc.

Memory

The patient's memory functions are assessed by comparing his account of his life with that given by others. It is important to test also for recent events—when he first attended hospital or when he was admitted, whether he had seen another doctor and, if so, whom and where the doctor saw him and when.

The patient may be given a name and address to remember and then asked to recall it three or five minutes later. He can be given a series of digits to repeat forwards, then others to repeat backwards.

Grasp of General Information

Questions regarding general information should be varied according to the patient's educational level, his experience and interests. He should be asked the name of the monarch and the immediate predecessors, the Prime Minister, the capitals of France, Germany, Italy, Spain and the United States; the date with the beginning and the end of World War II. He should be asked to name six large cities in England. He should be asked to carry out the serial-7 test, i.e. subtraction of 7 from 100, and note the answers given and the time taken.

The purpose of these tests is to give a general idea whether there has geen any falling off in a person's former presumptive level of knowledge and intellectual capacity.

Insight and Judgment

What is his attitude to his present state? Is his attitude and assessment of it reasonable for his intelligence and experience? Does he regard himself as being ill or as suffering from a nervous or mental illness or whether he needs treatment? How does he regard his present difficulties or deficits? What is his opinion regarding his previous attacks of mental illness if any?

EXAMINATION OF STUPOROSE OR NON-CO-OPERATIVE PATIENTS

The difficulties of getting information from non-co-operative or stuporose patients should not discourage the student from making and recording observations, which can be made without difficulty and which may be of great importance in presenting a record of the clinical state at the time in case the patient's clinical condition should change suddenly.

Observations can be made under the following headings:

(1) *Posture and general reactions:* whether his posture is natural or awkward; whether he maintains his limbs when they are placed in awkward positions; whether his behaviour is negativistic, evasive, irritable, apathetic or obedient; whether he exhibits any spontaneous actions; his behaviour with regard to dressing, eating and personal hygiene. Describe his facial expression—whether it was vacant, placid, perplexed, depressed, distressed, any tears, flushing etc.; whether the eyes are open or closed; if the eyes are closed whether they resist attempts to having the lid raised; reaction to sudden approach or threat to touch the eye.

(2) *Reactions to commands.* The patient should be asked to show his tongue, close his eyes, open his eyes, move limbs, shake hands. Notice whether there is negativism, echopraxia, echolalia or automatic obedience.

(3) *Muscular functions.* Note whether muscles are tensed, rigid or show waxy flexibility.

Test how the patient reacts to passive movements of the head and neck and of the limbs, and whether it is possible to influence these reactions by commands or distractions.

PHYSICAL EXAMINATION AND SPECIAL INVESTIGATIONS

It may cause surprise to include physical examination as an important part of treatment. Physical examination and any additional investigations that may be necessary must be carried out thoroughly, not only to detect, assess or exclude the presence of organic disease but, also, to give weight and conviction to the reassurance and explanation given by the physician at the appropriate time to the patient concerning his illness. The patient will be impressed by a thorough physical examination and, thus, more likely to accept the physician's opinion about his physical state.

It will only antagonise a patient to tell him there is nothing wrong with him. He may be told that there is nothing physically wrong but this must be followed by an explanation of his symptoms, in terms suitable to his intelligence and his personality.

Similarly, when special investigations are necessary, the reasons and nature of the investigations should be explained to the patient beforehand. Wherever possible, he should be told about the outcome of these results, otherwise feelings of anxiety and apprehension will be fostered.

Once a physician is reasonably satisfied with a patient's physical state, he should avoid repeating the physical examination unless this is dictated by the patient's medical condition. Repeated examination usually has a harmful effect on the patient, suggesting to him that the doctor is not sure of his case and reinforcing his fears that there may be something seriously, physically wrong with him. Prolonged and exhaustive clinical and laboratory investigations also may make the patient very apprehensive. Special investigations, when necessary, should be reduced to the minimum and always given with adequate explanation and, when possible, strong reassurance.

CHAPTER FIFTEEN

PRINCIPLES OF AETIOLOGY

Aetiology is the science or the philosophy of causation of disease.

Throughout the ages attempts have been made to determine the causation of mental illnesses and psychiatrists, like other physicians, have been tempted to look for a single cause for each disease. This approach, however, was found to be inappropriate and unhelpful and nowadays it is necessary to consider a complex interaction of forces within the individual and between the individual and the environment.

The search for causality in medicine always involves a concept of factors, each of which has as good a claim to the title of cause as any other. For example, if we stated that the tubercle bacillus is the cause of tuberculosis, this implies that the presence of the tubercle bacilli in the body is a sufficient condition for the occurrence of the disease tuberculosis but, as is well known, this is not so.

A person can experience the invasion of tubercle bacilli into the body without developing the disease tuberculosis. On the other hand, we could not say that the person was suffering from tuberculosis if he did not, or never had, any tubercle bacilli in his body. It may be said, therefore, that the presence of tubercle bacilli in a person's body is a necessary condition but we cannot say it is a sufficient condition for the development of the disease tuberculosis. It may be termed *a* factor or *a* cause but not *the* cause.

It is known that a variety of factors may determine whether invasion of the tubercle bacillus into the body will develop into the disease tuberculosis. Nutritional state, overcrowding, stressful experiences and many other conditions may determine the actual development of the disease tuberculosis at a particular time. These factors are the *sufficient* causes; the tubercle bacillus itself is the *essential* cause.

Thus, the aetiology of diseases may be discussed in terms of essential causes, without which a disease could not develop, and sufficient causes which enable the essential cause to be clinically manifested as the disease.

One may also regard causes as predisposing and precipitating.

In studying the causes of illness, there are three fields of observation.

(1) The field of the person, which includes observations on the characteristics of the person before he becomes ill.

(2) The field of the environment, including observations on the

features of the environment which the person met at, or just before, the time he became ill.

(3) The field of mechanism; this includes observation on the structural, physical, chemical and psychological mechanisms brought into action by the encounter of the individual with his environment which, ultimately, brings about the particular mode of behaviour which we refer to as illness.

Aetiology is therefore concerned with ascertaining which features of the individual are relevant and causal, which features of the environment are relevant and causal and which mechanisms in the body are involved in the illness.

We need to know the factors which determine the onset of the illness, the factors which determine the course of the illness and the factors which determine its outcome.

One can therefore discuss the aetiology of onset, an aetiology of the course of the illness and an aetiology of the outcome of the illness.

We can ask a number of questions about anybody who becomes ill:
(1) Why has he become ill?
(2) Why has he become ill in the way in which he has become ill?
(3) Why has he become ill at this time of his life?

Thus, we can consider intrinsic causes residing in the individual and extrinsic causes arising from his environment.

Intrinsic causes may be classified as follows:
(1) Genogenic.
(2) Constitutional.
(3) Personality.
(4) Critical stages of development.

Extrinsic causes, include psychosocial stresses, infections trauma etc.

A psychiatric illness is the resultant of the interaction of a number of factors residing within the individual (intrinsic factors) and in the environment (extrinsic factors).

Multiple causation is the rule. The relative importance of intrinsic and extrinsic factors varies according to the type of illness as well as the individual.

There is a continuous interaction between intrinsic and extrinsic factors.

Genetic Factors

As discussed in the Chapter 16, a number of psychiatric illnesses are genetically determined, some with a specific predisposition determined by a single gene.

Certain minor disorders and personality disorders appear to be determined by a large number of genes of small effect, i.e. they are multifactorially determined.

It should be remembered that more than one type of predisposition

MULTIFACTORIAL AETIOLOGY OF PSYCHIATRIC ILLNESS

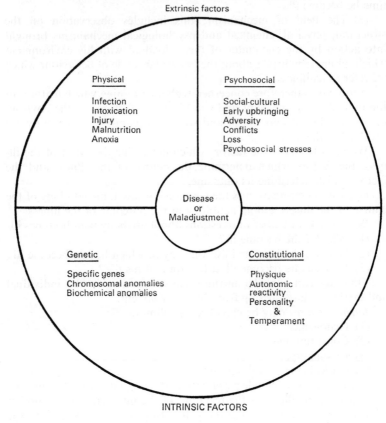

FIG. 7

to mental illness may occur in the same person, e.g. a person may carry the gene for schizophrenia as well as that for endogenous depression.

Genes are influenced by the genotypic milieu as well as by the internal environment of the body, in addition to the effect of environmental influences.

Genes produce their effects by controlling enzyme systems and, therefore, the chemical status of the body and it is believed that many of the severe psychiatric illnesses like schizophrenia and depressive illness would probably be demonstrated to have an underlying biochemical disturbance, and possibly many different types of disturbance for the subtypes of schizophrenia and depressive illness.

Certain changes in the internal environment occurring at puberty,

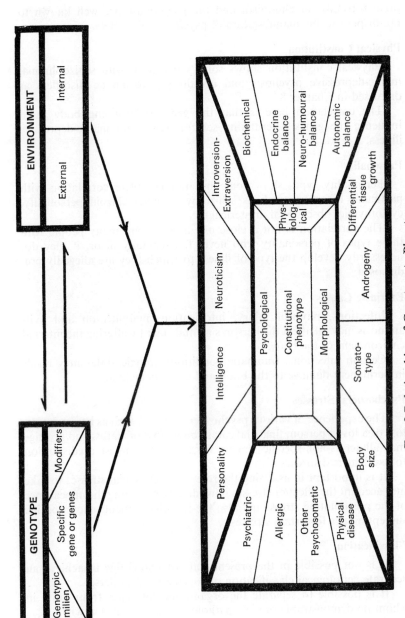

Fig. 8 Relationships of Genotype to Plenotype.

premenstrually, at childbirth and the menopause are well known to pre-dispose to the manifestation of psychiatric disorders.

Physical Constitution

Physical constitution shows some correlation with schizophrenia, manic-depressive psychosis and certain psychosomatic disorders as discussed in Chapter 8.

The correlation here is that the genes determining body build influence the genes determining schizophrenia and manic-depressive illness.

Personality

Personality types show some but not complete correlation with particular disorders, such as schizothymic and schizoid personality, cyclothymic, obsessional, hysterical etc.

The correlation is not a close one as there are many people with these types of personality who never fall mentally ill or, if they do, necessarily develop the type of illness to which they are allegedly pre-disposed.

Extrinsic Causes

Infections, physical injury, intoxication, malnutrition and avitaminosis may all affect the person's mental state by altering the internal environment of the body.

Certain infections, traumatic conditions, anoxic states may result in permanent damage to the brain and cause dementia.

Psychosocial Stresses

The experience of various psychosocial stresses such as bereavement, loss of a loved person, financial catastrophe, loss of status, and prestige may all act as non-specific stresses for making manifest predispoition to psychiatric disorders.

It is important in assessing the role of psychosocial stresses to take into account the effect of stresses immediately preceding the appearance of the precipitating stress, and also the fact that patients show specific susceptibilities to certain stresses.

Classification

It is not possible in the present state of knowledge to achieve an accurate aetiological classification of psychiatric disorders.

It is possible to separate the organic mental states from those in whom no demonstrable organic pathology is at present known.

The acute organic mental states (toxic infective mental states) comprise the syndromes, Delirium, Subdelirious state, Korsakow's syndrome and neurasthenia.

The next group are the organic dementias in which there is damage to the brain due to a variety of causes.

In the acute organic mental states the predominant clinical feature is disturbance of consciousness and confusion. In the dementias the predominant feature is loss of mental capacity mainly affecting memory functions.

The remaining disorders are often subdivided into psychoses and neuroses. The term psychosis refers to the more severe mental illnesses such as schizophrenia, manic-depressive psychosis, whereas the neuroses refer to conditions such as hysteria, obsessional state etc.

The distinction between whether an illness is psychotic or neurotic is not very sensible and serves no useful purpose, and very often the term psychotic is loosely used synonymously with schizophrenia. What the users of these terms usually have in mind is that the psychotic may lack insight into his illness and may need care in a psychiatric hospital, whereas the neurotic is alleged to have reasonable insight into his illness and can be cared for in the community; but these criteria are by no means satisfactory because some schizophrenics have good insight and can be cared for in the community, whereas some hysterics lack insight and may need institutional care. There would be no loss to psychiatry if these terms were discarded.

With regard to personality disorders, these may occur as problems by themselves or may occur in any psychiatric illness. Similarly, intelligence of all ranges may occur in all varieties of psychiatric illness.

CLASSIFICATION OF PSYCHIATRIC DISORDERS

1 **Psychosomatic and Somatopsychic interactions.**

2 **Organic states.**

Acute—Delirium, Korsakow's syndrome, subdelirious state.

Chronic—Including Dementia due to degenerative, infective, cardiovascular, neoplastic, traumatic, demyelinating epilepitic or metabolic disorders; drug and other intoxicants.

3 **Affective Disorders.**
Depressive illness.
Hypomanic and Manic states.
Anxiety states.
Phobic states.

4 **Schizophrenia.**
5 **Hysteria.**
6 **Obsessional states.**
7 **Personality abnormalities.**
8 **Psychopathy.**
9 **Psychosexual anomalies.**
10 **Mental subnormality.**

CHAPTER SIXTEEN

GENETICAL ASPECTS

The fruitless discussions of the past as to whether a particular disease or attribute was either genetically determined or due to environmental influences has been superseded by the modern concept of a continuous interaction between genes and the environment.

Genes may be influenced by three distinct environments:

(1) External environment.

(2) Interior environment of the body (milieu interieur).

(3) The environment of other genes, collectively called the genotypic milieu.

The observable manifestation of an inherited attribute is referred to as the phenotype. The phenotype is the resultant of interaction of the genetic make-up of the individual (genotype) and environmental influences.

GENES

The gene is the basic unit of heredity and consists of large and elaborately constructed molecules of desoxyribonucleic acid (DNA).

Genes are transmitted from one generation to the next unchanged unless altered by mutation.

Mutation is a rare and rather haphazard event and may occur spontaneously or brought about by chemicals, radiation or physical agents. Genes exert their effects through their control of biochemical reactions, accelerating some and retarding others, or inhibiting some reactions until the chemical environment is such as to set it into action.

Although genes are transmitted as independent units, it is necessary to think of the genetic constitution (genotype) as acting as a whole, with the cumulative effects of minor influences of many genes sometimes being just as important as the major effects of single genes.

Genes can only act in the framework of their environment and their effects will be influenced to a greater or lesser degree by environmental factors.

Genetical research aims at discovering how much of the total variance occurring in a given population can be attributed to genetical and how much to environmental factors.

CHROMOSOMES

Genes are found in chromosomes which are contained in the nucleus of the cell. In the human being there are 23 chromosome pairs. Every cell in the body has its full complement of chromosomes except for the sex cells, which contain only half the normal number.

Chromosomes exist in pairs, each member of which is homologous to the other. The genes of which they consist are also homologous and paired. Each member of a pair is either chemically identical with its partner or differing slightly.

Chromosomes are, in appearance, thread-like structures with the genes ranged along their length. In experimental animals, it is possible to identify the individual gene by its position in a particular chromosome.

Chromosome Abnormalities

During recent years, there has been a great expansion of research on human chromosome abnormalities. In 1949 *Barr* and *Bertram* discovered the sex chromatin body in the nucleus of cells of females. Later sexual dimorphism was also found to be expressed in the configuration of the polymorpho-nuclear leucocytes, a club-like attachment nucleus being seen in cells of females but rarely, if ever, in males.

The discovery of nuclear sex led to enquiries regarding the possibility that the anatomical expression of sex, i.e. the sexual phenotype could, in some clinical states, be at variance with the sex of the individual person as determined at conception.

This line of enquiry, coupled with the discovery of techniques of chromosome analysis, led to the discovery of a number of sex chromosome abnormalities in the human.

The normal number of chromosomes in somatic cells is 46, consisting of 2 sex chromosomes and 22 pairs of autosomes specifically associated with sex determination. Ova and sperm contain half this number of chromosomes, that is 22 autosomes and a single sex chromosome. In ova the sex chromosome is the same and is known as the X-chromosome, whereas half the sperm contains an X-chromosome and half a Y-chromosome. Thus, the sex chromosome complement of a male zygote is X-Y and that of a female zygote X-X.

Many of the chromosome abnormalities are results of errors of cell division and chromosome partitioning, either during gametogenesis during cleavage of zygote or, occasionally, later.

Mitosis is the regular repeated cell division which leads to the formation of tissues in organisms and animals from a single original cell. Meiosis, on the other hand, is the process involved in preparing the gametes, each of which will contain half the chromosome number of the original mother cell and takes place only in the gonads.

Its objective is achieved through two cell divisions, the first of which halves the chromosome number by separating the homologous chromosomes from each other into two daughter cells.

The abnormal phenomena whereby two chromosomes migrate together to the same part of the dividing cell and are both included in one daughter cell and excluded from the other is called non-dys-junction.

Sex chromosomes may be abnormal in number or in structure.

The first anomalies to be discovered were Klinefelter's syndrome, (i.e. chromatin positive males,) and Ovarian dysgenesis, (i.e. chromatin negative females).

Abnormalities of the Autosomes

Mongolism is associated with and due to a special chromosome anomaly, namely trisomy (three chromosomes instead of two) of one of the small satellited chromosomes identified as No. 21 in the Denver system. The general frequency of mongolism is 1 in 600 births.

Dominant Genes

A dominant gene is one which will transmit characteristics even in heterozygotes. 50 per cent of children of a parent with a dominant gene inherit that gene.

Recessive genes only transmit the inherited characteristic if they are homozygous for the gene, and an abnormality due to a recessive gene usually appears out of the blue in the family tree and will not, appear to be handed on from parent to child but may easily strike more than one member of a sibship.

SEX-LINKED INHERITANCE

One of the 23 pairs of chromosomes is anomalous, in that the two members of the pair are not the same size and hence not strictly homologous. These are the sex chromosomes of which the X-chromosomes are full-sized, whilst the Y-chromosome is hardly more than a fragment containing very little genetic material in proportion. The female can only produce ova of one kind with one X-chromosome, whereas the male can produce two kinds of spermatozoa—one with an X and one with a Y chromosome. As the X-chromosome is so much bigger than the Y-chromosome, the greater part of it in the male has no matching partner. Any gene, dominant or recessive, in this part of the X-chromosome will have its full effect in the male but, if recessive, will be liable to be repressed in the female.

Conditions determined in this way have a very characteristic pedigree, with transmission occurring through the female but manifestation being confined to males. Examples are red-green colour blindness.

MULTIFACTORIAL (POLYGENIC) INHERITANCE

Some characteristics show quantitative variation and usually are distributed along the normal frequency curve, as in the case of intelligence, height, weight, body build etc.

These are usually due to a large number of genes and, in fact, it may be said that when we find distributions of a normal frequency type we should think of multifactorial inheritance.

METHODS OF HUMAN GENETIC RESEARCH

In the past the principal method of studying heredity was the investigation of isolated family pedigrees. This was of value only for marked abnormality transmitted by dominant genes having a high penetrance and the method is quite unsatisfactory for studying the inheritance of common disorders.

The main methods used nowadays for investigating the inheritance of psychiatric illnesses and other common disorders are:

(1) *The Statistical, Genealogical Proband Method*

This method involves taking a random sample of patients suffering from the disease to be studied genetically, which are referred to as probands, and the incidence of the disorder is ascertained in the relatives of the probands. This is compared with the incidence in the relatives of a normal control group of probands of similar age and sex distribution which will give the incidence of the disorder in the general population.

If the results show a statistically significantly higher incidence of the disease among the relatives of the disease probands than among the relatives of the normal probands, it is highly probable that the disease is due to inherited factors in the absence of exogenous differences between the disease probands and the control probands series.

(2) *Twin Studies*

Genetic twin studies are based on the fact that the genetic equipment is uniovular twins is the same and that any differences found between the pairs are considered to be due to environmental influences. In binovular twins, as the genetic equipment is different, any intrapair differences could be due either to heredity and/or the environment. Stated in another way, the high degree of similarity among pairs of uniovular twins for a specific trait indicates a heredity factor. Binovular twins, on the other hand, are no more alike than ordinary siblings as regards genetical endowment.

INTELLIGENCE

Intelligence, in the normal population, is distributed along the normal frequency curve and is considered to be of multifactorial (polygenic) inheritance.

Mental subnormality, with I.Q.s above 50, represent the lowest part of the normal variation in intelligence and here the mental subnormality is also multifactorially determined.

Below an intelligence quotient of 50, mentally subnormal patients cannot be accommodated into this scheme and, in these instances, the mode of inheritance is by means of single major genes.

This is borne out by the fact that the correlation of intelligence between siblings and the mental defective whose I.Q. was above 50 was +0·5 which corresponds to the correlation for the general population, whereas in the low grade mentally subnormal patients, i.e. with an I.Q. below 50, the correlation was zero.

PERSONALITY, CHARACTER AND NEUROSIS

Animal breeding experiments provide strong evidence of a genetic basis for behavioural characteristics in mice, rats, dogs and rabbits, particularly differences in aggressiveness, emotional stability and temperament.

Identical twins have been studied by means of tests of intelligence, personality and autonomic nervous system functioning. The results showed that intelligence, autonomic lability and extroversion-introversion was genetically determined; extroversion is determined by heredity to as large an extent as intelligence.

Uniovular twins brought up apart still show a significant similarity, even when they are brought up by dissimilar types of parents—dissimilar in mode of upbringing, attitude and personality.

Family studies of the relatives of patients suffering from anxiety states, hysteria and obsessional states had a significantly higher incidence of neurosis than corresponding normal control groups.

Studies on identical and binovular twins revealed that about 80 per cent of individual differences in neuroticism was due to heredity and 20 per cent to environment.

It has also been found that uniovular twins were twice as likely as binovular twins to have a similar degree of difficulty in adjustment.

PSYCHOSOMATIC DISORDERS

It has been found that peptic ulcer patients had a higher incidence of narrow physique and autonomic imbalance than control groups and there was good reason to believe that they had existed before the onset of illness.

Genetic studies revealed a preponderance of similar personality traits in the near relatives of ulcer patients. The evidence suggests that the predisposition to duodenal ulcer is associated with certain personality characteristics and a narrow physique.

There is also evidence that the predisposition to peptic ulceration is correlated with a high level of pepsinogen in the blood; pepsinogen level is considered to be genetically determined.

Careful genetic studies carried out in Sweden have revealed that specific dyslexia, or *congenital word blindness*, is transmitted by a single dominant gene with a manifestation of practically 100 per cent.

Nocturnal enuresis has also been studied genetically in Sweden and was found to be aetiologically heterogeneous but that there was probably a group of patients in which it was genetically determined, although subject to environmental influences.

The mode of inheritance is not clear; it may be a simple dominant with reduced penetrance or polygenic.

Mental Subnormality

The genetical aspects of mental subnormality are dealt with in Chapter 28.

Various forms are determined by antosomal recessive or dominant genes, a variety of cytogenic aberrations and associated biochemical disorders as well as the important high grade group which is mainly multifactorially determined.

MENTAL ILLNESS.

The role of genetic factors is discussed in the text on each disorder. The following Table gives a summary of the mode of inheritance of some mental disorders:

Single Dominant	Single Recessive	Multifactorial
Endogenous Depression	? Schizophrenia	Intelligence
Manic-Depressive illness.		Personality
? Schizophrenia		Neurosis
Huntingdon's chorea		Physique
Pick's presenile dementia		Senile Dementia
Congenital Dsylexia		Alzheimer's presenile
Asthma		dementia
Migraine		Some forms of
Some forms of		Nocturnal enuresis
Nocturnal enuresis		

CHAPTER SEVENTEEN

EPIDEMIOLOGY AND SOCIAL PSYCHIATRY

Epidemiology is the study of health and disease in the community.
The uses to which epidemiology can be applied are as follows:
(1) To delineate the historical trend of diseases.
(2) To estimate the incidence of diseases in the population.
(3) To assess the working of Health Services.
(4) To estimate the risk of the individual of developing a particular disease.
(5) To complement the clinical picture of disease of which only a part is visible to the clinician.
(6) To describe and distinguish syndromes and search for causes of diseases.

The principles of aetiology as a science were established over a century ago by *Snow* who demonstrated that cholera was conveyed by sewage-contaminated water.

The application of epidemiological methods to non-infectious diseases were also applied to non-infectious diseases, e.g. the discovery that pellagra was due to a dietary deficiency and, more recently, the discovery of a causal relationship between cigarette smoking and lung cancer.

MEASUREMENT OF PSYCHIATRIC MORBIDITY

In order to ascertain the prevalence of mental illness in a community, three steps are required:
(1) To define what shall be meant by a case of mental illness.
(2) To define the population at risk.
(3) To ascertain the number of cases in that population Morbidity data are obtained from the following sources:
(a) Hospital statistics.
(b) Information derived from those on sickness benefit collected by the Ministry of Pensions and National Insurance.
(c) Surveys to ascertain the number of patients mentally ill in a random sample of the population using either (a) the birth register method which consists of studying all persons or a sample of them, born in an area during a certain period of time or (b) census or cross sectional method which is the study of the population of a particular area at a point in time or during a defined period of time.

HOSPITAL STATISTICS

This is the simplest method of obtaining information relating to the prevalence of mental illness. It concerns information on patients admitted to psychiatric hospitals or to psychiatric beds in general hospitals.

Hospital statistics give a lower figure for prevalence than studies in the community and need to be supplemented by data from other sources.

There are 211,939 psychiatric beds in England and Wales which cost £104,301,340 per year to run.

Psychiatric hospitals and hospitals for mental subnormality constitute nearly half of all the hospital beds in England and Wales.

In 1957, 90,000 people were admitted to mental hospitals, 48,000 for the first time. First admission rates give some indication of the inception rate of mental illness in the community.

In general, those for single persons exceed those for persons who have been married at some time. There is a striking increase in admission rate with increasing age. 1956 first admission rate at all ages was 100 per 100,000 but, at age 75 and over, it was three times as much. It was estimated in 1956 that of all people aged 65 and over, one in 109 was resident in a mental hospital.

In any one year, one person in every 1,000 is admitted to a mental hospital for the first time in England and Wales.

Out of every 100 persons born who do not die young, 6 or 7 will at some time be admitted to a mental hospital.

SURVEYS OF GENERAL PRACTICES

Neurosis

In a series of general practices in various parts of Great Britain, there was general agreement on the prevalence rate of neurosis. Out of every 1,000 registered persons, 50 consulted each year for a complaint diagnosed as neurosis. This rate was twice as high in females as in males.

The yearly prevalence rate for neurosis is 5 per cent in the general population. The incidence is higher in urban than in rural areas.

Psychoses and Subnormality

For psychoses and mental subnormality the expectancy rates are 1 per cent for schizophrenia, 1 per cent for manic-depressive psychosis, 5 per cent for all psychoses and a further 1 per cent for mental subnormality.

Logan and *Brook* (1957), from a nation wide survey of sickness covering a ten-year period, found the monthly prevalence rate for all types of mental and nervous illness to be 6·5 per cent for males and 16·3 per cent for females.

Out of every 1,000 days of incapacity in men, psychoses accounted for 43, neuroses 38 and, in women, the corresponding figures were 45 and 69. For both sexes combined it is 47 per 1,000 for psychoses and for neuroses.

Forty-one and 72 for male and female respectively per 1,000 days of incapacity. This means that 1 in 20 of all men and women incapacitated on a particular day were recorded as psychotic and 1 in 25 men and 7 in 100 women were recorded as neurotic. It has been estimated that psychiatric patients account for 10 per cent of a general practitioner's work and the average attendance of a psychiatric patient was 5 consultations per year, compared with 3 for the non-psychiatric patient.

Suicide

Statistics from the World Health Organisation have recently shown that suicide rates tend to remain relatively constant for each country, although differing considerably between different countries.

The rate per 100,000 population in England and Wales is roughly 11·5, Sweden 17, the United States 10·5, Northern Ireland 5, Republic of Ireland 3·2, Israel 6·4, Australia 11·9, France 15·9, West Berlin 37, Hungary 24, Japan 20.

It has been shown that the incidence of suicide in various London boroughs was correlated with indices of social isolation, mobility, divorce and illegitimacy but not with unemployment or overcrowding.

Suicide rates are higher in the upper social classes except in the older age groups when the rate is greatest in the lowest social classes. This suggests that different factors operate in the older groups where social isolation has been shown to be an important factor.

Psychosomatic Disorders

It has been estimated that a man aged 35 will run the risk of 1 in 8 chances of coronary heart disease, 1 in 10 from peptic ulcer; 33 per cent of men reaching 35 will die before they reach 65 compared with just over 20 per cent of women.

Epidemiology can sometimes help in the identification of syndromes. This was shown clearly in the case of peptic ulcer; mortality rates in different social classes showed that there were two conditions to be studied, namely gastric ulcer and duodenal ulcer.

Coronary disease has a particularly high mortality in Class 1. Although diet was considered to be the important factor, recent investigations have suggested that the differences are the product of a connection between coronary heart disease and physical activity of work. The higher the status the more light the job.

The class distribution seems to be mainly dependent on the proportion of light and heavy workers in each class; the reduction of muscular work was one of the stiking features both of industrial revolutions and the part of the change underlying all other changes.

Social Class

It has been known for many years that schizophrenia is relatively more common in unskilled workers than in professional or business men. It has been found in U.S.A. that the rate of schizophrenia was ten times as great in the lowest as in the highest social class. The figures for England and Wales for first hospital admissions indicate that schizophrenia is four times greater than in the highest social class.

The two possible reasons for this association are that the strains and stresses associated with the conditions in Social Class 5 are conducive to the development of schizophrenia or that schizophrenic patients, as they deteriorate, drift into these areas.

The main evidence of an individual downward drift is the ability of schizophrenic patients to win places in Grammar Schools, although they end up in semi-skilled or unskilled jobs.

The discrepancies in social performance between father and son could be mainly attributable to the effects of the disease process.

The social drift appears to affect the highest and lowest social classes most severely.

The findings suggest that gross socio-economic deprivation is unlikely to be a major aetiological factor in schizophrenia.

Marital Status

It has been shown that there is a higher proportion of single people amongst those admitted to mental hospitals as compared with the general population, with a considerable proportion of this excess due to those admitted with a diagnosis of schizophrenia.

There are two possible explanations for this; firstly that the pre-admission states of the disease militate against marriage or that marriage protects the individual against the psychosis.

Culture and Mental Disorder

It is tempting to associate the incidence of mental disorder with the complexity of civilisation and this is related to the idea that the 'noble savage' is free from mental disease.

Investigations of the Hutterite communities in North America suggested that the incidence of mental disorder was lower than that in the general community. Hutterite communities are relatively stable and isolated communities living under peaceful agricultural conditions with firm religious convictions but, in fact, a detailed study of mental health showed that the incidence of severe mental disorders is similar to that found in other population surveys. There is a relatively high proportion of manic-depressive illness and a low incidence of schizophrenia, but genetic factors may be responsible for this as most of the Hutterites were derived from a group of people who came from Russia in the late 19th century.

Epidemiological studies have shown that the valid differences in suicide rates in different countries appear to have a bearing on social pressures relating to the act of suicide.

The incidence of major psychosis such as manic-depressive illness and schizophrenia is remarkably similar in different countries and different cultures. This suggests that factors other than social factors play a substantial part in the genesis of these conditions.

It seems probable that schizophrenia and pre-schizophrenic states have a selective influence on a persons' choice of occupation, mobility between one country and another, a decision whether to marry or not, and that a large proportion of schizophrenics are to be found among low status occupations, emigrants and the unmarried. Schizophrenics tend to move down the social scale and into socially disintegrated areas of cities.

There is thus little evidence that the major mental illnesses are significantly correlated to the complexity of civilisation.

FURTHER READING

Aspects of Psychiatric Research edited by D. Richter, J. M. Tanner, Lord Taylor and O. L. Zangwill. Oxford University Press, London.

CHAPTER EIGHTEEN

PSYCHOSOMATIC DISORDERS

DEFINITIONS

The term psychosomatic has two main usages:

(1) It is applied to an approach to illness in general, in which the physician pays due attention to psychological and social as well as physical factors. Used in this sense the term is applicable to all illnesses.

(2) The term psychosomatic is also applied to denote a group of disorders in which emotional factors have a demonstrable role in aetiology. These are disorders manifesting a physical lesion in which emotional and physical factors may exert a causative role.

CHARACTERISTICS

A list of these disorders is given in the Table below. They have certain features in common:

(1) Emotions precipitate attacks of the illness; this may be demonstrable by clinical observation or reproduced under experimental conditions. Emotional changes may increase the severity of an attack, if already present, or prolong its duration.

TABLE 2

SOME COMMON PSYCHOSOMATIC DISORDERS

(1) **Respiratory Disorders**
    (a) Asthma
    (b) Vasomotor rhinitis
    (c) Hay fever

(2) **Gastro-intestinal Disorders**
    (a) Peptic ulcer
    (b) Colonic disorders

(3) **Skin Disorders**

(4) **Disorders of Muscles and Joints**
    (a) Rheumatoid arthritis
    (b) "Fibrositis"

(5) **Endocrine Disorders**
    (a) Hyperthyroidism
    (b) Diabetes mellitus

(6) **Cardiovascular System**
    (a) Essential Hypertension
    (b) Coronary disease

(7) Disorders associated with Menstrual and Reproductive Functions
    (a) Amenorrhoea and Oligomenorrhoea
    (b) Dysmenorrhoea
    (c) Menorrhagia
    (d) Premenstrual tension
    (e) Menopausal Disturbances

(2) A correlation is observable between the occurrence of stressful life experience and the onset of these disorders, or with recurrence of attacks during the course of the illness.

(3) They exhibit a differential sex incidence. For example asthma before puberty is twice as common in boys as in girls, whereas after puberty it is more common in women than in men. Chronic urticaria and thyrotoxicosis are more common in women; peptic ulcer, coronary thrombosis and arterial hypertension more common in men.

(4) Psychosomatic disorders often run a phasic course.

(5) Most of the disorders fulfilling the above criteria show evidence of a genetic and constitutional predisposition. Not infrequently other members of the family suffer from the same or allied conditions.

RESPIRATORY DISORDERS

Asthma, Hay Fever and Vasomotor Rhinitis

Asthma is characterised by recurrent attacks of dyspnoea, with difficulty and prolongation of the expiratory phase and accompanied by wheezing and, usually, with intervening periods of freedom.

The mechanism underlying an attack is a narrowing of the lumen of the smaller bronchi, arising either from constriction of the circular muscle of the bronchus and/or swelling of the bronchial mucosa. An additional factor in some patients is increased muscular tension of the muscles of the larynx and chest wall, which can also influence the degree of dyspnoea.

Studies of a random sample of asthmatic patients of all ages reveal a multiplicity of causal factors, the three most important being:

(1) *Infections*, particularly of the upper and lower respiratory tract.

(2) *Allergic factors*. In asthma the allergens commonly found are house dust, pollen and sometimes ingestants and injectants. A convenient method of investigating the role of suspected allergens is to measure the patient's respiratory movements with a spirometer and to introduce the allergen by means of an aerosol. If ventilation is reduced by more than 10 per cent, it is diagnostic of an attack of asthma.

(3) *Psychological factors*. Emotional tension is the most important of the various psychological factors. It may be of any form—anxiety, indignation, resentment, humiliation, grief, joy, laughter and even pleasurable anticipation of going out on a desired social occasion.

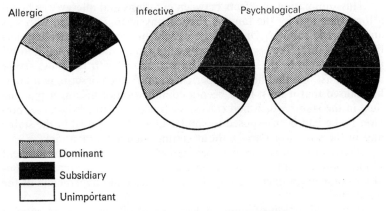

Allergic   Infective   Psychological

▨ Dominant
■ Subsidiary
☐ Unimportant

FIG. 9 Aetiological factors in Asthmas

Vasomotor Rhinitis

Vasomotor rhinitis is characterised by paroxysmal attacks of rhinorrhoea with sneezing and nasal blockage. During the attack there is profuse secretion of the glands of the nasal mucosa, increase in thickness and vascularity of the mucous membrane.

As with asthma, the three most important factors are allergens, infections and emotional factors and multiplicity is the rule.

Hay Fever

Hay fever is an allergic disorder par excellence. It is, by definition, an allergic reaction to pollen on the part of the nasal mucous membrane, conjunctivae and mucous membranes of the pharynx and upper respiratory tract. It is seasonal and the attacks are closely correlated with the amount of circulating pollen.

Allergy and Emotions

Under experimental conditions, subjects have been investigated in a specially prepared room in which a constant amount of pollen was circulated by means of a fan and the nasal mucosal reactions were recorded by objective methods including vascularity, thickness and amount of secretion. It was found that the reaction to a given amount of pollen was greater if the patients were in an emotionally tense state or if they had a preceding infection.

Similar observations have been demonstrated in asthma, when a known allergen was introduced by an aerosol and the reactions measured by a spirograph.

The reaction to a given amount of allergen is much greater when the patient is tense than when his is relaxed.

This summation of effects between emotions and allergy was noted a long time ago by the famous French physician *Trousseau*, who was an asthmatic sufferer. One day he caught his coachman stealing oats from his stable; Trousseau was very angry and wanted to tell him off but was unable to do so because he was seized with the most severe attack of asthma that he had experienced and, when describing it later, he realised that it must have been a combination of his anger plus the dust in the stable which had caused such a severe attack because, previously, he had been exposed to similar quantities of dust in the stable and in the streets of Paris without getting such a severe attack.

Interrelationships also exist between emotions and the development of infections and it has been demonstrated experimentally that emotional tension can produce swelling, hypersecretion and hyperaemia of the nasal mucosa.

Prolonged action of emotional factors results in a boggy, swollen state of the nasal mucosa, with impairment of ciliary activity and lymphatic stasis. These changes are conducive to the development of a superimposed infection.

Sometimes patients will develop attacks of asthma due to the combined effect of infections with emotional stress. One of my patients, a girl aged 10, who had suffered repeated attacks of bronchitis for many years without any wheezing or asthmatic attacks, developed her first attacks of asthma when she was suffering from bronchitis and a burglar broke into the house, causing her alarm and fright.

Thus, allergy, infections and emotions can interact in various ways, creating vicious circle effects which can result in a continuous disease process.

The Role of Suggestion and Conditioning

Many published accounts of asthma tend to describe the role of suggestion as being one of the most important of the psychological factors operating in asthma.

Suggestion very often can have potent effects; it can both relieve attacks and precipitate attacks. Similarly, various stimuli associated with allergic precipitation of asthmatic attacks may subsequently produce asthmatic attacks themselves, even without the allergen.

For example, people who were sensitive to pollen have been known to visit an art gallery and when they saw a painting of a cornfield they had an immediate attack of hay fever or hay asthma.

Other patients, sensitive to dust, have been known to develop an attack of asthma when watching a cowboy picture in which a stampede of buffaloes produced a dust storm. Others, sensitive to flowers have gone into a room and had an attack of asthma, only to discover later that they were artificial flowers.

Suggestion may sometimes relieve attacks. There is the well known example of a physician who suffered from asthma and who went to stay in a remote hotel in the countryside one weekend. He woke up in the middle of the night with a severe attack of asthma; he groped for the electric light switch but was unable to find it and, in desperation, caught hold of his shoe, felt for the window and, on feeling glass, smashed it. He breathed in deeply, the attack passed off and he had a peaceful night, but he was horrified to find in the morning when he woke that he had broken the mirror instead of the window.

There are now many authenticated cases of asthma developing as a conditioned response to stimuli originally associated with direct precipitants of asthmatic attacks, such as allergens.

Pathogenetic Mechanisms

The neural mechanisms mediating the effect of emotional tension in precipitating attacks of asthma, vasomotor rhinitis or aggravating hay fever are parasympathetic pathways.

Parasympathetic over-activity produces all the local changes which form the pathophysiological basis of the attacks. For example, a stellate ganglion block on one side will produce swelling, hyperaemia and increased nasal secretion on the same side. Interruption of the parasympathetic nerve supply on one side will stop the manifestations.

GASTRO-INTESTINAL DISORDERS

Peptic Ulcer

Clinical observations for many years have shown that peptic ulcer symptoms may arise or be precipitated or exacerbated by emotional changes in the patient or by the experience of various stressful conditions.

The first reports of direct correlations between the reactions of the stomach and emotional changes were made by *Beaumont* in his celebrated patient Alexis St. Martin, who has a gastric fistula resulting from an old gunshot wound. *Beaumont* described the course of digestion of various articles of diet under different conditions and various emotional states.

More recently, work of outstanding importance was carried out by *Wolf* and *Wolff*, who carried out a study of gastric functioning on a gentleman called Tom, who is now famous throughout the world. He had a gastric fistula which enabled Drs. *Wolf* and *Wolff* to carry out observations and investigations on the functioning of the gastric mucosa of the stomach under various conditions. On one occasion, as part of a planned experiment, Tom was in a round about was accused of overcharging for some work he had carried out for his employers; he resented this accusation greatly but, being an employee, was unable to express his resentment outwardly to those responsible and went around in a state of bottled up indignation and resentment. During this emotional state it was observed that the gastric mucosa became redder due to greater engorgement with blood and that gastric juice was produced in higher volume and of greater acidity. The gastric mucosa in this state when touched with a glass rod was found to be very friable and bled easily.

These changes are precisely those which are conducive to the development of chronic peptic ulceration. Thus, emotional changes can produce changes in the function of the stomach which are conducive to the formation of peptic ulcers. The increased friability, which is conducive to the development of acute ulcers or abrasions with mechanical stimuli when acted upon by the gastric juice produced in greater volume and greater acidity are prevented from healing, tending to make them chronic.

Emotional factors are not the only ones concerned in the genesis of peptic ulceration. For example, recent work by *Mirski* showed that the level of pepsinogen excretion was much higher in patients with peptic ulcer. It was found that the level of blood pepsinogen tended to remain relatively constant and was determined early in life and may be predominantly genetically determined.

In a study of many thousands of individuals called up for the United States Army, it was found that ulcers tended to develop in persons with a sustained high rate of gastric secretion, as indicated by the level of serum pepsinogen together with the presence of certain conflicts, personality difficulties or environmental circumstances which evoke emotional reactions which, in turn, affect autonomic, neuro-endocrine mechanisms.

The Large Intestine

Certain disorders of the large intestine, such as irritable and spastic colon, have been shown to be largely determined by psychogenic factors. Direct observations on the functioning of the large intestine in patients who had colostomy or . . . caecostomy have demonstrated the marked changes which occur in vascularity and lysozyme secretion during certain emotional states.

One series of experiments showed that certain emotional states increased motility in the bowel, increased vascularity and increased the production of the enzyme lysozyme, which has been suggested by some workers as a possible factor. Lysozyme, by depriving the colonic mucosa of its protective layer of mucus, makes it more vulnerable to other noxic agents, including infective, mechanical factors. Others have suggested that prolonged spasms of the muscles of the colon, resulting from emotional tension, produces an ischaemia of the colonic mucosa and, on relaxation of the muscular tension, a necrosis of the epithelium results in bleeding.

Other theories are that the liquid contents of the small intestine are

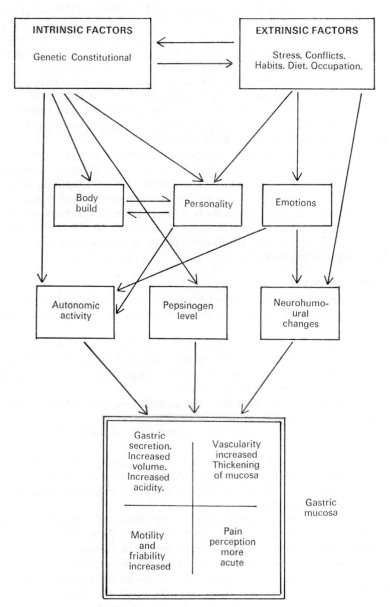

FIG. 10. Factors involved in the development of a peptic ulcer.

carried into the colon as a consequence of emotionally induced hyper-motility of the small bowel, that the enzymes of this liquid have a greater digestive action than normally and that anything which lowers the natural protective powers of the colonic mucosa could lead to diges-tion of its surface, permitting bacterial invasion and ulceration.

Although the evidence is very clear that emotional factors can aggravate ulcerative colitis, the relationship between emotional and other aetiological factors has not been fully elucidated. The aetiology of the condition remains obscure and infective, allergic, nutritional and psychological factors have all been implicated.

It is, however, clear that anything which can relieve the patient's emotional distress can be of potential therapeutic value in the manage-ment of ulcerative colitis and that some physicians have reported in the early stages that group psychotherapy has apparently been beneficial but, in many instances, particularly when the disease has been present for a long time, tissue changes may occur to such an extent that they become irreversible and psychotherapeutic measures then can have little therapeutic effect.

Anorexia Nervosa

Anorexia nervosa is a disorder which is almost confined to young women; it occasionally occurs in older women and, exceptionally, in men.

The term anorexia is a misnomer. At first there is usually a deliber-ate restriction of eating; the patient takes minimal quantities usually of the most slimming foods and will secretly dispose of food or vomit it afterwards or hide it in various places.

Anorexia nervosa often does not come to medical attention until the patient has lost 2 st. or more in weight.

With the decrease in food intake anorexia will occur but, even so, at times the patients often have ravenous appetites and occasionally will gorge large amounts of food, then feel very guilty and either vomit what they have eaten or take a great deal of exercise to work it off.

Progressive loss of weight makes the patients emaciated and some look like victims of Belsen.

They however remain characteristically active and energetic. Some-times a growth of fine, downy hair appears over the body which is similar to that found in other types of intense starvation.

Amenorrhoea is characteristic and the basal metabolic rate is low.

The onset of the disorder is usually associated with some emotional conflict, the most common being conflicts about accepting the female role or, during the engagement period, if the paitent has conflicts about accepting the responsibilities of marriage. Other conflicts relate to the parents, particularly the mother. Often the restriction in diet starts because the girl regards herself as too fat and may have been teased about her weight. More rarely the condition starts in a setting of depressive illness.

Differential Diagnosis

The condition superficially resembles Simmond's disease but, in practice, the differential diagnosis between the two conditions is not difficult. The loss of weight in Simmond's disease is not marked. Simmond's disease usually comes on after childbirth. In anorexia nervosa, the 17-ketosteroid excretion will not be decreased to a level 2–3 mgms. per 24 hours. Similarly, the marked insulin sensitivity found in Simmond's disease is not found in anorexia nervosa.

Treatment

Admission to hospital is essential and skilled nursing care, with one nurse assuming responsibility for the patient's supervision who should personally assist at every meal and, by persuasion, encourage the patient to eat.

With skilled nursing, weight can be gained with ordinary food but, sometimes, highly concentrated foods in small bulk are helpful in recovering lost weight.

Chlorpromazine is a useful drug for relieving tension and facilitating regain in weight. Recently Amitriptylene has been even more helpful.

When weight has been regained, psychological investigation and treatment may be necessary and may be indispensable in order to achieve lasting recovery. In some patients, in whom the motives for losing weight were mainly for appearance's sake and with no deeper conflicts, psychotherapy may not be necessary.

The first essential step in treatment is the regain of lost weight and then the need for psychotherapy will have to be assessed in each individual on the merits of each case.

In practice, one cannot be satisfied that recovery has occurred until the menstrual periods return.

Without treatment, or after unsuccessful treatment, the patient's condition may become extremely serious and death can occur due to inanition or intercurrent infection, such as pneumonia or tuberculosis.

SKIN DISORDERS

It is everyday knowledge and observation that emotional factors affect the skin as shown by the blushing of embarrassment, the pallor of fear and the pallor or redness of rage, depending on the subject and his emotional state. Experiments have demonstrated that emotional states can affect the following, which are of direct relevance in the aetiology of certain skin disorders:

(1) Control of vascularity of the skin.
(2) Control of sebaceous gland secretion.
(3) Control of sweat.
(4) Influencing of the degree of exudation.
(5) Influencing of the tendency to pruritus.

In urticaria, for example, it has been demonstrated that acetyl choline and histamine are involved in the production of the characteristic wheals and constitute the final common pathway for a large number of causative agents such as physical stimuli, infections, allergic reactions, emotional factors and certain changes in the internal environment. Emotional tension by increasing vascularity, exudation and itching can exacerbate the majority of skin disorders. The itching mechanism is of particular importance, as pruritus tends to lead to scratching which in turn stimulates the itching mechanism in the skin further, thus creating a vicious circle.

In skin disorders emotional factors are only one of many causative factors. Constitutional predisposition, allergy, mechanical factors, dietetic, hormonal and many others can all play a part in determining the onset and the course of these illnesses.

DISORDERS OF MUSCLES AND JOINTS

Fibrositis and muscular rheumatism are rather vague diagnostic labels which probably cover a variety of conditions. They are characterised by a dull aching and stiffness which is worse in the mornings and tends to wear off during the day. Sharp twinges of pain are brought on by sudden movements or by pressure on particular spots.

Undoubtedly a proportion of these patients are mainly psychogenically determined. They are often local manifestations of tension in a strained, tense, anxious individual. They may also occur in depressive states, whereas some pains are hysterical. In pains due to localised increased muscular tension, it is possible to demonstrate this objectively by measuring action current potentials in these muscles.

Rheumatoid Arthritis

Whether rheumatoid arthritis should be regarded as a psychosomatic disorder is still controversial. *Selye* has shown that arthritis can occur as a result of an imbalance between the mineral corticoids and the glucocorticoids, and it is possible that rheumatoid arthritis may develop as a result of prolonged stress leading to the changes of the general adaptation syndrome with an imbalance of the various fractions of adrengenal corticoids as described by *Selye*.

The role of emotional factors, is, however, obscure and further research is necessary in order that they may be elucidated.

ENDOCRINE DISORDERS

Hyperthyroidism

In patients suffering from hyperthyroidism, psychosomatic and somatopsychic effects are often intermingled. Although some patients have been emotionally disturbed before developing hyperthyroidism, once the thyroid becomes over-active the patient's emotional instability is increased and anxiety symptoms, tension and various bodily manifestations similar to those of anxiety are very frequent. These effects of hyperthyroidism often lead to increased interpersonal tensions and problems, thereby increasing the patient's emotional difficulties and again worsening the condition.

For very many years physicians have reported the development of thyrotoxicosis following emotional upsets, stresses and shocks of various kinds. A variety of psychosocial stresses may be associated with the onset of thyrotoxicosis, e.g. bereavement, financial, domestic, marital problems and crises, traumatic experiences etc.

Although there is strong evidence that psychosocial stresses and emotional disturbances can exert a precipitating action at the onset of thyrotoxicosis, this does not necessarily mean that the concatenation occurring in thyrotoxicosis can be reversed by psycho-therapeutic measures. The immediate need in treatment is to diminish thyroid over-activity by medical or surgical means. It has often been found that patients who have been so treated and now have their thyroids functioning normally, still suffer from a large variety of emotional, autonomic symptoms and still may have considerable disability. Psychotherapy at this stage can, of course, be valuable.

DIABETES MELLITUS

Physicians, supervising the treatment of diabetics by insulin, diet etc., have observed that the balance in the patient can be readily disturbed by emotional disturbances. This is a comparatively new field but the possible mechanisms involved are:

(1) The autonomic nervous system, through the sympathetic which is mediated by adrenalin which increases the level of blood sugar, or the parasympathetic through the vagus nerve, stimulating the production of insulin which lowers blood sugar.

(2) Neuro-endocrine mechanisms, particularly the adrenal cortex. Many of the hormones of the adrenal cortex are concerned with carbohydrate metabolism.

Another possible factor is the effect of diuresis provoked by stressful anxiety, which can occur in normal as well as diabetic subjects. In diabetic subjects the diuresis can lead to marked loss of sugar, ketones and chlorides, accompanied by a marked decrease in the fixed base and in glycogen storage. These effects can lead to acidosis, particularly when the anxious patient neglects his dietetic regime or other treatment, as he often does.

CARDIOVASCULAR SYSTEM

Essential Hypertension

High blood pressure when not due to arterial disease or kidney disease or to other physical causes is known as essential hypertension. In some cases it can be demonstrated that emotional factors can play an important role. Clinical and experimental observations demonstrate the effect of emotions on blood pressure. Every physician knows that the first blood pressure reading is usually much higher than subsequent ones because of the patient's state of apprehension initially. States of bottled up anxiety, tension, aggression, hostility, resentment and many others can result in a sustained rise of blood pressure.

The mechanisms responsible include:

(1) Stimulation of the sympathetic division of the autonomic nervous system.

(2) Prolonged emotional tension evoking manifestations of the General Adaptation Syndrome which, in certain circumstances, results in disorders such as arteriosclerosis, hypertension and thrombosis of the coronary and cerebral vessels.

(3) Noradrenaline release from the adrenal medulla with emotions and stress.

(4) All the above mechanisms can produce constriction of the arterioles of the kidney giving rise to ischaemia and release of a chemical substance which is now believed to play an important role in the development of hypertension.

John Hunter, the celebrated physician, suffered from hypertension and used to declare that his life was in the hands of any fool who cared to annoy him.

Cerebro-vascular Accidents

Cerebral haemorrhage and cerebral thrombosis are determined by multiple factors, one of which can be emotional tension arising in response to difficulties, conflicts or stresses.

The interrelationships between psychosomatic and somatopsychic processes can be seen clearly in the development of stroke and associated disabilities.

Coronary Disease

Coronary thrombosis and angina pectoris are disorders of great medical and social importance by virtue of the frequency with which they cause suffering, disability and death. The role of emotional factors in the development of coronary disease is still rather controversial.

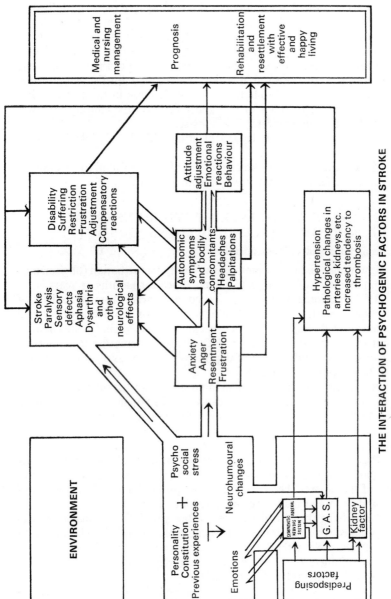

THE INTERACTION OF PSYCHOGENIC FACTORS IN STROKE

FIG. 11

Other factors such as the amount and type of fat in the diet, the level of blood cholesterol, the amount of exercise engaged in by the individual and the amount of atheroma of the arteries have been implicated.

Many authors have reported that the onset of coronary heart disease is not infrequently preceded by severe strain associated with occupational, domestic or financial anxiety. Studies in which a group of persons were observed working under great intellectual pressure revealed a rise in serum cholesterol with decrease in the clotting time of whole blood. In times of rest and relaxation the clotting time was normal and serum cholesterol was lower.

These changes were independent of individual variations in weight, diet and physical activity.

An increase in serum cholesterol has also been found to accompany the mental and emotional stress of examinations.

DISORDERS ASSOCIATED WITH MENSTRUAL AND REPRODUCTIVE FUNCTIONS

Amenorrhoea and Oligomenorrhoea

Emotional disturbance may cause scanty menstruation (oligomenorrhoea) or may cause complete amenorrhoea for months or years.

The emotional factors are varied and arise from a variety of psychological stresses such as illness, injury or the death of a loved person; a frightening experience, accidents, radical change of environment or occupation, fears of pregnancy after intercourse in unmarried persons, as a manifestation of depressive states or as a result of addiction to morphia or heroin.

Amenorrhoea can occur in an interesting disorder known as Pseudocyesis or false pregnancy which can occur in young women and at all ages including women approaching the menopause. The disorders provides a striking illustration of the powerful action of psychological factors on female behaviour and endocrine function.

Pseudocyesis is characterised by a cessation of menstruation accompanied by nausea, vomiting, enlargement and sometimes pigmentation of the breasts. The patient reports quickening and has swelling of the abdomen and may have simulated labour pains.

Underlying the disorder there is often a wish for pregnancy, sometimes linked with a desire to please her husband or to retain his attention and affection. Sometimes the wish for pregnancy is motivated to prove her youthfulness or health and, more rarely, it occurs in unmarried people as an attempt to force marriage.

The diagnosis is made by repeated negative pregnancy tests, absence of an abdominal tumour on examination of the abdomen, disappearance of the abdominal swelling under anaesthesia and a normal size uterus on bimanual examination.

Functional Dysmenorrhoea

Primary functional dysmenorrhoea starts with menarche and seconary functional dysmenorrhoea develops after the establishment of normal menstruation.

A number of factors are usually involved, e.g. a lowered pain threshold, emotional tension, intolerance of discomfort or pain. Other possible factors are the greater intensity of muscular uterine contractions due to hormonal or other causes during menstruation.

Menorrhagia, in some cases, may be determined by stress and emotional tension.

Pregnancy and Childbirth

During early pregnancy, if there is conflict or doubt about having a baby or if definitely unwanted, a reactive depression or an anxiety state may precipitate attempts at suicide or self-induced abortion.

There is little evidence that the incidence of psychiatric disorders, apart from those reactive to the pregnancy, is significantly greater than what would be expected by chance.

Post-partum reactions, however, are not common and some are very severe.

Post-partum psychiatric illnesses must not be confused with the 'maternity blues' which is very common and occurs usually within the first week after delivery. It consists of transitory depression and tearfulness lasting a few days only. This, in my experience, occurs in about a third of normal women and does not cause any significant disability.

There is a group of women who get depression following childbirth which continues for weeks or months but is of mild degree and does not necessarily come to medical attention or necessitate treatment.

Surveys carried out on all deliveries in the general population show that the incidence of severe post-partum psychiatric illness is about 1 per 1,000 deliveries.

In Bristol, a survey revealed an incidence of 1·7 per 1,000 deliveries. 1 per 1,000 were sufficiently ill to require admission to a mental hospital.

Most post-partum illnesses start within 6 weeks of birth and the large majority appear before the end of the third week after birth, the peak incidence being between 7–20 days after birth. There is usually a latent period during which the patient may appear normal. A smaller number of patients develop their symptoms within the first few days after birth.

The most common types of post-partum psychiatric illness are depressive states, schizo-affective states, schizophrenia and only rarely nowadays a toxic confusional state.

Even patients who eventually turn out to be suffering from schizophrenia may initially show symptoms and signs of depression and it is only after two or three weeks' observation that the underlying schizophrenia becomes more clearly manifest.

The Registrar General has shown that post-partum patients constitute about 1 per cent of all female admissions of all ages to mental hospitals, and that post-partum patients tend to stay in hospital 4–6 months as against an average length of stay of 2·2 months for all admissions.

In general, post-partum psychiatric illnesses do well, recovering either spontaneously or with treatment with electroconvulsive therapy in the case of depressions and schizo-affective disorders. In the Schizophrenic illnesses, combined therapy by phenothiazines and E.C.T. gives good results. Some regrettably remain ill for years and prove resistant to all forms of treatment.

The author has observed a subgroup of patients suffering from post-partum psychiatric illnesses who, having recovered completely from their post-partum psychiatric illness, subsequently, when the periods become re-established, develop a premenstrual recurrence of their post-partum psychiatric symptoms similar qualitatively but quantitatively less marked. In post-partum schizophrenic patients, for example, the same delusions may re-eappear but are less marked, less disturbing and they appear about 7–10 days before the menses and usually clear up at the onset of the period, the patient remaining free from psychiatric manifestations until the next period. This premenstrual recurrence following a post-partum psychiatric illness in many cases spontaneously clears up during the course of a year or so or responds to progestogen therapy.

Follow up studies have shown that the chances of a further post-partum illness with subsequent births are of the order 1 in 5 to 1 in 7.

Treatment of Post-Partum Psychiatric Disorders

The treatment of these disorders will depend on the type of illness and its degree of severity.

Depressive illnesses will respond to antidepression drugs but, if severe, electroconvulsive therapy will be needed.

Schizophrenic illnesses will require phenothiazine drugs, with or without electroconvulsive therapy.

Large doses of progestogens have been tried but the results have been, on the whole, disappointing.

For premenstrual recurrence of post-partum illnesses, the treatment is that for premenstrual tension syndromes.

Premenstrual Tension

Premenstrual tension is a syndrome occurring during the second half of a menstrual cycle and consisting of a number of mental and physical symptoms. The syndrome is composed of feelings of anxiety, tension and irritability, with one or more of the following symptoms: Depression, bloated abdominal feelings, swelling of the subcutaneous tissues, nausea, fatigue, painful swelling of the breasts, headaches, dizziness and palpitations. Less frequently there may be increased sex desire, excessive thirst, increased appetite and hypersomnia.

The symptoms usually start about seven to fourteen days before menstruation and pass off soon after the onset of the period, although some patients continue to have symptoms throughout the period.

The aetiology of the condition is still obscure. The most generally accepted view is that it is due to the unantagonized action of oestrogens resulting from faulty luteinization. Oestrogens produce many of the manifestations of the premenstrual syndrome and oestrogens given to ovariectomised women after the menopause will produce similar symptoms.

Diagram gives, schematically, various factors entering into the premenstrual tension syndrome. The syndrome is somatopsychic rather than psychosomatic but there is a complex interplay between psychological factors and physical factors.

It is interesting to note that, in many women, their conflicts and problems become manifest during the premenstrual phase and at other times of the cycle may not significantly affect them.

The syndrome can occur in normal, stable women but when it co-exists with neurosis it is more severe the more neurotic the woman.

Treatment

Dehydration therapy consisting of restriction of salt and water and giving diuretics produces some relief particularly in physical comfort, but does not help emotional symptoms significantly. Treatment by progesterone injections or orally active progestogens gives the best results.

MENOPAUSAL DISTURBANCES

It is well known that in many women the menopause is associated with a variety of nervous symptoms and manifestations of emotional instability. Increased nervousness, irritability, depression, hyperaesthesias, paraesthesias, vertigo and many other symptoms associated with a lowered threshold of nervous stimuli resulting in an increase in emotional tension and organ response. The autonomic nervous system is more labile, particularly the vascular apparatus, giving rise to hot flushes, night sweats, chills, fainting, palpitations and cardiac arrhythmias.

The most striking feature is the hot flush. The woman suddenly experiences a sensation of heat, more or less violent which sweeps like a wave over her body to her head. This may come on spontaneously or may be provoked by emotional upsets. Along with the subjective sensation of heat there is an intense flushing of the face. Following this there is a feeling of depression accompanied by pallor and profuse sweating, especially on the head, sometimes so copious that sweat drops from the skin. Finally, there may be cold or shivering sensations.

The syndrome, therefore, is a rushing of warm blood to the skin, particularly face and neck and the upper part of the body i.e. the areas which are particularly concerned with controlling heat loss by the body.

A number of factors will precipitate the attacks. Flushes will be aggravated by physical effort, by eating or drinking warm foods or beverages, by intense emotions, by excitement by warm environment, too many bedclothes at night or heavy clothes in the day. All of these factors are ones which give rise to excessive heat production or retention. It is believed that the hot flush is hypothalamic in origin and represents a disturbance of the heat regulating mechanism.

SOMATOPSYCHIC SEQUENCES

We have considered the role of emotional changes and stress in the production of lesions and dysfunctions in psychosomatic disorders where the sequence is a psychosomatic sequence.

We now need to consider the effect of an illness, disorder or disability on the person's reactions, i.e. Somatopsychic sequence.

Even in those psychosomatic disorders which have important psychogenic factors, with emotions or stress exerting a demonstrably contributory role in their aetiology, somatopsychic sequences may also be important.

This is well exemplified in the case of Stroke due to a cerebral vascular accident.

A patient's reations and the consequent psychological burden he has to carry with regard to a Stroke derives from three main sources: (1) The symptoms, i.e. the sudden onset of paralysis, sometimes aphasia, dysarthria and sensory defects is naturally a frightening, perplexing and frustrating experience. (2) The threat inherent in the diagnosis of the underlying cause of the Stroke, e.g. high blood pressure and/or arteriosclerosis. (3) The strain imposed by the limitations due to his physical disability resulting from the Stroke and which evoke increased anxiety, depression, anger or frustration.

Such reactions are important as they evoke emotional changes which by different mechanisms can, by a psychosomatic sequence, worsen the disorder. For example:

(1) Stimulation of the sympathetic nervous system, by increasing heart rate and causing arterial vasoconstriction, causes an increase in blood pressure.

(2) Prolonged states of emotional tension evoke the General Adaptation Syndrome and, under certain conditions, the adaptive mechanisms

of the syndrome fail which may result in arteriosclerosis, hypertension and thrombosis.

(3) The mechanisms described under (1) may result in a decrease in the blood supply to the kidney, releasing a chemical factor now known to play an important role in the development of arterial hypertension.

(4) Emotional tension and stresses are known to increase coagulability of the blood and, therefore, increase the tendency to cerebral thrombosis.

The psychosomatic and somatopsychic mechanisms involved in a stroke are shown in Figure 11.

Reactions to Onset of Symptoms and Diagnosis

The patient's reactions will, in part, depend on his personality make-up and, in part, on the suddenness or unexpectedness of the development of symptoms and, also, the threat to security which may be caused by the onset of an illness and by knowledge of the diagnosis.

Anxiety is the most frequent reaction. Anxiety arises because the illness threatens the patient's bodily safety and security. The illness incapacitates him temporarily or for a long period from his usual work; this may lead to financial worries.

Other patients react to illness by becoming apathetic with loss of interest; this may sometimes cover an underlying anxiety.

Some patients will resent the enforced dependency due to an illness and they particularly resent being in a position of being looked after by other people and may react to this by becoming tense, anxious, irritable or even aggressive, truculent and generally awkward.

To other people, illness and bed rest satisfy their dependency needs and they almost welcome the opportunity of being dependent.

Thus, the reaction to a diagnosis, to disability and to enforced dependency may evoke in some people anxiety, in others hostility and in others an increase in dependency needs. In some, a non-acceptance and non-recognition of the diagnosis or the illness.

Undesirable forms of reaction to a disability may take the form of:

(1) Developing rebellious, aggressive attitudes and unwillingness to conform to medical regimes and treatment. This attitude impairs the chances of successful rehabilitation and its emotional effects may aggravate the disorder or, at least, the degree of disability associated with it.

(2) The patient may react by becoming vindictive, spiteful and tending to belittle other people in order to elevate himself or he may succumb to the disability, using it as an excuse for avoiding responsibility or failure.

In general, patients when they come into hospital are anxious and frightened about three things. First of all what is wrong with them, secondly, what is going to be the outcome of the illness and thirdly, what residual effects are likely to occur after the illness or following the operation.

Patients sometimes give the impression that they do not want to know anything about the illness and that they are happy to remain ignorant; but this is only applicable to a small number of patients and the majority, and sometimes even those who pretend they do not want to, in fact, wish to know something about the illness. They want to know how long they are going to be in hospital, because they have to make necessary arrangements, and they want to know what implication the illness has on them for the present and for the future.

Communication between doctors and nurses is an important need to alleviate patients of these anxieties. It is important for a patient to be treated as an individual, as a person; one should remember his name and one should take him into one's confidence with regard to the various procedures, diagnostic or therapeutic, which are going to be carried out to help him.

If the patient can express his various fears this, in itself, is often a great relief. So the nurse or doctor should listen and give whatever comfort possible to the patient.

PRINCIPLES IN TREATMENT AND MANAGEMENT OF PSYCHOSOMATIC DISORDERS

The first step is the thorough investigation of each patient to assess the relative importance of various physical as well as emotional factors.

In asthma, for example, infections and allergy and other factors may play a dominant or subsidiary role to psychogenic factors. Team work is important and every method of treatment to deal with as many factors as possible is the correct approach.

In some patients emotional factors may be playing a very important part, and, in these, special consideration has to be given to what extent these can be helped.

It is necessary to study each patient to assess which personality attributes are conducive to the development of states of tension which may precipitate attacks of the psychosomatic disorder under consideration. The next step is to ascertain the setting in which the attacks occur and the third step is to help the patient to understand how the relationship between his personality disposition, his life situation, his conflicts and emotional problems make him react in the way he does and predispose to the arousal of an emotional state which leads to an attack of migraine.

Patients suffering from psychosomatic disorders are not necessarily unstable or neurotic in the usual sense and frequently are well adjusted, successful persons. However, certain personality characteristics which are common in psychosomatic disorders tend to lead to emotional states which, in turn, can produce the various manifestations.

Psychosomatic patients are often tense, anxious, self-driving persons who are rigid, ambitious, perfectionistic, always highly competitive in their outlook, always trying to do better than their fellows. They are usually reliable, conscientious persons and, in such instances, responsibilities and duties are thrust on them and characteristically they may have great difficulty in delegating responsibility.

Such patients readily become resentful when they cannot keep up to their own expectations or what others expect of them. The inevitable outcome is the development of tension, fatigue and exhaustion.

Psychotherapeutic Management

The interview is the medium whereby the patient, with the help of the physician, gains an understanding of the factors and situations which form the setting for the occurrence of attacks of the psychosomatic disorder the patient suffers from.

Attacks may be precipitated by sudden traumatic experiences or may be the result of a gradual build-up of tension due to everyday problems and difficulties, determined largely by the patient's attitudes and personality make-up.

The direct relationship between attacks and stressful experiences is important but it is also necessary to realise that some disorders such as migraine, urticaria and asthma may occur during the 24–48 hours immediately following a stressful period.

The patient needs to be advised to modify his attitudes; he must avoid becoming extremely perfectionistic and avoid imposing on himself expectations to get greater amounts of work done in a given time. He should aim at getting three quarters of the work that he usually attempts done in a given period of time. He has to learn to delegate responsibilities and to have adequate periods of rest and recreation. He should be encouraged to deal with each day as it comes, rather than to anticipate problems and meet them half way. He will need frequent and strong reassurance and it will probably be some time before he realises that greater spontaneity, productivity and effectiveness will come with less anxiety and tension.

In the case of children with asthma or other psychosomatic disorders, the best way of helping the child is usually to devote one's main attention to the parents, particularly if they exhibit over-anxious, over-protective, perfectionistic or rejecting attitudes.

The best way to get the parents' co-operation is not to condemn them or pass judgment but to try to get them to discuss their problems freely, with the interviewer adopting an accepting, listening attitude. This often results in their spontaneous realisation of the effect of their attitudes on the child's well-being and attacks of asthma.

The over-anxious parent can be turned to the advantage of the child because often the mother is quite willing to learn how to manage the child more satisfactorily. By letting the parents speak, express their feelings regarding the child—sometimes aggressive feelings, sometimes anxiety or fear—they increasingly come to realise the effect that their attitudes have and therefore to realise their importance and this may help to achieve a modification in attitude and upbringing.

Improvements in the child, when such attitudes can be improved, are sometimes quite dramatic.

FURTHER READING

Psychosomatics by M. Hamilton. Chapman and Hall, London (1955).

CHAPTER NINETEEN

ORGANIC MENTAL STATES

Organic mental disorders are a result of anatomical and physiological disturbance in the central nervous system caused by physical disease, trauma, intoxication or degeneration.

Organic states may be conveniently subdivided into:

Acute and Subacute Organic States
    (a) Acute Delirium.
    (b) Subacute.
        1. Dysmnesic syndrome (Korsakow).
        2. Subacute delirious state.

Chronic Organic Mental States
These are classified according to the underlying pathogenetic processes, e.g. inflammatory, degenerative, traumatic etc.

DELIRIUM
The following are the characteristic features of delirium:

(1) Varying degrees of clouding of consciousness. This is associated with (a) disorientation for time, place or person, (b) difficulty in grasping what goes on in the environment.

(2) Attention is disturbed and it is difficult to secure the patient's attention for more than a short time. The patient is easily distracted by stimuli, moving objects, shadows and noises which he often misinterprets.

(3) Disorders of perception, such as illusions and hallucinations, particularly visual hallucinations.

(4) Mood varies from mild unease to frank terror and perplexity. Fear and suspicion are the predominant aspects.

(5) Mental content. Sometimes thinking is disconnected and speech is incoherent. Occasionally talk and actions are concerned with daily tasks; this is referred to as occupational delirium—the bus conductor calling for fares and handing out imaginary tickets.

(6) Misidentification of people.

(7) There is a tendency for the symptomatology to become more marked as darkness falls.

(8) Sleep is disturbed. There is a tendency for the patient to be drowsy during the day and to be awake as night comes on. Occasionally there is marked restlessness by day and night.

(9) On recovery from delirium, the patient's memory for the period is vague or sometimes absent. This is because attention and registration have been significantly impaired during the acute phase.

Diagnosis

The diagnosis of acute delirium usually presents no difficulties. Occasionally acute mania and acute schizophrenia may appear to be like delirium but there is no clouding of consciousness and the patient's awareness of his surroundings is usually intact. The main problem of diagnosis is to ascertain the underlying toxic metabolic infective or other factors responsible for the delirium.

A large number of illnesses may be complicated by delirium, e.g.

(1) Systemic infections.

(2) Inflammatory conditions of the central nervous system, such as tubercular cerebro-spinal meningitis, cerebral abscess, meningo-vascular syphilis, etc.

(3) Non-inflammatory lesions of the brain, such as concussion, contusion, neoplastic deposits, raised intracranial pressure, haemorrhage, embolism, hypertensive encephalography, senile and presentile dementia, epilepsy.

(4) Barbiturates, bromides, amphetamines, hyoscine, atropine, cocaine, hashish, alcohol. Tofranil, Amitriptyline and Nortriptyline in elderly patients.

(5) Sudden withdrawal of drugs such as barbiturates, narcotics and alcohol.

(6) Cerebral anaemia due to any cause.

(7) Metabolic and endocrine conditions. Uraemia, liver failure, ketosis, alkalosis, vitamin deficiency, acute porphyria, hyperinsulinism, hypoglycaemia, thyrotoxicosis and hypopituitarism.

The severity of delirium is determined by the patient's constitutional make-up and by the severity of the toxic, infective or other noxic agent. Some patients will become delirious with an infection of the finger. Children and elderly patients more readily become delirious, probably due to difficulty in maintaining homeostatic mechanisms.

Two approaches have been made to analyse and interpret the manifestations in terms of cerebral function:

(1) Certain elements of the delirium may be viewed as reflecting dysfunction of particular parts of the grain such as agnosia, dysphasia, amnesia, auditory and visual hallucinations.

In the Korsakow syndrome, the confusional state is notable for the breakdown in memory mechanisms and the orientation of memory in correct temporal sequence; the hypothalamic region and its interconnections with the frontal lobes are usually involved. Thus, a lesion in this situation should be considered when temporal disorientation is a distinct feature of delirium.

Subdelirious State

The conditions which may give rise to delirium may also give rise to states which do not amount to delirium, in which the degree of clouding of consciousness is less marked and less constant.

A striking feature of a subdelirious state is incoherence of thinking. The patient is more interested and eager to get into contact with his environment than with delirium and awareness fluctuates considerably. The patient, during his more lucid moments, realises that he is unwell and is perplexed and anxious about his symptoms, particularly disorders of perception such as illusions or hallucinations.

Korsakow Syndrome

Here the memory difficulty is the characteristic feature and the disorder is sometimes included under the general term Dysmnesic Syndrome.

There is great difficulty in retaining recent events and faulty orientation, particularly with regard to time and place and person. Memory for past events is usually satisfactory. The patient tends to fill in the gaps in his memory by confabulation.

Korsakow syndrome may follow a delirious state, head injury or may be due to alcohol, in which it is first described in association with polyneuritis. It is also found in poisoning with lead and carbon monoxide and with uraemia, vitamin B deficiency, arteriosclerosis and cerebral syphilis.

Post-Infective Depression

This may follow any severe infection, especially virus infections.

The patient complains of weakness, headaches, irritability, hypersensitivity to light and noise, tendency to be anxious, unduly reactive to noise and to have lack of concentration. Emotional lability, depression and retardation are common.

The duration of post-infective depression shows little correlation with the course of the underlying infective illness and depression and hypochondriasis may continue for months after all signs of bodily illness have cleared up.

DEMENTIA
Definition

The term Dementia denotes a loss of mental capacity due to organic damage to the brain.

It is characterised by:

(1) A failure of memory mainly for recent events at first, and subsequently for remote events as well.

(2) Difficulty in grasp and comprehension.

(3) Emotional instability with emotional outbursts on minor provocation.

(4) Difficulty in forming judgments.

Classification

The dementias may be classified on an aetiological basis into:

(1) *Primary degenerative conditions*, e.g. Senile Dementia, Huntingdon's Chorea, Pick's Disease and Alzheimer's Disease.

(2) *Cardiovascular disorders* including Arteriosclerotic Dementia and Hypertensive Encephalopathy.

(3) *Inflammatory*, e.g. Cerebral Syphilis, other forms of Encephalitis, Encephalomyelitis etc.

(4) *Demyelinating disorders.*

(5) *Neoplastic.*

(6) *Metabolic, endocrine and nutritional disorders.*

(7) *Intoxications, poisoning and anoxia*, e.g. Carbon Monoxide poisoning or arrest or decrease of blood supply to the brain.

(8) *Traumatic.*

Clinical Features of Dementia in General

The loss of mental capacity and deterioration may be diffuse as in senile dementia or focal as in arteriosclerotic dementia. It may be gradually progressive or it may be arrested, with a limited degree of improvement; or may be rapidly progressive.

Dementia denotes deterioration of a person's mental capacity affecting mainly memory, comprehension and judgment and, secondarily, affecting feeling and conduct; due to damage to the cerebrum.

We have noted that different pathological agencies can produce dementia and the clinical picture will vary, (1) according to the nature of the underlying pathological condition (2) the age of onset (3) the previous personality (4) the localisation of lesions (5) the rate of progress.

The following are the principal manifestations of dementia:

(1) *Memory impairment*—recollection of recent events is first affected and usually the condition becomes progressively worse and more remote events are affected as well. The memory failure is mainly due to difficulty in retention.

(2) *Judgment and reasoning.* Impaired judgment and the failure to grasp the situation as a whole and hence the failure to react to it appropriately, may be an early sign of dementia.

(3) *Emotional reactions.*—emotional instability manifested by irritability, impulsive conduct, occasional acts of violence, alcoholic excess or sexual aberration can occur.

A variety of mood change can occur in dementia, e.g. euphoria, depression, anxiety and perplexity. In some patients apathy predominates.

(4) *Disorientation.* This occurs mainly at night but also depends on the underlying condition; for example, it is more common in arteriosclerotic and hypertensive disorders because of interference to the blood supply of the brain.

(5) *Delusions* are the outcome of the impairment of judgment, the defective appreciation of reality and the person's emotional state. The form of the delusion is often influenced by the person's previous personality.

(6) *Personal care*—carelessness in dress, cleanliness and, finally, complete disregard for personal cleanliness and hygiene with incontinence occurs.

(7) *The physical concomitants* will depend on the underlying causal disorder, but there is usually a general physical deterioration with loss of weight and depression of endocrine functions.

PRIMARY DEGENERATIVE DISORDERS

OLD AGE

During the past 50 years the proportion of elderly people in the general population has steadily increased, and the incidence of psychiatric disorders has shown a disproportionately greater increase.

Senescence

The term senescence is applied to the normal process of growing old and is characterised by a gradual falling off in mental and physical capacity, a decrease in ability to cope with new situations, a tendency to become rigid and fixed in outlook, movement becoming slower, more tremulous, less accurate and a decreased tolerance of physical effort. Gradually there develops some impairment of memory for recent events and an increasing tendency to dwell in the past; a narrowing of interests, a decrease in adaptability and a tendency to become possessive and rigid.

It should be noticed that there is considerable variation between people in the rate at which normal processes of senescence take place. Although many people lose speed and ability to adapt to new situations this is often offset by gains in persistence and quality as well as accuracy of performance. This is particularly relevant to the question of employment of elderly people.

Senile Dementia

In senile dementia the changes of senescence develop to such a degree that it interferes with a person's well-being and adjustment. Senile dementia is characterised by a progressive deterioration of memory, thinking and stability by blunting, lack of responsiveness in emotional reactions and reduction in interest and initiative.

Senile Dementia is a disease with a fairly well defined course and, when the diagnosis has been made, it carries a prognosis of death within a period of a few years from clinical onset.

The onset is gradual and later becoming more rapidly progressive. The keystone of the understanding of senile dementia is that memory for recent experience is impaired, whilst the person retains the ability to remember remote experiences. This failure of memory for recent events tends to recede progressively backwards until ultimately it involves early life.

There is a decrease of interest and the person become increasingly egocentric, irritable and difficult, intolerant of any change and suspicious of things which are modern. Judgment is defective, emotions tend to be generally blunted and the patients tend to be irritable and quarrelsome. At night there is a tendency for confusion to develop and the patient will wander about the house, often causing domestic difficulties by turning the taps on and then forgetting about them by turning the water taps on and possibly flooding the house, turning the gas taps on and sometimes lighting a fire and forgetting about it. These are the ways in which the person with senile dementia often cause problems at home. The patient has difficulty in grasp and comprehension, he tires easily and finds it difficult to follow conversation, particularly when it deals with new or unfamiliar topics. Patients may become deluded because of difficulty in comprehending and grasping what goes on around them. Delusions that people are stealing their property or possessions are a common form. Any sudden change in the environment, such as moving house or a new domestic servant, may precipitate severe ideas of persecution.

Huntington's Chorea

Huntington's Chorea was first described in 1872 by George Huntington in America and is characterised by progressive dementia associated with choreoathetoid movements.

There is evidence that at least some of the American families with Huntington's Chorea came from Suffolk.

It has been reported in many parts of the world in different races.

Huntington's Chorea is transmitted by a single dominant gene with a manifestation rate of practically 100 per cent. Therefore 50 per cent of the children of one parent with Huntington's Chorea will develop it if they live sufficiently long.

The onset occurs between the ages of 30 and 50 years but sometimes it starts earlier.

Psychiatric anomalies often precede the development of neurological manifestations. The patient becomes irritable, moody, ill-tempered, quarrelsome and very sensitive and may develop delusions of persecution. Occasionally the illness may first present itself as dullness, apathy, lack of initiative and occasionally as depression. The onset of the physical symptoms are gradual and subtle; the patient appears fidgety but he soon develops the characteristic jerking, abrupt movements which usually start in the face, hands and shoulders. Sometimes the movements are choreic but more often are a combination of slow, writhing movements combined with a jerking movement, i.e. chorea-athetoid movements.

Speech becomes abrupt and staccato. Involvement of the diaphragm causes irregularity of breathing. Involvement of muscles concerned with swallowing may sometimes cause choking.

The most common psychiatric syndromes associated with it are (1) depression, which may be associated with impulsive suicidal attempts (2) paranoid tendencies and (3) sometimes a definite paranoid psychosis. It has been stated that some patients who develop the disease earlier show evidence of Parkinsonism as well as the choreo-athetotic movements. The average duration is 10 to 15 years.

The pressing problem with Huntington's Chorea is to find some means of ascertaining the carrier of the dominant gene.

Investigations have been directed towards studies of premorbid personality, electroencephalogram and other abnormalities which might be associated with the carrier of Huntington's Chorea.

Management

Recently it has been demonstrated that the phenothiazine drug thiopropazate is helpful in the care and management of patients with Huntington's Chorea. The patient becomes calmer, more tranquil and more amenable. Usually after three weeks of thiopropazate administration the involuntary movements decrease.

PRESENILE DEMENTIA

Alzheimer's Disease

Alzheimer's Disease usually develops in the fifties or sixties but sometimes earlier.

The average duration of the disease is about seven years.

Alzheimer's Disease usually starts with memory failure for recent events. Marked lack of spontaneous activity and lack of initiative is common in the early stages.

Quite frequently extra-pyramidal manifestations or akinetic hypotonic symptoms occur. Reading difficulties occur and there is marked disorientation in space, whereas orientation in time is not so much affected. The loss of spatial orientation causes patients to wander and lose themselves, even get lost in the house in which they live.

There is a tendency for patients to stare with a forward gaze which is associated with a marked inability to change the position of their eyes.

After two or three years dementia becomes well established and focal symptoms appear in the form of aphasia, apraxia and agnosia. Gait disturbances become noticeable, gait being slow, unsteady and clumsy.

The terminal stages of the illness are characterised by a very severe dementia and a vegetative existence, with progressive deterioration in speech and a rapid physical deterioration with flexion contractures, bed sores and cachexia. Forced grasping and groping sometimes occur and also the sucking reflex. The genetic basis of Alzheimer's Disease is considered to be multifactorial.

Neuropathology

Diffuse atrophy occurs mainly in the frontal and temporal lobes and sometimes in the parietal lobes. There is a marked loss of ganglial cells, particularly in the outer parts of the cortex and degenerative changes which are characteristic of a disease and referred to as Alzheimer's fibrillary change together with argentophile plaques.

Pick's Disease

Pick's Disease is a form of presenile dementia which is transmitted by a single dominant gene.

It has an average age of onset between 52 and 57 years and an average duration of the disease of 6 to 7 years. In the early stages there is lack of initiative and drive and memory failure for recent events, with a tendency to be fatuous and to have diminished control over impulses and behaviour.

Later there is severe progressive dementia with aphasia. Patients do not show the typical disturbance of gait found in Alzheimer's Disease.

The final stage is one of marked dementia, the patient being bed-ridden with contractures of the limbs and cachexia similar to Alzheimer's Disease. Spatial disorientation occurs much earlier than in Alzheimer's Disease.

Pathologically there is a marked atrophy of the frontal and/or temporal lobes with narrow sulci. There are no Alzheimer's fibrillary changes or senile plaques and the parietal lobe is very rarely affected.

HYPERTENSIVE AND ARTERIOSCLEROTIC DEMENTIA

Hypertension does not necessarily cause any psychiatric symptoms. In those cases who ultimately develop signs of dementia there is usually a history of episodes of disturbances of consciousness, which may vary from transient interruptions of consciousness to periods of confusion or twilight states.

Eventually symptoms of dementia with memory failure and difficulty in comprehension supervene. Bouts of hypertensive encephalapathy with vomiting, loss of vision, epilepsy and monoplegia may occur.

Arteriosclerotic Dementia usually starts in the sixth decade but may occasionally begin in the forties or fifties.

The presence of arteriosclerosis in itself, even in the fundal arteries, does not mean that the patient is suffering from arteriosclerotic dementia.

The diagnosis of arteriosclerotic dementia must first be made on the evidence of dementia and secondly the characteristic features of arteriosclerotic dementia itself.

If it is remembered that underlying pathology is an ischaemia of parts of the brain causing anoxia and necrosis. As the disorder is vascular, the characteristic features are its fluctuating course, with periods of exacerbation and intervening periods of improvement. At first the personality is well preserved with good insight into the condition. The memory loss for recent events tends to be transient, variable, patchy and lacunar.

There are periods of loss of consciousness, which may be transient or last days.

The presence of focal neurological signs clinches the diagnosis, e.g. paralysis, aphasia and apraxia.

Epileptiform seizures occur in about 20 per cent of cases. The fluctuating course of the disease is maintained until a late stage.

Eventually there is a disintegration of personality with marked dementia.

INFLAMMATORY

Cerebral Syphilis

Neurosyphilis occurs in some 10 per cent of persons infected with Spirochaeta pallida.

Psychiatric symptoms may occur with other manifestations of neurosyphilis, e.g. severe meningo-vascular syphilis may give rise to clouding of consciousness or delirium. Mental disturbances sometimes accompany tables and are due to the syphilitic changes in the brain.

The most important condition in clinical practice is general paralysis.

General Paralysis of the Insane (G.P.I.)

G.P.I. is three times as common in men as in women and the incubation period ranges from 10 to 24 years after initial infection.

The most common type of disorder is a simple dementing form;

other types are the manic-expansive-grandiose type and the depressive variety. Negative blood W.R.s are found in 8 per cent but the W.R. is always positive in the C.S.F.

Early diagnosis and prompt penicillin treatment produces clinical improvement and ability to return to work in more than 80 per cent and has nearly eliminated deaths from neurosyphilis. Even in severely affected patients needing treatment in a mental hospital, there is a 1 in 3 chance of improvement and re-ablement for work.

However, in very few cases is recovery complete; impairment of judgment, insight and speech usually persist.

A total of 6,000,000 units of penicillin is usually adequate.

Further courses of penicillin are indicated if clinical improvement is followed by deterioration or if the C.S.F. cell count was greater than 5 per cubic millimetre in the first post-treatment year.

The pre-treatment C.S.F. findings are of some value in forcasting the response to treatment. A marked increase in the cell count, indicating an active inflammatory process, will tend to improve with treatment, although there might be residual symptoms due to damage of the brain before treatment was started. Absence of pleocytosis in the C.S.F. indicates a relatively static process and is less likely to be improved by treatment but also less likely to deteriorate.

Encephalitis Lethargica

During the acute phase of the illness the patient may exhibit involuntary movements of the choreiform and athetoid type, and show insomnia and mild delirium.

Usually some years after the initial attack various extra-pyramidal phenomena occur, including parkinsonism and oculogyric crises. Patients with these extrapyramidal conditions are often slow and may develop a reactive depression on account of their disability and its long duration.

Encephalitis lethargica affecting children and young adults often results in marked personality difficulties. The patients may become social problems, be cruel, show lack of restraint in sexual or aggressive and social behaviour. If it occurs very early in childhood it may cause an arrest of development of the mind and cause mental subnormality.

Sydenham's Chorea

The early symptoms of Sydenham's chorea are irritability, disobedience and misbehaviour and sometimes unusual placidity, apathy and lack of attention; emotional lability varying from depression to hilarity, distractability, absent-mindedness.

Following the illness tics, twitches and compulsive utterances may persist into adult life.

DEMYELINATING DISORDERS

Disseminated sclerosis may be associated with emotional instability, hysterical tendencies and, extremely rarely, may lead to dementia.

Schilder's disease causes marked dementia along with blindness, deafness, aphasia and agnosia.

NEOPLASTIC

Cerebral Tumour

Cerebral tumours may produce effects as a result of increased intracranial pressure when the common symptoms are headaches and vomiting, both being worse in the morning and associated with papilloedema.

The effects of infiltration of the tumour into the brain will vary according to the area affected but certain symptoms are common. A change of personality, a lack of control and suppressed earlier tendencies, such as homosexuality, may now become manifest, sometimes hysterical mechanisms are released. The development of hysteria for the first time in middle age or later should make one suspect an underlying organic lesion.

If the tumour is rapidly growing disturbances of consciousness, clouding of consciousness or the dysmnesic syndrome may occur; dementia, loss of mental capacity with memory failure, difficulty in comprehension also occur.

Tumours in the frontal lobe tend to be associated with fatuousness and cheerfulness, but this can occur with other cerebral tumours as well. The patient tends to be inattentive, distractable, dull and apathetic.

Temporal lobe tumours may give rise to temporal lobe epilepsy and behavioural and emotional changes which are referred to in Chapter 20.

Parietal lobe lesions produce defects at the highest levels of sensory and perceptual integration.

METABOLIC, ENDOCRINE AND NUTRITIONAL DISORDERS

Vitamin Deficiency

Thiamine (Vitamin B_1, Aneurin).

Thiamine plays an important part in the oxidation of carbohydrates and has a fundamental role in the processes of oxidation in the living cell.

Thiamine deficiency may result in the following syndromes:

(1) *A neurasthenic syndrome:* this is the earliest and most frequent manifestation of thiamine deficiency. Anorexia, fatigue, insomnia are common; irritability, mild depression etc. may also occur.

(2) *Wernicke's encephalopathy*. This syndrome often has an abrupt onset and may occur with alcoholism or as a terminal complication of diseases, particularly chronic gastro-intestinal disorders such as gastric carcinoma.

The features include clouding of consciousness, varying ophthalmoplegias and ataxia. The clouding of consciousness may vary from drowsiness or apathy to delirium or coma. There is paralysis of conjugate eye movements nystagmus is often present, polyneuritis of the lower limbs is common.

(3) *Korsakow's syndrome*

(4) *Delirium Tremens*.

Treatment is the provision of a balanced highly nutritious diet of natural unrefined foods and the administration of the missing factor.

For mild cases the dose should be 10 mgms.–30 mgms. a day, for severe cases with polyneuropathy the dose may vary from 10 mgms.–100 mgms. twice daily, for Wernicke's encephalopathy 50 mgms.–100 mgms. three times daily for 7 days.

Nicotinic Acid

The following syndromes occur with nicotinic acid deficiency:

(1) *A neurasthemic syndrome*.

(2) *Pellagra*. The diagnostic triad of dermatitis, diarrhoea and dementia is out of date. The features of pellagra are mental abnormality, loss of weight, stomatitis, glossitis, dermatitis, porphyrinuria, diarrhoea, tachycardia, peripheral neuropathy and vomiting, in relative order of frequency.

(3) *Encephalopathy*, characterised by clouding of consciousness, cogwheel rigidity in the extremities and uncontrollable grasping and sucking reflexes.

Treatment includes an abundant high-calorie diet together with the specific vitamin.

In the early stages, owing to painful mouth lesions and gastric disturbances, milk and meat juices may have to be the mainstay.

Nicotinamide is given in a dose of 15 mgms.–30 mgms. every hour for 10 hours a day. The addition of Brewer's yeast 15 g.–30 g. daily is advisable, owing to the danger of precipitation of latent deficiencies in other B factors such as thiamine or riboflavine.

A maintenance dose of 25 mgms.–50 mgms. three times a day should be given for a prolonged period, in addition to the continued enriched diet.

ANAEMIA

Sometimes a disturbed mental state may precede evidence of megaloblastic anaemia. An abnormal E.E.G. is one of the positive findings.

Much larger doses of Vitamin B_{12} are needed in treating this type of case and care must be taken to ensure that an associated encephalopathy is not missed in a patient who presents with severe anaemia.

Severe iron deficiency anaemias may result in fatigue, irritability and mild depression.

THYROID DISORDER

Hypothyroidism

The features of hypothyroidism are mental torpor, lack of spontaneity, retardation in thinking and motor activity, intense fatigue associated with emotional lability.

In some patients marked memory difficulties may occur and in others delusions and hallucinations and disturbances of behaviour may be present. The most frequent accompaniment is depression and retardation.

Hyperthyroidism

Hyperthyroidism is associated with excessive activity, emotional instability, difficulty in interpersonal relationships due to irritability, excitability, impatience and liability to explosive rage.

In predisposed subjects a schizophreniform picture may occur, which is usually of short duration. Depressive and manic states also occur.

MISCELLANEOUS INTOXICATIONS

Bromide

Bromide intoxication is an iatrogenic disorder which is often unrecognised.

Delirium, confusional states with delusions of persecution, amnesic states with emotional lability are the usual forms. Acne and physical signs of intoxication are not always evident.

Diagnosis is made by the history of administration of medicine containing bromide and a level of blood bromide greater than 50 mgms. per 100 cc.

Treatment consists in withdrawal of the drug and giving large quantities of sodium chloride to promote its excretion.

Lead Poisoning

The mental symptoms associated with lead poisoning may be acute or chronic.

Acute poisoning may cause delirium, tremors, visual hallucinations and delusions.

In the chronic progressive form apathy, depression, memory impairment, speech difficulties and Korsakow's syndrome may occur.

Mild intoxication may give rise to a clinical picture of irritability, weakness and dizziness.

S.T.P.—6

Mercury Poisoning

This includes irritability, loss of confidence, anxiety symptoms and depression. There is a coarse tremor of the lips, tongue and hands.

Manganese Poisoning

Prolonged exposure to manganese gives rise to parkinsonism and uncontrollable laughing and crying.

Carbon Monoxide Poisoning

This may occur accidentally as a result of improperly burning combustion stoves, inhalation of exhaust gases from petrol engines and working in coal mines.

Acute poisoning occurs with suicidal attempts with coal gas. A gradual onset of carbon monoxide poisoning leads to lowering of efficiency and self control without insight, leading eventually to loss of consciousness.

Acute poisoning results in disorientation, confusion, amnesia, headache, giddiness.

Only about 50 per cent of cases recover completely. In some chronic symptoms may follow directly on the acute intoxication, whereas others develop symptoms after an interval of 1–3 weeks; they then become disorientated, confused, amnesic with headaches, giddiness, pains in the extremities and sometimes a parkinsonian syndrome develops.

TRAUMA (HEAD INJURY)

A patient who suffers from immediate unconsciousness as a result of head injury on recovering goes through stages of stupor and confusion before regaining clear consciousness. Though this recovery can be complete in a matter of minutes or it can take hours or days.

The term concussion should not be confined to instances in which there is immediate loss of consciousness with rapid and complete recovery, but should also include the very many instances in whom the initial symptoms are the same but subsequently have a long continued disturbance of consciousness which is often followed by residual symptoms.

Concussion in this wider sense depends on the diffuse injury to nerve cells and fibres sustained at the moment of the accident. The effects of such an injury may or may not be reversible.

Acute Stage following Brain Injury

It is customary to divide the symptoms in the acute stage into those seen in mild cases, moderate cases and severe cases.

In the mild case the patient loses consciousness for a few seconds to an hour or so, or he may be dazed and walking around in a confused manner with amnesia for the accident and just before it. Within a few hours the mental symptoms will have disappeared in most cases.

In the moderate case unconsciousness lasts for several hours and, before awakening, the patient shows clouding of consciousness followed by a dysmnesic state. Sometimes acute delirious states occur before recovery.

In severe head injury unconsciousness lasts for several hours to several days. The delirious and dysmnesic stages may last for days or weeks. Mortality in severe injury is high.

The severity of the injury can be gauged from the duration of post-traumatic amnesia, which is best measured from the time of the injury to the time of the occurrence of continuous awareness. The longer the post-traumatic amnesia, the longer the period of convalescence before return to work. If the post-traumatic amnesia is greater than seven days it usually takes four to eight months for the person to get back to work.

Chronic Stage

The following disabilities can occur: Post-concussional syndrome, dementia, epilepsy, chronic subdural haematoma, focal neurological lesions and precipitated endogenous illnesses or organic mental disorders.

The post-concussional syndrome starts within a few days or a week or more after the accident. The syndrome consists of headache, giddiness and nervous instability with undue fatigue of body and mind, intolerance of noise and light, insomnia, anxiety and depression.

The manifestations of the post-concussional state are similar to those of anxiety states. Psychological factors and predisposition to psychiatric breakdown as well as compensation factors, may influence the symptomatology.

Nevertheless, the syndrome would appear to have some organic basis which is often reversible and variable in severity. The severity of the disability is largely influenced by the patient's predisposition together with the influence of psychological and environmental stresses.

Post-traumatic Dementia

The degree of the loss of mental capacity of dementia shows infinite variation from mild forgetfulness, impaired concentration and lack of spontaneity to severe dementia with personality change, sometimes showing evidence of the frontal lobe syndrome when the patient becomes disinhibited, tactless, expansive, jocular and euphoric.

Post-traumatic Epilepsy

This is more common with penetrating wounds, particularly where there is penetration of the dura.

Patients who develop epileptic fits soon after the injury do not usually have recurrent attacks, whereas epilepsy starting months or years afterwards tends to persist. Grand mal attacks are the most common but other forms can also take place.

Chronic Subdural Haematoma

This is a late sequel of head injury and occurs after some weeks or months. The injury is often slight; the patient is sleepy and his condition fluctuates in severity.

Focal Neurological Lesions may also occur as sequalae to head injury.

FURTHER READING

Clinical Psychiatry by W. Mayer-Gross, E. Slater and M. Roth. Cassell, London (1960).

CHAPTER TWENTY

PSYCHIATRIC ASPECTS OF EPILEPSY

Epilepsy may be defined as a disorder of the brain, expressed as a paroxysmal cerebral dysrhythmia. This dysrhythmia is symptomatic and is associated with seizures composed of one or more of the following recurrent and involuntary phenomena:

(1) Loss or derangement of consciousness or memory.
(2) Excess or loss of muscle tone or movement.
(3) Alteration of sensation, including hallucinations.
(4) Disturbance of the autonomic nervous system.
(5) Other psychic manifestations, including abnormal thought processes and moods.

It should be noted, however, that a person with clear cut seizure discharges in the E.E.G. but without these symptoms is a potential epileptic but not, in fact, an epileptic. Genuine epileptics may have normal brain-waves on some occasions when recording of the electroencephalogram is taken and repeated e.g. examination may be necessary to record the epileptic dysrhythmia.

CLASSIFICATION OF EPILEPSY

Classification of epilepsy on clinical grounds is traditionally into Petit mal, Grand mal and psychomotor seizures. Lennox gives detailed classification:

(1) *The petit mal triad*
    (a) True petit mal.
    (b) Jerk.
    (c) Atonic.
(2) *Convulsive triad*
    (a) Generalised (grand mal).
    (b) Focal (localised, partial).
    (c) Jacksonian (Rolandic).
(3) *Temporal lobe triad*
    (a) Automatic.
    b) Subjective.
    (c) Tonic focal.
(4) Autonomic.
(5) Unclassified.

The Petit Mal Triad

The three varieties classified under petit mal include an absence or true petit mal, a jerk and a fall (atonic form).

They frequently co-exist in a given patient. They all show a spike wave in the electroencephalogram and improve with forms of medication which are not effective for convulsions. They also are characterised by marked frequency, brevity, an abrupt onset and ending; and occur predominantly in childhood. In the pure petit mal (absence) the period of unconsciousness varies between five and thirty seconds. Muscular movements take the form of small, rhythmic clonic movements. Facial movements are usually twitching and extremities are usually in the form of jerks. The twitch and the jerk coincide with the spike of the electroencephalogram and occur at the rate of three per second.

The Convulsive Triad

1. *Grand Mal Epilepsy*

The tonic phase of the convulsion lasts twenty seconds, the clonic phase forty seconds, the period of relaxation one minute and recuperation three minutes.

2. *Focal or Partial Convulsions*

Represented by convulsive movements confined to one side of the body. Movements may be limited perhaps to the facial muscles of one side or to an arm or leg. Muscles with bilateral innervation, as those of the chest, are not involved unilaterally. Consciousness is usually retained if movements remain unilateral.

3. *Jacksonian or Rolandic Epilepsy*

This is a focal seizure characterised by a march of spasm or sensation with preservation of consciousness; however, some authorities use the term Jacksonian to cover all forms of focal seizures. The march of the spasm or sensation usually appears in distant portions of the extremity and travel upwards.

Temporal Lobe Epilipsy

Temporal lobe seizures vary in severity and complexity. They vary according to the situation of the epileptic focus within the temporal lobe, according to the violence of the local epileptic discharge and the extent to which it spreads, not only within the temporal lobe but to other regions of the brain.

Auras in temporal lobe epilepsy may be of various kinds:

(1) Crude perceptual disturbances including epigastric sensation like the 'stomach turning over', sudden crude sensations of smell or taste of

an unpleasant character, experience of roaring, rushing or ringing noises or sudden disturbance of balance.

(2) Emotional phenomena, sudden change in mood such as fear, anger, excitement or pleasure.

(3) Perceptual disturbances based on memory mechanisms. Here the patient may experience a sudden feeling of familiarity with surroundings or, conversely, a sudden unreality or strangeness. He may be in a dreamy state in which surrounding objects seem small and receding or appear unduly large and near. He may suddenly feel that he is witnessing a scene which has already taken place before, viz. the 'deja vue' phenomenon.

(4) Auras arising from adjacent regions of the brain.

Sometimes, before losing consciousness, the patient with a lesion of the temporal lobe exhibits symptoms which indicate that the epileptic discharging process has already spread into adjacent regions of the brain, e.g. the occurrence of twitching movements, numbness of one side of the face or body, aphasic difficulties.

Varieties of Temporal Lobe Seizure

(1) Minor seizures without loss of consciousness.
(2) Amnesic attacks without convulsions.
(3) Major convulsive seizures.

1. *Minor seizures*

These are usually sudden and transient sensory auras and usually lasting for one or two seconds.

2. *Amnesic attacks without convulsions*

The patient is dazed and exhibits confused or semi-purposive behaviour but not by generalised convulsions. The E.E.G. at the onset of these amnesic seizures usually shows a suppression of electrical activity over both hemispheres for a few seconds, followed by more or less symmetrical and rhythmical bilateral 6–8 cycles per second waves. The motor phenomena are usually masticatory, grimacing or semi-purposive movements of the limbs.

3. *Major convulsive seizures*

Unless the initial aura has been witnessed, these major convulsions may be indistinguishable from grand mal attacks resulting from lesions in other parts of the brain. These have a particular tendency to occur during sleep.

Investigation of Suspected Temporal Lobe Epilepsy

It should be noted that the recent appearance of temporal lobe seizures may signal the presence of a cerebral tumour. The diagnosis becomes clear if neurological signs or evidence of increased intercranial pressure are present. In cases in which the fits are of long standing and there is nothing obvious in the clinical picture that would suggest tumour, an attempt should be made to control the seizures by drugs such as phenobarbitone and Epanutin. In cases in which the fits cannot be properly controlled and are disabling, or in which there is severe personality disorder, recourse should be made to full neurological, radiological and E.E.G. investigations. The electroencephalographic examination which is most likely to give the decisive answer and may help to be repeated over a long period is that during induced sleep records using sphenoidal electrodes.

A history of intractable epilepsy and an E.E.G. demonstration of an epileptic focus which is confined to one temporal lobe or, if bilateral, predominantly on one side constitute the usual indications for temporal lobectomy.

EMOTIONS AND EPILEPTIC ATTACKS

Both petit mal and grand mal attacks may be precipitated by emotional changes.

Petit mal may be precipitated as an immediate response to sudden unpleasurable emotions such as surprise, embarrassment or the arousal of competitive feelings.

Temporal lobe epileptic attacks may also be precipitated by stress but usually the stress period is more prolonged than in petit mal.

Emotions may also be aroused by the epileptic process and there is a clear relationship between these and focal abnormalities in the temporal lobe.

The commonest emotions are depression, anxiety, pleasure and displeasure. The emotions are vivid and seem to arise automatically and are, as it were, foreign to the patients; they do not feel them to be a part of their normal emotional reactions; they are simple rather than complex. Pleasant emotions are uncommon but unpleasurable emotional states are very common. The emotions appear to be experiences which are unrelated to the external world of reality or the person's internal world.

It must also be realised that the epileptic's various difficulties, caused by fits or other unrelated factors, and involving his relationships and social interactions, may, by arousing emotions which can precipitate attacks, influence this frequency.

Aetiology of Epilepsy

Epilepsy is of varied and multiple aetiology with genetic influences, brain damage, biochemical and psychogenic factors all having a potential role.

Precipitants of Attacks

It is well known that hydration increases cerebral dysrhythmia and increases the tendency to produce epilepsy. This is the basis of the water pitressin test for epilepsy.

Overbreathing may also precipitate attacks in the epileptic person. Various photic stimuli and, in some, music may precipitate attacks. Alcohol also increases the tendency and the frequency for epileptic attacks to occur.

Epilepsy and Schizophrenia

Recent work has shown that there is often a close link between schizophrenic-like disorders and epilepsy.

This occurs more often with temporal lobe epilepsy and that the psychotic onset occurs more often with a decrease in fit frequency rather than with a rising fit frequency.

The onset of the illness was often insidious. Delusional beliefs in clear consciousness were present in all but two. Compared with the ordinary run of schizophrenic patients, the epileptic group showed less catatonia and more normal affective responses.

Abnormal Behaviour in Relationship to Fits

Abnormal behaviour occurring during the actual fit (ictal) is usually spontaneous and the result of the epileptic disturbance of the brain tends to be stereotyped, short-lived and without relation to circumstance.

Post-ictal activity, whether restlessness, aggression or a fugue, is due to the state of confusion so it is simple in form. evoked by stimulation and when purposeful, primitive or stupid its form is often determined by past experience. It appears automatic.

The confused person walks and fumbles with clothes, undresses routinely or blindly, resists help or interference.

It can be said that there is no real purpose in the ictal activity and that the purpose in the post-ictal activity is immediate and very crude.

No prolonged elaborate and intelligently purposeful fugue state is epileptic.

It may be said that in status epilepticus, focal or general; abnormal states of movement, sensation or consciousness may last for many hours.

It is usually possible to recognise the individual attacks of the status and so establish the responsibility of epilepsy for a prolonged behavioural disorder. Prolonged amnesic states, fugues, stupor, coma or aggressive or antisocial behaviour are unlikely to be epileptic in the absence of status, for even post-ictal confusion lasts for minutes only rather than hours.

S.T.P.—6*

It should be noted that activity which is motivated, which uses past learning cannot be epileptic.

The soldier absent without leave who finds his way home by road and rail with no memory of the process could not have done so in an epileptic attack. Neither can a criminal who has amnesia for an act of violence directed against a selected subject with an appropriate weapon, however obscure the motive or violent the act.

Employment of Epileptics

Surveys of epilepsy in general practice have revealed that three quarters of all chronic epileptics are fully employed; 12 per cent are in sheltered employment and 6 per cent unemployed for reasons other than epilepsy and 8 per cent unemployed because of the fits or social difficulties arising from epilepsy. Sixteen per cent of all cases presented a social problem.

The importance of suitable employment for the epileptic cannot be over-emphasised. If unemployed the epileptic tends to become depressed, morose, apathetic, aggressive and demoralised. Work helps to bring financial security, provides interests and fosters a suitable sense of independence and responsibility which facilitates proper social adjustment.

Certain occupations are unduly hazardous for the epileptic; for example, those associated with fire, water, vats, ladders, e.g. painting and window-cleaning, machinery, motor driving. The question should be asked, are serious hazards likely to be met if there is sudden loss of consciousness?

It is usually advantageous for the epileptic to register under the Disabled Persons Act 1944. He will then benefit from the services provided by the Ministry of Labour.

FURTHER READING

Epilepsy and related disorders by W. G. Lennox and M. A. Lennox. (2 vols.)
    Churchill. London (1960).

CHAPTER TWENTY-ONE

SCHIZOPHRENIA

Under the term schizophrenia are included those illnesses, in all age groups, which are characterised from the outset by fundamental disturbances in personality, thinking, emotional life, behaviour, interests and relationships with other people.

Schizophrenia involves a tendency for the person to withdraw from the environment and to show an internal disintegration of thinking, feeling and behaviour, resulting in an incongruity between his emotional state and his thoughts and actions, a tendency to form characteristic associations in thinking and a tendency to morbid projection.

The disintegration of mental functions in schizophrenia is 'molecular' and quite different from the 'molar' dissociation found in hysteria and multiple personality.

It is convenient to describe the clinical features of schizophrenia under the following headings:

(1) Withdrawal.
(2) Splitting
    (a) Thought disorder
    (b) Emotional disconnection
    (c) Conduct disconnection.
(3) Paranoid disposition.
(4) Abnormalities of perception.

Withdrawal

The withdrawal in schizophrenia includes a generalised loss of interest in the environment and a diminution in response to external impressions, particularly in affective responses.

There tends to be loss of natural affection for relatives and friends and the patient may react to happenings of great importance as if they were of no concern.

Answers to questions are brief and uninformative.

Inertia towards external activities and general failure of will with lack of drive and initiative are other manifestations of withdrawal.

The most marked form of withdrawal is stupor, in which the patient shows marked decrease in responses to stimuli. There is lack of spontaneous thought and action but with awareness of passing events. Consciousness is clear and registration and retention of memories is unimpaired.

Thought Disorder

Disorder of thinking is a characteristic feature of schizophrenia. The patient in the early stages of the illness may exhibit a general vagueness and woolliness in his speech which tends to lack coherence and to be uninformative. After talking to a patient for some considerable time, it becomes apparent that very little information has been given by him. There is a feeling of a glass wall between one's self and the patient or, in other words, a difficulty in establishing rapport.

Thoughts and ideas tend to be disconnected and the patient seems unable to continue a normal sequence of his thoughts and speech.

Replies to questions may be irrelevant.

Thought blockage, which makes the patient stop in the middle of a sentence or sometimes in the middle of a word also may occur. This may be described by the patient as thought deprivation, i.e. as if his thoughts are suddenly taken away.

There is a general paucity of ideas and repetitive and stereotyped themes may continue throughout the conversation. Thought interpolation may occur whereby the patient feels as if thoughts are inserted into his mind as if from outside. He may also experience a 'crowding in' of many simultaneous thoughts which interfere with his conversation and with the course of his thinking.

Associations may be determined by sounds, clang associations, alliteration or any chance irrelevant connection.

Some patients show relative loss of conceptual (categorical) thinking with a tendency to think in concrete terms. This can be shown by interpretation of proverbs, which tends to be literal with the patient having great difficulty in seeing the deeper meaning or wider application of the proverb. It may also be seen in his difficulty in categorising objects into a particular class; he tends to see them all separately. It may also show itself in literalness, in that he tends to take everything quite literally and will transform metaphors into their literal meaning. Concrete thinking and literalness may not be present in all patients or may be only observable in the patient at certain times but when they are present, in combination with other manifestations of schizophrenic thinking, they are of considerable diagnostic importance.

Sometimes condensation occurs; a number of different concepts, ideas or words may be fused together.

Cause and effect may be interchanged; things linked by chance association or by any characteristic are taken to be the same. Associations may appear not to proceed in a straight line but may jump from one course to another, exhibiting what has been referred to as the 'Knight's move' in association. The patient has a tendency to talk in riddles; he counters a question by asking another question and deals with things in a rather philosophical and mystical approach, e.g. when asked about the health of his mother, he may reply by asking some philosophical question about what is meant by health or the understanding of relationships between people.

The patient may invent new words (neologisms) to describe experiences or the way he views things. In some schizophrenic patients, particularly paranoid schizophrenics, the characteristic thought disorder may only become manifested after a long interview and only when they become emotionally disturbed when talking about their delusions. At other times they may show little evidence of thought disorder in ordinary conversation.

Change in Affect

The patient tends to become emotionally flattened and to show a loss of natural affection and appropriate emotional reactions to people he formerly loved. He may become insensitive, inconsiderate or even callously indifferent to other people's feelings and experiences. He takes slights and offence readily and tends to isolate himself from his environment and increasingly develops a state of apathy.

Emotional incongruity is one of the most important aspects of the disturbed affect in schizophrenia. There is a lack of agreement between what the patient says and thinks and behaves and how he feels. He may describe intense persecution in a state of indifference or even with cheerfulness. He may show in his facial expression and demeanour a picture of dejection and misery and yet he may feel happy, elated or may have no feeling at all.

Schizophrenic patients may also experience an extremely rapid change of emotion within a matter of seconds or minutes; they may be angry, depressed, perplexed, ecstatic and anxious all in rapid sequence. Emotional responses may be quite inappropriate, the patient may smile fatuously in a far-away dreamy state. A knowing smile gives the impression that he understands things that the interviewer knows nothing about.

Emotional reactions may be disproportionate and inappropriate to the stimulus and sometimes severe emotional outbursts may appear spontaneously and without any apparent provocation. These may take the form of anger, violence or marked terror and characteristically come out of the blue without warning.

Ambivalence may also be found; the person may hold contrasting and antithetical feelings to the same person or object, concurrently or within a short space of time, e.g. he may have feelings of love and hate for a person at the same time.

Disturbances in Behaviour and Motor Functions

The general demeanour of a schizophrenic patient is often awkward, abrupt and gauche. The patient may show grimacing, twitchings and stereotyped movements of various parts of the body.

In some patients there may be a marked absence of activity, so-called akinetic states, which may last for a few seconds or longer.

Conduct may be disconnected from other aspects of the patient's mental life and one may get evidence of automatic obedience, in that the patient may show waxy flexibility (flexibilitas cerea) in which he will maintain imposed postures for periods of time. He may repeat actions carried out by the interviewer (Echopraxia) or repeats things that are said to him (Echolalia). He may impulsively utter things in a meaningless fashion. He may exhibit spontaneous fixed attitudes and expressions or exhibit a stereotopy of speech and conduct. He may show negativism, i.e. doing the opposite of what is requested. Some patients show typical negativism in operation when one goes to shake hands with them; they withdraw their hand and, when one puts one hand down, they bring their hand forward and so on.

Delusion Formation and the Paranoid Disposition

A delusion is a false belief which is not amenable to persuasion or argument and which is out of keeping with the patient's cultural and educational background.

Delusions are characteristic of schizophrenia; they may be primary or secondary. Primary delusions are almost pathognomonic for schizophrenia and characteristically appear suddenly, fully developed and immediately carrying a strong and overwhelming feeling of conviction. They occur in a setting of clear consciousness and the patient is convinced that a particular happening or stimulus is of great significance. For example, a patient on going into the house, on perceiving that the window was left partly opened, considered that this indicated that he was Jesus Christ and that he was destined to save the world.

Secondary delusions may occur on the basis of primary delusions or may arise as delusional interpretations of symptoms, such as feelings of passivity or other manifestations of intellectual, emotional or conduct abnormalities found in schizophrenia.

In its strict sense the term paranoid refers to a disturbance of the individual's relationship to the world, so that it would include both delusions of persecution and delusions of grandeur but there is a tendency, generally, among psychiatrists to use the word paranoid as being equivalent to persecutory.

The paranoid disposition is the tendency to attribute to the outside world things which really arise from within the person.

Morbid projection is the basis of the paranoid disposition, i.e. the attribution of something to the outside which arises from within the person, and is a fundamental tendency in paranoid schizophrenia and in the genesis of paranoid delusions.

Morbid projection may vary in form and degree from ideas of reference, to complete systematical delusions the person may believe that he is the subject of special reference, either in people's conversations or from what is said on the wireless or seen on television. Delusions of reference are when these beliefs are held with conviction.

Delusions of persecution may be changeable and fleeting or they may be partly systematised to form a system of delusions around a central theme, e.g. that the person is being persecuted by the Jesuits, the Freemasons, the Communists, the Co-operative Society, the Police, M.I. 5 etc. The systematisation may be partial and variable, to a fully systematised fixed series of delusions as seen in some forms of paranoid schizophrenia.

It is often stated that delusions of grandeur are compensations for delusions of persecution but there is no evidence for this. They may arise spontaneously without delusions of persecution and, even when both are present, a relationship is often assumed rather than demonstrated.

Hypochondriacal delusions are very common in schizophrenia and are characteristically bizarre. Sometimes sensations of bodily change, feelings of passivity or interference and other bodily sensations form the basis of hypochondriacal delusions.

Hypochondriacal delusions based on hallucinatory phenomena are diagnostic of schizophrenia.

The patient's complaints are often bizarre but, in assessing bizareness, it is important to remember the patient's cultural background and intelligence. For example, a depressed mental defective may express hypochondriacal complaints which are extremely bizarre.

In the management of a patient suffering from delusions, the appropriate manner of dealing with him is to do nothing which would confirm the delusions; on the other hand, it is useless trying to argue with the patient about his delusional beliefs because it only tends to make the patient antagonistic and resentful and make him lose faith in the doctor.

Disorders of Perception

Hallucinations, particularly auditory hallucinations, are among the commonest schizophrenic symptoms. Auditory hallucinations in a setting of clear consciousness are characteristic of schizophrenia.

The auditory hallucinations in schizophrenia vary in clarity, frequency and duration. They may be continuous, completely dominating the patient's attention or may be intermittent. More or less continuous hallucinosis is more characteristic of schizophrenia.

The patient states that he hears voices talking to him; sometimes the voices are clearly audible giving clear communications in the form of remarks or commands. Patients vary with regard to the tendency to be influenced by their hallucinatory voices; some patients feel impelled to carry out the commands of their hallucinatory voices; whereas other patients describe the voices as being vague, incoherent or a lot of rubbish.

The voices very frequently are abusive. In men, voices often refer to them as homosexuals, rakes, thieves or other uncomplimentary things. In women that they are prostitutes or are unclean or suffer from venereal disease.

Sometimes the patients feel compelled to answer their voices back and become angry in response to their hallucinations. They often adopt listening attitudes and sometimes smile, sometimes get puzzled and at other times get angry.

The origin of the voices may be located by the patient outside the body, e.g. as coming through the floorboards, from the ceiling or from elsewhere, or may be located inside the body, sometimes inside the head but occasionally from other parts of the body, e.g. from the stomach, from the hands, from the feet etc.

Sometimes patients have an experience in which they can hear their own thoughts spoken aloud and this is highly characteristic of schizophrenia.

Visual hallucinations are uncommon; they are often fragmented in contrast to the complex visual hallucinations one sees in some hysterical states.

Bodily hallucinations, tactile sensations, passivity feelings, sensations of heat, cold, pain, electricity, sexual interference are not infrequent in schizophrenia.

Olfactory hallucinations sometimes occur, e.g. patients complain of odours of decomposition, chemicals, rotting substances, gas etc., These experiences may be woven into their delusional experiences, believing that they are being persecuted or drugged.

VARIETIES OF SCHIZOPHRENIA

It is customary to classify schizophrenia into the following forms:
(1) Simple
(2) Hebephrenic
(3) Catatonic.
(4) Paranoid.
In addition, there are the following clinical varieties:
(5) Schizo-affective.
(6) Pseudoneurotic.
(7) Periodic catatonia.
(8) Late paraphrenia.

The use of customary subtypes—simple, hebephrenic, catatonic, paranoid—has become well established in clinical practice but it is clear that the boundaries between these types are not clear and that an individual patient may change from one subtype to another during the course of the illness.

Simple Schizophrenia

This is characterised by an insidious onset, with a gradual deterioration socially and very often a difficulty in establishing the exact time of onset because of its insidious development.

Clinically, it takes the form mainly of withdrawal of interests from the environment, apathy, difficulty in making social contacts, poverty of ideation, a decline in total performance with marked sensitivity and ideas of reference.

Simple schizophrenics go downhill socially and may become tramps, beggars, thieves or dupes for criminals; women may become prostitutes.

It is distinguished from schizoid psychopathy by the fact that it is an illness with an onset and a definite change and deterioration in personality, whereas schizoid psychopathy has been present throughout the patient's life.

Hebephrenia

This also has an insidious onset in early life and is characterised by thought disorder and emotional abnormalities.

Characteristically the affect is inappropriate and fatuous, with meaningless giggles and often a self-satisfied smile. Thought disorder and delusions, which are often changeable, are common. Hallucinations occur, particularly auditory hallucinations. Behaviour is often silly, mischievous, eccentric, showing much grimacing, mannerisms and the patient may be inert and apathetic.

Catatonic Schizophrenia often has an acute onset and the clinical picture is dominated by disturbance of behaviour and motor phenomena.

The onset is in adolescence or early adult life, but occasionally in the fourth decade or later.

The course of the illness often shows extreme alterations in behaviour, varying from stupor to excitement.

Catatonic schizophrenia provides the best examples of disconnection in conduct, ranging from mannerisms, constrained attitudes, automatic responses to stimuli including automatic obedience, echolalia, echopraxia; spontaneous over-activity, the maintenance of imposed postures, negativism.

Hallucinations, delusions, thought disorder and emotional disorder are also present but are less prominent than motor phenomena.

Paranoid Schizophrenia is characterised by the development of delusions, particularly delusions of persecution.

It usually has a later age of onset and patients have a better preservation of personality than in other forms of schizophrenia.

The delusions are most often persecutory but grandiose delusions and hypochondriacal delusions may occur.

The delusions may be variable, transient and poorly held in some patients and in others systems of delusions which are highly complex and relatively fixed.

It was customary in the past to regard Paraphrenia and Paranoia, which are really subtypes of paranoid schizophrenia, as distinct diseases.

Paraphrenia is characterised by a late age of onset with the existence of semi-systematised delusions occurring with hallucinations, thought disorder becoming more apparent when the patient talks about his delusions or when he gets emotionally disturbed.

Paranoia was the term given to patients showing a fixed delusional system without evidence of thought disorder and without hallucinations and good preservation of personality.

Follow-up studies of patients so diagnosed usually revealed that they later became transformed into clear cases of schizophrenia, with thought disorder and hallucinations.

Schizo-affective Disorder

This term tends to be over-used and ill-used and is sometimes used for cases of schizophrenia with an affective component to the clinical state.

The term schizo-affective disorder should be confined to those cases in which depression or mania occur concurrently with schizophrenia in the patient.

Pseudoneurotic Schizophrenia

This variety of schizophrenia characteristically presents as a neurosis but with certain anomalous features.

Anxiety is prominent which pervades all aspects of the patient's life (pan anxiety). The neurotic manifestations are usually varied, showing many symptoms of a neurotic illness at the same time (so-called pan-neurosis).

Gross hysterical mechanisms, somatic manifestations of anxiety, anorexia, vomiting, palpitations, phobias, obsessions, compulsions etc. may be present. The neurotic manifestations constantly shift but are never completely absent.

Short-lived psychotic episodes with clear schizophrenic symptoms may be distributed throughout the illness. Ideas of reference, hypochondriacal delusions, depersonalisation as well as sexual perversions may be present in pseudoneurotic schizophrenia.

Periodic Catatonia

This is an interesting condition in which Gjessing found clear correlations between metabolic disturbances and the onset of psychiatric symptoms.

The illness is characterised by phases of stupor or excitement and the metabolic changes are nitrogen retention followed by excretion.

Late Paraphrenia

This occurs more frequently in women than in men and more often in widows or spinsters living alone. Twenty-five per cent have some defect of sight or hearing.

Delusions of persecution, for example of being raped and gassed or being affected by strangers, are frequent. Hallucinations of smell, hearing and visual phenomena are common.

AETIOLOGY OF SCHIZOPHRENIA

Heredity

Strong evidence that the predisposition to schizophrenia is inherited is provided by data revealing that the chance of developing the illness increases directly in proportion to the closeness of the blood relationship to the relative suffering from schizophrenia (*vide* Table 3, page 172).

The mode of inheritance of the predisposition to schizophrenia has been a matter for controversy. Some consider that recessive transmission is the operative one. They claim that the heterozygote is a schizoid psychopath and that the homozygote is a schizophrenic.

The criticisms of the recessive theory include the finding that the incidence of schizophrenia in the children is higher than in siblings of schizophrenic patients.

Other authorities believe that the results obtained from family studies are best explained by the action of a single dominant gene with only 25 per cent penetrance, i.e. three quarters of the patients who bear the gene for schizophrenia and should be schizophrenic avoid this, either by environmental influences or the action of modifying genes.

As the frequency of schizophrenia is about 1 per cent, the total frequency of the schizophrenic gene must be 4 per cent.

Physical Constitution

Kretschmer in 1921 propounded his hypothesis that there was a biological affinity between manic-depressive psychosis and the pyknic or relatively broad and rounded physique, whereas schizophrenia had a biological affinity to narrow types of physique—athletic and certain dysplastic physiques.

A great deal of research has been carried out to test Kretschmer's hypothesis and the results indicate that schizophrenics, in general, tend to be narrower in physique than normal controls and manic-depressives, that the pyknic or physique of manic-depressives is in part due to increase in age but that the age factor does not entirely invalidate Kretschmer's theory.

There is also some evidence that the narrower the physique the more marked are the manifestations of disconnected thinking, the earlier the age of onset and the more insidious the type of onset.

An explanation of the effect of the correlations between physique and schizophrenia and its course and prognosis probably rests in the fact that the genes determining body build exert an influence on the operation of the gene or genes determining schizophrenia.

Endocrine and Metabolic Factors

As is well known, genetically determined conditions are manifested or are brought about by the control of chemical systems in the body by genes.

For many years research workers have been searching for the biochemical abnormality or abnormalities which are presumed to exist in schizophrenia.

The most striking finding is that of *Gjessing* on a rare type of schizophrenia named periodic catatonia, and these findings have been confirmed by other workers in other forms of recurrent schizophrenia.

Gjessing carried out painstaking studies on patients with periodic catatonia who, because of the development of attacks of stupor or excitement at a definite point in time with intervening periods of normality were admirable for study as they could serve as their own controls. It was found that the onset of the abnormal phase, whether stupor or excitement, was correlated with changes in nitrogen metabolism. Furthermore, Gjessing found that if these patients were kept on a low protein diet and given adequate doses of thyroid, the nitrogen retention-excretion balance became normal and the patients remained symptom-free.

This provides a possible look into the future when the precise nature of biochemical abnormalities in schizophrenia etc. are discovered and when means are found to control and correct these.

The fact that many of the hallucinogenic drugs, which produce syndromes somewhat similar to schizophrenia, contain an indole nucleus, led to the belief that an abnormal metabolite with an indole nucleus may be a factor in schizophrenia and a number of workers have recently isolated an indole fraction from schizophrenic patients' serum which, when transferred to another person, produced evidence of the disease. This work is still too early for adequate evaluation.

Other investigators have shown that the whole range of biochemical and endocrine functions tend to be outside above or below the normal range in schizophrenia and that, with recovery, the endocrine status tends to return to normal limits.

At one time it was believed that testicular atrophy or gonadal atrophy was a feature of schizophrenia but nowadays this is usually found to be secondary to chronic disease and inanition, rather than a causative factor.

Early Mother-child or Parent-child Relationships

Some workers have claimed that maternal deprivation is more common in schizophrenics than in the general population and that faulty parental attitudes such as over-protection, rejection by the mother, broken homes, divorce of parents are more common in schizophrenia than in the general population.

It is possible that these influences are non-specific as they may be found in other disorders too, such as childhood asthma and, in any event, if the matter is to be studied only the parents of young schizophrenics can be investigated. Schizophrenia very frequently starts after the age of 30 and may even start in the 60's or 70's.

Social Class

There is an excess of schizophrenic patients in Social Class 5. Forty-five per cent of the total number of schizophrenics come from Social Class 5 which has only 18·4 per cent of the total population.

Recent work has shown that this correlation with social class is an effect of the illness rather than a cause. Late paraphrenia or paranoid schizophrenia has a high correlation with social isolation and physical factors.

Extrinsic Factors

A large number of extrinsic factors may serve to precipitate schizophrenia in a person so predisposed. Among these are:

(1) Physical illnesses.
(2) Head injuries.
(3) Childbirth.
(4) Psychosocial stresses.
(5) Alcoholism.

Conclusion

Schizophrenia is probably a genetically determined biochemical disorder which is influenced by other constitutional attributes. In other words, the genetic predisposition to schizophrenia may be influenced (1) by the genotypic milieu (2) by the physical constitution of the person and other aspects of human constitution.

Environmental experiences may hinder or help to make the predisposition to schizophrenia; these include unfavourable early experiences, abnormal parental attitudes, physical illness, head injury, intoxications, loss of weight and various psychosocial stresses.

In other words, the essential cause of schizophrenia appears to be genetic and constitutional but a large variety of factors may act as the sufficient causes which make the predisposition manifest in illness at a particular time in a person's life.

TABLE 3

EXPECTANCY RATES OF SCHIZOPHRENIA IN RELATIVES OF THE SCHIZOPHRENIC PATIENT

	per cent
General population	1
Half siblings	7–8
Full siblings	5–15
Parents	5–10
Children with one parent schizophrenic	18–60
Children with both parents schizophrenic	53–86
First cousins	2
Grandchildren	3–4
Nephews and nieces	3
Parents	5–7
Siblings	5–15
Children	7–16
Dizygotic twins	14
Monozygotic twins	82.6

Diagnosis

The diagnosis of schizophrenia depends on the recognition of the anomalies described above in the patient and their evaluation against the general background of the development of the illness and their relationship to other symptoms. In the matter of schizophrenic diagnosis, one swallow does not make a summer and the presence of isolated manifestations such as thought blockage, ideas of reference, in themselves would not necessarily indicate schizophrenia; but, if they occur in a setting of a definite change in the patient's personality, in the form of increasing withdrawal and deterioration their diagnostic significance is much greater.

Any marked change is probably of much greater importance than the presence or absence of a particular sign. Sudden change in religious persuasion or philosophical outlook without adequate preparation, sudden increase of introversion may also be a danger signal. Patients may show lack of propriety and new fads or mannerisms, particularly if there is less firm contact with reality.

It is very important that schizophrenia be diagnosed in its early stages, before it becomes clearly apparent to medical and lay people. Schizophrenia often occurs in people of introverted personality; the important thing to look for is (1) a change in this type of personality, which is one of the normal forms of personality, as shown by withdrawal, merging into apathy and blunting of affect. (2) Acute anxiety, panic and perplexity, particularly in unfamiliar surroundings. (3) Inappropriate emotional reactions: (a) An increasing tendency to dreaminess (b) fleeting smiles, fatuous laughter, sometimes a knowing smile is highly characteristic. A tendency to think concretely and to take things literally, increasing ideas of reference and persecution, revaluation of religious and political beliefs without due preparation, lack of propriety in behaviour, development of mannerisms.

It must be remembered that, in diagnosing schizophrenia, all these signs of abnormality are particularly important when they appear in the setting of a definite change in personality characterised by a falling off in efficiency, effectiveness and increasing withdrawal.

Prognosis

Schizophrenia is a serious disease and a proportion of patients fail to recover, some only make a partial recovery but, many patients can recover fully from attacks of schizophrenia.

The prognosis always has to be assessed in each case on its own merits.

Follow-up studies on the outcome of schizophrenia indicate that certain features are helpful prognostic indicators. The following are favourable prognostic indicators:

(1) An acute onset of illness.
(2) Precipitation by environmental or physical factors.
(3) Well-adjusted, stable previous personality.
(4) The presence of true affective components in the illness.
(5) A pyknic (Eurymorphic) physique.
(6) A history of previous attacks from which the patient has made a complete recovery.

Features which indicate a poor prognosis are:

(1) Long duration of illness, over two years.
(2) A gradual onset.
(3) An unstable, ill-adjusted previous personality
(4) An early age of onset.
(5) Marked leptomorphic physique.
(6) Absence of clear precipitating factors.
(7) A gradual onset.

Certain features are of little value such as:

(1) Family history.
(2) Type of symptom.

Follow up studies on hospital patients over a 15 year period reveal that about a quarter of all cases end in severe deterioration, another quarter end showing a marked personality defect, a third quarter end in a mild personality defect and a fourth quarter recover completely, without any residual symptoms or defects. This does not include cases of schizophrenia who have not been admitted to hospital and in these it is probable that the prognosis and outcome may be much better.

TREATMENT OF SCHIZOPHRENIA

General

Social and psychological treatment are important both for patients cared for in hospital or in the community.

Hospital patients should be allocated to nurses and frequent discussion groups in the ward are desirable. An active daily regime is essential.

Work therapy and occupational therapy are important in promoting recovery and preventing deterioration.

Physical Methods of Treatment

Insulin coma therapy, which used to be the first line of treatment in schizophrenia, is now largely of historical interest as it has been superceded by the use of new psychotropic drugs.

Electroconvulsive therapy is useful for relieving depressive symptoms in schizophrenia and many of the florid manifestations of schizophrenia.

The first drug to be used in the treatment of schizophrenia, in the new series of psychotropic drugs, was Reserpine but there were disadvantages in that it took many weeks to produce its beneficial effects, there were phases of turbulence and sometimes severe depression occurred as a side-effect.

The phenothiazine derivatives have now taken pride of place in the drug treatment of schizophrenia.

For the acute and disturbed schizophrenic patient, Chlorpromazine is still the drug of choice. For inert, apathetic schizophrenics, the piperazine derivatives such as Stemetil or Stelazine are to be preferred; Stelazine appears to be effective in the treatment of paranoid schizophrenia.

Chlorpromazine is still the drug of choice for the treatment of the majority of schizophrenic patients. The dose necessary will probably be between 300–600 mgms. a day and will need to be continued for up to two years after initial treatment.

Treatment with the phenothiazines can be supplemented with electroconvulsive therapy.

With regard to the rehabilitation of the patient after discharge from hospital, it has been found that some schizophrenic patients are unable to tolerate demanding or emotionally intense personal relationships and that some do better in lodgings or hostels than with near relatives.

Early diagnosis and prompt treatment with phenothiazines and, if necessary, supplemented with E.C.T. or other drugs appears to offer the best prospect for the control of schizophrenia.

The community should be provided with adequate resources and facilities to support the partially disabled schizophrenics in their midst.

Among other things, the general practitioner has to ensure that the patient remains on adequate doses of drugs until the symptoms show a true remission.

FURTHER READING

Schizophrenia by F. Fish. J. Wright, Bristol (1965).

CHAPTER TWENTY-TWO

AFFECTIVE DISORDERS

Affective disorders are illnesses in which mood change is the primary and dominant feature.

The mood change is relatively fixed and persistent and is associated with characteristic changes in thinking, attitude and behaviour.

The main varieties of mood change are Anxiety, Depression and Hypomania (and Mania) and the corresponding disorders are termed Anxiety state (Anxiety Neurosis), Depressive State and Hypomania (Mania if severe).

A comparison of depression, anxiety and hypomania is given in the following table.

DEPRESSIVE ILLNESS

Definition

A depressive illness is one in which the primary and dominant characteristic is a change in mood consisting of a feeling tone of sadness which may vary from mild despondency to the most abject despair. The change in mood is relatively fixed and persists over a period of days, weeks, months or years. Associated with the change in mood are characteristic changes in behaviour, attitude, thinking, efficiency and physiological functioning.

Depression, as a symptom, may occur in many psychiatric and physical illnesses and is a subsidiary or secondary part of the clinical picture. Depression can be a normal feeling and is characteristic of mourning and grief.

In distinguishing the normal reaction from pathological depression, a quantitative judgement has to be made. If the precipitant seems in adequate, the depression too severe and too long lasting, the condition is regarded as abnormal. In addition, the severity and incapacity in depressive illness differs qualitatively as well as quantitatively from depressed feelings which are a part of normal experience.

Depression in Depressive illnesses affects the whole organism: feelings, energy drive, thinking, bodily functions, personality and interests, and tends to influence every sphere of a person's life.

TABLE 4

Feature	Depression	Hypomania	Anxiety
Appearance	Pale, dejected posture. Muscular tone poor.	Looks well. Good complexion and posture.	Tense, strained facies. Posture tense, movements awkward.
Speech activity	Under-active unless agitated.	Pressure of talk	Rapid, high-pitched voice.
Motor activity	Reduced except when agitated.	Pressure of activity.	Restless, over-activity, inability to relax, poorly integrated.
Speed of thinking and decision-making.	Difficult to think and make decisions.	Rapid	Mild anxiety facilitates. Marked anxiety hinders.
Mood	Sad.	Elated ± irritability.	Anxious, apprehensive, fearful.
Self-valuation	Deprecatory.	Over-values self, confident, even grandiose.	Uncertain, constantly needing reassurance.
Awareness. Response to outside stimuli.	Normal or decreased.	Alert and distractable.	Alert, irritable, jumpy.
Energy	Poor.	Conspicuous.	Fitful. Restless with sudden exhaustion.

Appearance and General Behaviour

The patient's appearance provides valuable clues to the diagnosis. Appearance and behaviour will be influenced by the degrees with which anxiety and agitation are concomitant.

In depression with retardation the patient is slow in movements. He has a heavy, tired gait and shows a decrease in bodily movement. He has a rigid, immobile face; sometimes the facial expression may be distressed and sorrowful, reflecting anxiety or despair. Sometimes agitation occurs instead of retardation; the patient is restless, often constantly wringing his hands with an anxious, distressed facial expression.

Mood

The affect in depressive states may vary in intensity from a mild feeling tone of sadness to the most intense, distressing misery. Patients describe their subjective state in such terms as 'feeling ill'; 'good for nothing' etc. Sometimes the patient has difficulty in expressing adequately the quality and intensity of his suffering.

Although every patient is aware of the presence of a feeling of dejection and sadness, few present this as their main symptom, particularly in the early stages of the illness. More usually they will present with physical symptoms such as lack of energy, bodily pains, loss of weight.

Output of Talk

This may vary from complete muteness to constant chattering. Often a tendency to reiteration and preoccupation with certain topics is a feature. Agitation and importunity are often associated with a greater output of talk.

Thinking

Patients complain of difficulty in thinking. They complain of inability to concentrate, difficulty in formulating their ideas and collecting their thoughts and making decisions.

Difficulty in thinking rather than slowness of thought is the characteristic feature of depressive illness, especially when thinking is directed to an end as in carrying out a particular intellectual task such as grasping and answering a question or deciding on a course of action or dealing with a problem. The end is either not attained or only achieved after a long period of effort.

Retardation

In some patients general slowness of motor activity is marked and in a minority it may be so severe that the patient is in a state of depressive stupor. In stupor, activity is reduced to a minimum and response to stimuli is diminished and facial expression is usually one of fixed despair.

Painful Thoughts

The depressed patient is self-concerned and, however much he dislikes, it, he tends to be preoccupied with himself and his difficulties. His thoughts are invariably painful and usually centred around difficulties and liabilities. He is quite unable to count his blessings. He may blame himself for errors of omission and commission and tends to be self-depreciatory and self-accusatory. He tends to magnify minor misdemeanours of the past and may magnify them to the extent of regarding them as unforgivable sins. He ruminates over his past and is filled with doubts about the correctness and morality of his actions.

Anxiety and Agitation

Some degree of anxiety is usually present. Severe anxiety associated with motor restlessness is termed agitation.

Loss of Interest

The patient finds that he has lost interest and enjoyment in his usual work and recreational activities. This may be a particularly striking change noticeable to the observer, especially in the early stages when other manifestations are not so obvious.

The loss of interest may apply to work, home, family, former hobbies and recreations and sometimes personal hygiene and appearance.

Derealisation and Depersonalisation.

These are often present; the patient complains that the environment appears different (Derealisation) or that he, himself, feels changed (Depersonalisation).

Hypochondriasis

Hypochondriacal preoccupation is common and varies in degree from mild concern with health on the one hand to the occurrence of delusions that he has diseases such as cancer, V.D. or that certain organs and functions have stopped functioning or are absent (Nihilistic delusions).

Disorders of Perception

Hallucinations are rare but when they occur are in keeping with the depressed mood. Illusions are not uncommon.

Sleep

Disturbance of sleep is characteristic of depression, early morning waking being the rule in endogenous depression and difficulty in getting off to sleep in milder depressive states associated with anxiety.

Loss of Appetite

This is very characteristic and sometimes weight loss may be dramatic, e.g. the patient may lose up to 2 stones in a matter of weeks.

Diurnal Variation

Most commonly the mood tends to be worse in the mornings. Occasionally patients feel worse towards the latter part of the day; this occurs especially if anxiety is a prominent part of the clinical picture.

Physical Symptoms and Signs

The patient may complain predominantly of physical symptoms such as headaches, vague bodily complaints such as pains, dyspepsia, tight feelings in the chest, giddiness, constipation, urinary frequency, palpitations, dyspnoea, blurred vision, dryness of the mouth and paraesthesiae. In women menstrual functions become disturbed and there may be amenorrhoea. Libido is diminished or lost.

Prevalence and Aetiology

Between 35 and 40 per cent of all psychiatric illnesses which come to medical notice are depressive. This was found in in-patient surveys in England and Wales and in surveys of various general practices.

In 1959 there were 20,000 new admissions with depression into mental hospitals in England and Wales and an equal number were re-admissions, that is a total of 40,000 admissions a year.

General practitioners' estimates of how frequently they see new cases of depressive illness vary from a figure of 1 and 5 cases per 1,000 registered patients per year, depending on the strictness of the diagnosis. A reasonable assessment would be that, in a general practice of 3,000 patients, a practitioner would see in any one year between 5 and 10 new cases of depression and about as many old ones. About 1 in 10 of such patients get referred to psychiatrists and, of these, about half are ad-mitted as in-patients.

The chance of any person developing a depressive illness during the course of his life is 1 per cent. About 1 person in every 100 is likely to get a depressive illness of such severity as to get admitted to a mental hospital. The number of people who go to general practitioners with depressive illnesses and are not admitted into hospital is probably about 2 per cent (1 in 50).

Depression is twice as common in females as in males. Age is the important factor regarding the onset of the first attack of depression. The onset increases towards middle age with a maximum onset in the 55–60 age group. It is quite different from schizophrenia where the rate of onset is highest in the 20–30 age group.

In the lowest social class (Social Class 5, unskilled workers) the rate for depressive illness is about double that in other social classes.

The incidence in first degree relatives of a patient who has a depression is about 15 per cent compared with 1 per cent in the general population.

It is believed that the predisposition to depressive illness is determined by a dominant gene with an incomplete degree of penetration.

Depressive illnesses are the resultant of the interaction of genetic and constitutional factors on one hand with environmental and other exogenous influences on the other. Those depressive illnesses which are predominantly determined by genetic-constitutional factors are usually referred to as endogenous depressions and are characterised by a typical diurnal variation, being worse in the morning and tending to improve later in the day, and an onset which may occur independently of adverse environmental circumstances. Depressive illnesses which are predominantly a reaction to environmental influences are referred to as

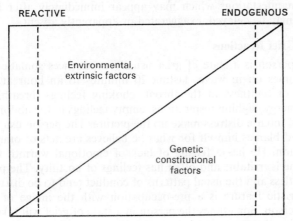

FIG. 12. Possible combinations of endogenous and exogenous factors in depressive states.

reactive depressions and are usually less severe and often fluctuate in severity according to external circumstances.

In a large number of depressive illnesses, however, both endogenous and environmental factors are present. In clinical practice an infinite variety of combinations of these factors are found as shown diagrammatically in Fig. 12.

Involutional Melancholia (syn. Involutional Depression)

This term is applied to severe psychiatric illnesses which are depressive but often with paranoid and hypochondriacal components; occurring for the first time in the involutional period, i.e. roughly between 45 and 65 years. The personality of patients before the illness is usually characterised by rigidity, ambitiousness, drive, perfectionism, high standards and exaggerated concern with health.

Hypochondriacal ideas are frequent and they vary from concern about health and the decline in physical strength and dexterity, which is common at this time of life, on one extreme, to delusions of a nihilistic and bizarre kind—for example, that the intestines are missing and that the head is empty.

Anxiety, tension and restlessness are common. Disorders of perception in the form of illusions which, when they occur, are in keeping with the anxious affect. Hallucinations may also occur but are infrequent; they are often tactile, especially genital in women. Auditory hallucinations can occur but are rare.

ACUTE GRIEF AND ITS MANAGEMENT

Acute grief is a definite syndrome with both physical and psychological manifestations which may appear immediately after bereavement or may be delayed, exaggerated or apparently absent.

Normal Grief Reactions

The person is a state of grief usually experiences somatic distress which comes on in waves lasting 20 minutes to an hour at a time. Feelings of tightness in the throat, choking feelings, breathlessness, lack of energy, sighing respirations, empty feelings in the abdomen and feelings if intense distress make up the picture. The person usually feels guilty and blames himself for what he believes are acts of omission or commission. He has a feeling of lack of emotional warmth to other people, he is irritable and often has feelings of hostility. The person is often restless and the usual patterns of conduct tend to be disrupted. A characteristic feature is a pre-occupation with the image of the deceased person. Sometimes the person in a state of grief will take on the personality traits, mannerisms or symptoms experienced by the deceased person in his terminal illness.

The duration of the grief reaction will depend on successfully going through the grief work which involves obtaining freedom from the bonds which tie and imprison the bereft person to the deceased person and the achievement of re-adjustment to the environment and the formation of new relationships.

Grief is painful and the patient will often try to avoid getting emotionally upset and mistakenly may be encouraged to hide his feelings by friends or even medical advisors. This advice is completely wrong and tends to prolong the duration of the grief reaction. It is imperative for the person to face the fact of bereavement and its discomfort and to deal, in memory, with the deceased person by discussing the loss with friends, relatives or the physician. This will produce relief of distress.

Morbid Grief Reactions

The following morbid grief reactions are distortions of normal grief reactions. They are treated by transference to normal grief reactions which are then more readily resolved.

(1) Delayed grief. Grief reactions, if not experienced soon after bereavement, may be delayed months or years.

(2) Overactivity without sense of loss.

(3) Acquiring symptoms of deceased person's illness.

(4) Disturbed interpersonal relationships.

(5) Intense feelings of hostility against doctors, hospital authorities or others.

(6) Severe agitated depression.

Prognosis in Depressive Illness

Prognosis may be considered for the attack and for recurrence.

Prognosis depends on:

(1) The inherited predisposition and the evidences of it in constitution and personality.

(2) The experiences which have moulded the patient and to which he is still exposed and responsive.

(3) The tendency of an emotional reaction to subside or to continue.

Prognosis therefore depends on heredity, on the environment and on the biological form of the illness.

With regard to heredity, the chances of complete recovery from an attack will be good where a typical affective illness, periodic or solitary has occurred in one or more of the patient's antecedents. If the patient has always been maladjusted, an attack of depression will increase his difficulties of adjustment and when he recovers from it he will still remain a maladjusted person. Recovery here is, therefore, a qualified one.

If psychosocial stresses on careful evaluation are important, this may be of some help in prognosis if they can be remedied or are unlikely to recur. Severe depressive illnesses usually subside; mild emotional states tend to persist autonomously.

The most satisfactory outcome occurs when the onset is abrupt, the clinical features are typical of classical depression and the previous personality healthy and well adjusted or a history of defined previous affective attacks without physical disease. Gross hypochondriacal ideas, nihilistic delusions and admixture of schizophrenic or other anomalous symptoms are unfavourable prognostic indicators.

In fairly well diagnosed and clear cut depressive illnesses, it is probable that 95 per cent will recover, 1 per cent will commit suicide and 4 per cent will remain in a state of chronic illness.

Depressive illness in general tends to be self-limiting with a natural tendency to recovery.

Principles of Management

One must constantly keep in mind that depressive illness causes disability and suffering.

The degree of disability will depend on the severity of the depression and persons with the greatest drive, productivity and creativeness may become completely ineffective during a depressive illness. Such effects are temporary, the patient reverting to his normal state with recovery from his illness.

It is important for the patient to accept the fact that depression does impose great difficulties in coping with everyday tasks and it is better for him to accept this rather than to make desperate efforts to carry on despite his symptoms, as this increases his burden because of the resulting frustration, anxiety and disappointment. He should be encouraged to do what he finds he is able to do during his illness but exhortations that he should pull himself together are absurd, the patient himself realising that if he could do this he would be the first person to do so.

It is important for those dealing with depressive illnesses to be friendly, to show interest and to give support. This is helpful in all types of depression. In severe depressions the effects of this may not be noticeable; nevertheless, it is important in all depressions and is appreciated by the patient and he will remember it with gratitude later.

It is important not to urge patients to try to undertake normal responsibilities, particularly when they are severely depressed, as they are quite unable to so do at that stage. As they improve they will automatically find it easier to do things. This is the time when encouragement, if needed, will help the patient to return to normal activities, to work and social pursuits.

The general practitioner should also realise the importance of keeping the family informed about the nature of the illness, so that they can be more understanding and not add to the patient's burden and frustration because depressive illnesses, as they affect a person's warmth in his relationships and sometimes bring out the worst traits in his personality, are treated with great intolerance by the family which does not provide the conditions conducive to the patient's improvement and rehabilitation.

If the depression is sufficiently severe to prevent him from working, this usually indicates that the illness is at least of moderate severity and may be severe. This criterion indicates the need of some active medical treatment.

The severity of the illness as well as the possible risk of suicide, social factors such as home conditions and the ability of the family to look after the patient will influence the decision whether a patient ought to be treated in hospital or not. Severely depressed patients, particularly those with suicidal preoccupations or intentions should, of course, be treated in hospital.

A further important point is management is to be able to assess the importance of what the patients say. They will often tell you that 'I am depressed because I foolishly did this or that when I was a child or in my teens' or they attribute the depression to something more recent which they feel guilty about; or they may say that they are depressed because of pressure of work or the attitude of their superiors or the attitude of their family, or that they find the work too much for them. All these, in fact, may be symptoms of depression and the things they believe have brought on the illness may be just the effects of the illness rather than the cause.

Another mistake, which is unfortunately only too frequently carried out, is to advise a severely depressed patient to take a cruise or a holiday, as this usually not only has no beneficial results as the illness prevents him enjoying himself wherever he is. If a patient says that he feels that life is not worth living and he would be glad if he were run over by a bus or if he did not wake up, or if he has feelings that he would like to take an overdose or gas himself, this should not be dismissed but should be assessed in the light of the patient's general condition.

The risk of suicide is usually associated with the intensity of suffering experienced by the patient and is often linked up with feelings of unworthiness, self-depreciation and guilt. The patient feels that he is no good, that life offers nothing for him and that he is unwanted. Elderly depressed patients, when they are socially isolated, carry a greater risk of suicide.

It is important to remember, too, that the risk of a successful suicidal attempt is present in the early part of the illness, before the danger has been recognised or sufficiently assessed, and again when the patient starts recovering from a severe depression, because during the depth of his depression he may be unable to carry out his suicidal wish into action but on relief of the retardation he may then put his wishes into a suicidal attempt.

DRUG TREATMENT

(1) *Central Nervous Stimulants.* These are of limited value in the treatment of depression. The amphetamine drugs and allied drugs such as Ritalin have a possible place only in the management of mild depressive states but have serious disadvantages and unpleasant side-effects and are of no value in severe depressive states.

They are mostly of value when the depression is limited to one part of the day, for example the early morning, and amphetamines may tide the patient over this period.

Amphetamines are drugs of addiction and, with a very high dosage psychotic states can occur.

(2) *Antidepressants.* The discovery of antidepressant drugs in the last 8 years has been a major advance in psychiatric treatment. (Vide Chap. 32.)

They are of two main classes:

1. The monoamine oxidase inhibitor drugs (*vide* Table 4, p. 283).

2. Drugs similar in chemical structure to phenothiazine and collectively referred to as the tricyclic antidepressants; these include Imipramine, Amitriptyline, Nortriptyline, Desimipramine.

Monoamine Oxidase Inhibitors (MAOI)

The quickest acting of the MAOI drugs is tranylcypromine (Parnate) which has a direct stimulant action on the central nervous system as well as its more prolonged action in inhibiting the enzyme, monoamine oxidase. It has also a marked tendency to produce side-effects which are referred to below.

Isocarboxazid (Marplan) is the safest MAOI drug but usually takes about three weeks to produce its clinical effects.

Phenelzine (Nardil) and nialamide (Niamid) have a greater tendency to produce side-effects than isocarboxazid (Marplan), but probably less so than tranylsypromine (Parnate).

The full effect of MAOI drugs is usually achieved by the end of three weeks' medication and if no significant improvement has occurred by the end of this time it is unnecessary and unwise to continue it further. **Precautions.** It has been shown that certain foods and beverages which contain tyramine may cause severe reactions in patients on MAOI drugs. The reaction usually consists of an intense headache starting at the back of the head and then extending to the front, and associated with an elevation in blood-pressure which fluctuates in severity. The severity of the symptoms often suggests a subarachnoid haemorrhage which has in fact occurred in some patients. Foods to avoid are cheese, Marmite, broad bean pods, certain wines like red Chianti, and strong beers.

Care has to be exercised with sympathomimetic amines such as amphetamine and ephedrine as sometimes a rise in blood-pressure with headaches may result. Drugs like pethidine and other narcotics are potentiated and must be avoided, and it is also important to remember that the MAOI potentiate the effects of sedatives, phenothiazines and alcohol.

If after MAOI therapy it is proposed to try a tricyclic antidepressant an interval of 10 to 14 days must elapse in view of the possibilities of adverse interaction. Some experienced psychiatrists successfully combine antidepressants but this is unwise in general practice.

Tricyclic Antidepressants

Imipramine is the antidepressant of choice in endogenous depression. The starting dose is 25 mg. t.d.s. increasing to 50 mg. t.d.s. after a week. In elderly patients a smaller dose must be given, 10 mg. t.d.s. increasing to 20 mg. t.d.s., because of the risk of producing states of confusion or delirium.

Desipramine was claimed to be more effective than imipramine but the available evidence does not support this.

Amitriptylene is of value in depressive states associated with anxiety or agitation.

Nortriptylene is of value in depressive states associated with apathy and lack of energy and drive.

The dosage of all tricyclic antidepressants is of the same order as that given for Imipramine. Administration for three weeks is generally sufficient, and if there is little or no improvement in that time, or at the most four weeks, the drugs should be discontinued as further improvement is unlikely to occur. If monoamine oxidase inhibitors (MAOI) are given after one of the tricyclic antidepressants a period of four to seven days should elapse before introducing them.

Indications for Tranquillizers, Tranquillo-Sedatives and Sedatives

Patients exhibiting marked anxiety and agitation in addition to depression may need drugs in this class as well as antidepressants. It is important to realise that tranquillizers such as chlorpromazine (Largactil) and other phenothiazine derivatives, tranquillo-sedatives such as chlordiazepoxide (Librium) and diazepam (Valium), and sedatives such as barbiturates do not significantly influence the degree of depression but are mainly effective in relieving associated anxiety and tension.

The MAOI drugs are mainly of value in depressions of mild or moderate severity and more in atypical than the typical endogenous depressions. In cases of severe depression none of the antidepressants is as effective as electroconvulsive therapy which may be given as an outpatient or as an inpatient depending on the needs of the case.

Electroconvulsive Therapy (E.C.T.)

This remains the most effective treatment available for severe depressive illness. (Vide Chapter 33.)

Other Physical Methods of Treatment

Another treatment sometimes used for depressive states is continuous narcosis, in which narcotics and sedatives are given to induce sleep for up to 18 hours a day. This method sometimes shortens a depressive illness. Patients with depressive states developing after prolonged stress and associated with marked loss of weight often benefit from modified insulin therapy. This treatment consists of giving intra-muscularly, gradually increasing doses of insulin to induce hypogly-caemia. In contrast to the insulin coma treatment for schizophrenia, the hypoglycaemia is terminated by glucose administration before it deepens sufficiently to cause loss of consciousness.

When all other methods of treatment have failed, prefrontal leuco-tomy or one of its modern modifications may have to be considered for patients with long-standing depression associated with marked emotion-al tension. The best results are obtained in patients with good previous personality and whose social and home circumstances are favourable for resettlement and rehabilitation after the operation.

HYPOMANIA AND MANIA

The clinical manifestations of hypomania and mania are the antithesis of those seen in depressive states.

Hypomania is characterised, as in other affective disorders, by a fixed change in mood which here is one of excitement and elation. The patient is optimistic, confident and has a general feeling of well-being and sometimes marked euphoria.

The determination of the onset of hypomania may be difficult. It is essential to know the previous personality of the patient and the ways in which his hypomanic state differs from his normal behaviour.

Patients show very marked pressure of activity which affects think-ing, speech and general activity. Patients usually talk a great deal and sometimes talk may be almost incessant. Pressure of talk and physical activity (psychomotor over-activity) is characteristic. The talk is replete with details and is circumstantial and easily influenced in trend and content by the patient's distractability to any stimuli he may encounter. In fact any stimulus or any association can influence content of speech.

In contrast to schizophrenia, hypomanic and manic states show flight of ideas, the patient going from one subject to another, such flights of ideas being determined by their inner pressure and by the patients' circumstantiality and by associations they form with what they say or with external stimuli. Nevertheless, they tend to reach the goal, though it may take a long time with a great deal of circumstantia-lity in speech on the way.

Hypomanic patients frequently make puns based on sounds, clang associations or other stimuli.

Ceaseless activity is the rule but the activity is easily distractable and patients change from one activity to another before finishing the task already started.

Mood is one of elation which is often infectious, a feature which distinguishes the elated state of hypomania from the elated state some-times found in schizophrenia.

In schizophrenia there is a characteristic glass wall between the observer and the patient and difficulty in establishing rapport. One may be tempted to laugh *at* some of the things the schizophrenic patient says but, with the hypomanic, one will laugh *with* them. Their enthusiasm wit and good humour have an infectious quality.

They are over-confident, lack reserve and feel that no obstacle is too great for them to overcome. They are often productive in ideas but often are unable to record them because they are too much in a hurry or too distractable.

Hypomanic patients are alert, notice many things. This, together with the increased drive and distractability, makes them go off tangentially in speech and actions but this is quite different from the disconnected speech and behaviour found in schizophrenia.

Hypomanics are expansive, friendly, interfering as they like to manage other people's affairs and are often a nuisance to others. They have little or no insight into their condition; they feel very fit and their ideas and plans are presented with enthusiasm and often convincing to others.

The following are the usual difficulties that persons with hypomania and mania get into:

(1) They spend a great deal of money, buy unnecessary things or enter into unwise legal agreements in business. They will sometimes issue cheques which cannot be met ('rubber cheques', as the Americans call them, as they bounce back).

(2) They often drink excessively or indulge in excessive or unwise sexual activity leading to venereal disease or pregnancy.

(3) When thwarted they tend to become angry or even violent.

Therefore disturbances of behaviour and social difficulties bring the patient into conflict with society and, as a result, to medical attention. Sometimes treatment has to be arranged compulsorily, e.g. when the patient is unwilling to accept treatment voluntarily and when behaviour or circumstances make admission necessary.

In the most severe forms—viz Acute Mania and Delirious Mania— all the above features already are shown in greater degree and severity with greater psychomotor activity and distractability and greater tendency to be involved in problems of social behaviour. Grandiose tendencies may take the form of delusions, e.g. delusions of great physical or intellectual strength and prowess or sometimes delusions of grandeur regarding possessions, birth and personal beauty.

The extreme form is Delirious Mania, which the psychomotor activity is so great that the patient's speech is incoherent, he is continually restless and leading eventually to exhaustion. There is a risk of a terminal pneumonia supervening on such a state of physical exhaustion.

Illustrative Examples

The following are pen sketches of two typical patients with attacks of hypomania:

(a) A lady aged 48; gets up early in the morning, is very cheerful, talkative, noisy, keeps singing in the bath and gets on with the housework quickly. She has completed the housework and has got her husband and family out of the house by 8 o'clock in the morning. She then dresses in her brightest clothes, puts on excessive make-up—slaps on plenty of lipstick and daubs on excessive eye shadow—and then goes visiting her friends to whom she talks incessantly, making jokes, puns and tries to manage their affairs, persisting to a degree which makes her a nuisance.

She will spend a great deal of money in buying flamboyant new clothes and hats which she does not need or cannot afford and in buying things for her family and friends. She is tireless, talking incessantly with great circumstantiality until the early hours of the morning.

(b) A male patient aged 56 with an attack of hypomania: He gets up early in the morning with a great deal of energy, is very active, singing in the bath, talking, a great deal of slapping people on the back, making jokes and puns. He may start decorating his house, e.g. he may start painting the front door and before finishing he will start dismantling his car and then start digging the garden, at the same time talking with rapidity to anyone nearby, giving advice and often interfering with their affairs.

He feels very fit, wants to be doing everything at once and is readily distracted by any external stimulus.

He will tend to go off buying things, things that he does not need or cannot afford; he may change his car unnecessarily or buy new outfits of clothes. He is excessively generous, giving away money by cheques that cannot be met. If anybody thwarts him he will get angry, even violent. He may go off to the local pub and drink excessively, standing everyone drinks, incessantly talking and making puns. He makes rash promises to do things for people and feels that nothing is impossible for him to achieve. Such a state of over-activity and drive continues through the day and until the early morning, as he regards going to sleep as a waste of time.

TREATMENT OF HYPOMANIA AND MANIA

General Management

The hypomanic and manic patient very rarely realises or admits that he is in any way unwell, as he feels euphoric, energetic and overconfident.

The dangers are that he may get into difficulties by over-spending, excessive drinking or due to heightened sexual activities are important keynotes to management.

Admission to hospital will depend on the severity of the hypomania or mania and on the patient's social behaviour. In very severe states of mania admission becomes imperative, due to the fact that ceaseless over-activity carries the risk of exhaustion which may endanger the patient's life due to the development of intercurrent infections.

Drug Treatment

The introduction of the new major tranquillising drugs (see Chap. 32) such as Chlorpromazine and Reserpine brought a new hope that these drugs would be effective in hypomania and mania. However, these drugs, although helpful in many patients, there are some who even on extremely high doses of Chlorpromazine continue to be hyperactive and continue to present problems of management.

The newer drugs in the butyrophenone series, such as Haloperidol, have proved to be more useful in the treatment of mania. Haloperidol is given in doses of up to 10 mg.–12 mg. daily.

Thioproperazine has also been claimed to be effective. Patients are given $7\frac{1}{2}$ mg. Thioproperazine intramuscularly three times a day at first, or twice a day for the first two or three days, after which a dose of 5 mg. three times a day by mouth is given. The dosage is then gradually reduced to 1 mg. or 2 mg. three times a day. Some patients are adequately dealt with by giving the drug by mouth only, starting with 10 mg. twice a day.

With both Haloperidol and Thioproperazine there is a high risk of producing parkinsonism but this can be controlled by the concurrent administration of Artane, Cogentin or Orphephenedrine (Disipal).

Lithium is also used in the treatment of mania. It is essential that the blood level should be determined regularly and that an adequate sodium chloride and fluid intake is ensured.

Surprisingly, E.C.T. is effective and necessary in some patients. E.C.T. given 3–5 times a week will sometimes terminate an attack of mania. It should be pointed out that the use of E.C.T. for mania, is not a matter on which there is general agreement.

In conclusion it can be said that the more potent major tranquillisers such as Haloperidol at present offer the best means for the control and management of attacks of hypomania and mania and that extrapyramidal drugs need to be given concurrently.

There is no evidence that medication fundamentally shortens course of the illness, so that medication has to be given sufficiently long for the attack to run its course.

ANXIETY STATES

Anxiety is a normal emotion which in moderate degree can be a helpful force by increasing effort and alertness. In excess anxiety impairs effectiveness and is a handicap.

The term anxiety state refers to a disorder in which anxiety is the primary and dominant part of the clinical picture, with the mood change being relatively fixed and persistent and of such a degree as to affect well-being, efficiency and normal adjustment.

Anxiety states vary in severity and duration. Thus they may be acute and mild or acute and severe or chronic mild or severe.

The Biological Significance of Anxiety

Throughout the animal kingdom, an animal in danger shows all the bodily and behavioural manifestations of anxiety.

Cannon has shown that, during such situations, the body becomes mobilised for action either for fight or flight and that the mechanisms involved include the autonomic nervous system, the locomotor system and other changes throughout the body which serve to increase the organism's ability to deal with the threat by action. The sympathetic part of the nervous system is predominantly involved but certain aspects of parasympathetic activity which would subserve the need for total mobilisation for activity, e.g. the sacral parasympathetic causing evacuation of the bladder and bowel.

Various changes which occur, alert the animal, increase awarenesss and responsivity to various stimuli and serve to bring about more effective blood supply to the muscles of locomotion, where it is most urgently needed during an emergency, so that the rate of respiration is increased to cope with the increased demands of oxygen by the muscles; heart rate is increased to pump the blood round to the muscles where it is needed. The blood vessels to muscles and heart tend to be dilated where as the arterioles to the skin and digestive tract, where food and oxygen are not urgently needed, are diminished, so that there is a redistribution of blood supply to the vital organs of circulation and locomotion. Muscular tone is increased so that the animal can go into action without delay. Dilatation of the pupils and increased alertness in response to stimuli also serve the organism in being effectively aware of the environment.

In some animals, pilo-erection makes the animal look more fierce. In man, anxiety just inconveniently produces goose pimples without serving any obvious beneficial effect, biologically or otherwise.

A knowledge of the physiological changes occurring with anxiety is helpful in understanding the symptoms of patients suffering from anxiety states.

CLINICAL FEATURES OF ANXIETY STATES

General Appearance and Behaviour

A person with an anxiety state has a tense, anxious, apprehensive attitude and demeanour. Increased muscular tension is shown in his facial expression, posture and his difficulty in relaxing, Characteristically he sits on the edge of the chair during an interview and jumps at any sudden noise.

When muscular tension is marked, tremors of the hands, knees and sometimes other parts of the body are noticeable. Palpebral fissures tend to be wide and pupils dilated; the mouth tends to be dry so that the patient can be observed licking his lips and moistening his tongue.

Mood

The patient is in a constant state of worry and usually looks apprehensively ahead, anticipating problems and crossing his bridges before reaching them, fearing that dangers and catastrophes lay awaiting him around the corner. He is apprehensive about his health, family, finances about his abilities and other aspects of his life. He seeks constant reassurance. His thoughts are concerned with worries for the present and the future. Speech, is often rapid and may exhibit stammering or hesitancy.

Bodily Concomitants of Anxiety

These are to be seen as changes in locomotor system sudomotor system and the autonomic nervous system of control of functions of various organs and systems. An understanding of the physiological basis of these will enable one to understand the patient's symptoms and to be in a better position to explain and reassure him effectively.

(1) *Muscular System*

Increased tension of the voluntary musculature is characteristic of anxiety states and has been referred to already. Symptoms directly referable to increased muscular tension include tremors, aches and pains in various muscles of the body—for example, pain in the back, limbs, neck and side of the head. One type of headache is due to increased tension of the scalp muscles.

A useful diagnostic test is that the pains arising from increased muscular tension disappear with a small quantity of intravenous 10 per cent sodium amytal; viz. one or two cc. injected intravenously slowly, the pain will go long before there is any interference with the patient's consciousness and occurs when the patient develops feelings of relaxation. Sodium amytal in this dosage has no analgesic effect and produces this by producing relief of anxiety, tension and, concomitantly, reduction of muscular tension.

(2) *Cardiovascular System*

Tachycardia and the subjective experience of increased rapidity and forcefulness of heart beat, palpitations are common effects of anxiety. The patient often becomes worried about this and develops fears of heart disease which further increases his anxiety, thus creating a vicious circle. Precordial pain is frequent which, again, the patient tends to assume is evidence of heart disease, but precordial pain in young people is invariably due to psychogenic factors. It has its origin in the inter-costal and pectoral muscles and, if it were necessary for this to be proved, an injection of local anaesthetic into these muscles would immediately abolish the pain.

Blood pressure is often increased, systolic pressure being mainly affected and it usually soon returns to normal. During physical examination, initial readings tend to be much higher than subsequent readings which provides evidence of the effect of anxiety and apprehension on level of blood pressure.

Pallor and cold, blue extremities are evidence of vaso-constriction in the arteries supplying the skin.

(3) *Respiratory System*

Anxious patients tend to have rapid, shallow breathing, sometimes frequent sighing and, in general, to show poor effort tolerance—much poorer effort tolerance than is characteristic of their normal state.

(4) *Gastro-intestinal System*

Decrease of salivary secretion gives rise to characteristic dryness of the mouth. Epigastric tremulousness nausea, dyspepsia, bowel urgency, frequency or diarrhoea are common.

In some patients, anxiety and tension produces spasm of the large bowel, giving rise to constipation.

It should be noted that, in some people, anxiety makes them eat more because eating gives them relief of tension and may serve a substitute for love and affection. As a rule appetite is diminished in anxiety states.

(5) *Sudomotor System*

The distribution of sweating in anxiety states is typically emotional in distribution, i.e. from the palms, the axillae and forehead. The cold, moist palm is typical of a person suffering from an anxiety state, in contrast to the warm, moist palm of a patient suffering from thyrotoxicosis.

Aetiology

The principle of multiple aetiological factors can be clearly seen in the genesis of anxiety states. Aetiological factors may be conveniently considered as (a) extrinsic or environmental and (b) intrinsic or constitutional, or they may be classified into (1) predisposing factors and (2) precipitating factors.

Genetic and Constitutional Predisposing Factors

It was demonstrated in World War II that a person's constitution determined the degree of environmental stress that he could cope with before developing a psychiatric illness, such as an anxiety state. The constitutional predisposition included genetic factors, probably a number of genes of small effect.

Genetic factors may be manifested in a number of ways:

(1) By determining the predisposition of breakdown.

(2) Determining, in part, personality type and stability.

(3) Determining physiological features such as autonomic imbalance and, possibly, certain neuro-endocrine mechanisms which may be important.

Genetic factors cannot be considered in isolation because parents and siblings with anxiety states or other psychiatric disorders may also exert a direct influence on the person and influence his personality disposition and may cause him to develop certain traits of personality which are conducive to the development of anxiety and distress, the tendency to be very sensitive, the tendency to be timid, apprehensive and unassertive and the tendency to emotional instability with minor frustrations. It has been suggested that people of introverted personality tend to develop conditioned responses more readily and tend to learn anxiety reactions more rapidly than extroverted persons.

Physical Factors

These include fatigue, exhaustion

(2) Infections, particularly virus infections which may leave depression and anxiety persisting for many weeks after the physical aspects of the infection have passed off.

Endocrine Factors

In hyperthyroidism, anxiety is a common feature. Similarly, changes in the hormonal balance of the body which occur at puberty, following childbirth and at the menopause may be associated with emotional lability and increased tendency to anxiety.

In some women, the various psychophysical changes comprising the premenstrual tension syndrome are particularly associated with development of anxiety and tension.

It should be remembered, too, that certain addicts develop very marked anxiety as a part of the withdrawal effects of the drugs. Originally, people may take barbiturates for the relief of anxiety but, if they take a sufficiently high dose over a long period of time, they become addicted and when the drug level of the barbiturate decreases, they develop marked anxiety which leads to the increase of further barbiturates, thus creating a marked vicious circle and increasing the problems of addiction.

Similarly, increased anxiety can follow the intake of alcohol and, again, one can get alcoholism developing as a part of this mechanism.

Psychological

Psychosocial stresses may be acute and severe or may be prolonged. Every person has his breaking point. Some people are more vulnerable to certain stresses—for example, financial, marital—whereas others are mainly affected by threats to their status and prestige. Severe stresses include accidents, frightening experiences, bereavement, prolonged stresses relating to interpersonal problems, to marital, financial and occupational worries and conflicts.

Stresses tend to have a cumulative effect and sometimes the experience of a series of stresses or prolonged stress combined, perhaps, with infections, fatigue, may be the culminating point which leads to the development of an anxiety state.

Conflicts relating to any sphere of a person's life may be associated with anxiety. Desires related to instinctive drives and the conflicts imposed by the person's standards or the requirements of society or, indeed, conflicts about any wish can lead to the development of anxiety.

Anxiety and tension may become a part of the life pattern of a successful business man. They live in a constant state of tension and over-activity and are unable to relax and some remain well for years without much rest or recreation. Others become increasingly fatigued and depressed and ultimately break down with a psychiatric or psychosomatic disorder.

In some persons, the relief of pressure of work, such as holidays or weekends, leads to increased anxiety unless they are able to channelise their energies into substitutive activities.

The Occurrence of Anxiety and Other Psychiatric, Physical and Psychosomatic disorders

Anxiety may occur in practically all psychiatric disorders but, here it is a part and not the main and predominant and primary component of the clinical picture.

For example:

(1) *Schizophrenia.* Anxiety may be prominent in many forms of schizophrenia; the diagnosis will rest on the discovery of features which are indicative of schizophrenia.

One type of schizophrenia, referred to as pseudo-neurotic schizophrenia, may cause difficulties in diagnosis. Here the anxiety is overwhelming. It is a state of pan-anxiety but careful observation will illustrate deterioration of personality, emotional incongruity and other features which indicate the true nature of the disorder.

(2) *Depressive States.* Anxiety is a frequent component in depressive illnesses. In those illnesses which are a reaction to environmental difficulty, anxiety is particularly prominent but it may also occur in

endogenous depressions and is particularly intense in agitated depressions.

In patients developing anxiety for the first time after the age of 40, in the absence of any organic disease, one should bear in mind the possibility that this may, in fact, be a depressive state in which the main manifestation to the observer is anxiety.

Anxiety occurs in acute organic states such as delirium; also in cases of organic dementia, including senile dementia and arteriosclerotic dementia, and is related to the emotional lability of these patients and also to the difficulties of adjustment which the dementia imposes on them.

(3) *Post-concussional syndromes* are often associated with anxiety and irritability.

(4) Anxiety symptoms are common in all psychosomatic disorders and in almost all physical disorders, depending on a variety of factors including the patient's reaction to the illness and the threat which it presents to him.

PROGNOSIS

This will depend on the strength of the predisposing factors and the personality of the patient, his habitual modes of reaction, the role played by organic and endocrine factors in predisposition and the extent to which they can be modified and, finally, the severity and nature of the stresses and the extent to which these can be modified.

Factors of good prognosis are an acute onset, short duration of symptoms, stable personality, good work record and good general previous adjustment. Factors of poor prognosis are family history of neurosis, neurotic traits in childhood, poor work record and other evidence of difficulties of adjustment, unstable personality and the extent to which various vicious circles have developed in the perpetuation of symptoms, such as worry about somatic effects of anxiety and, in the case of phobias, avoiding situations which were previously associated with phobias.

Treatment

The steps in treatment include:

(1) First of all, taking a full history.

(2) Thorough physical examination.

(3) Discussion, explanation and positive reassurance.

(4) General support and management, giving further explanation, encouragement and guidance in coping with their problems (V Chap. 30).

(5) Social measures dealing with problems of work and home, as far as they can be modified.

(6) Symptomatic treatment—the use of anti anxiety drugs to relieve

symptoms and to encourage resumption of normal activities. (V Chap. 30).

(7) Psychotherapy if indicated and according to the needs of the case.
  (a) shorter supportive.
  (b) prolonged and intensive psychotherapy.
  (c) group therapy.
(8) Behaviour therapy for certain phobic symptoms (V Chap. 31).

FURTHER READING

Depressive Disorders in the Community by C. A. H. Watts. J. Wright, Bristol (1965).

CHAPTER TWENTY-THREE

HYSTERIA

Hysteria is defined as a disorder in which the patient develops symptoms and signs of illness (mental, physical or both) for some real or imagined gain without being fully aware of the underlying motive.

Frequently the term hysteria is misapplied for histrionic or uncontrolled behaviour, whereas it should be reserved for psychogenic illnesses having a motive of gain.

Hysteria is protean in manifestation and may stimulate any disease.

The mental mechanism underlying the formation of hysterical symtoms is a process of dissociation whereby certain dynamically related facts of experience (usually psychic traumata) become separated from the mainstream of consciousness in predisposed individuals under conditions of stress. The development of the hysterical symptom usually enables the patient to escape from a difficult situation. It is on account of the gain resulting from the illness that hysteria has been confused with malingering.

A malingerer is a person who claims he has symptoms when he knows he has none, whereas the hysteric has genuine symptoms.

FORMS OF HYSTERICAL REACTION

The varied manifestations of hysteria can conveniently be classified into three main groups:

(1) **Dysmnesic**
- (a) Amnesia.
- (b) Fugues.
- (c) Somnambulism.
- (d) Twilight states.

(2) **Conversion Symptoms**
- (a) *Motor* e.g. paralysis, paresis, tremors, rigidity, abnormal gait, ataxia, fits.
- (b) *Sensory General*—anaesthesia, paraesthesia, hyperalgesia and pains.
  Sensory Special—visual difficulties, blindness, deafness, loss of taste, loss of smell.
- (c) *Visceral* e.g. vomiting, retention of urine, constipation.

(3) **Miscellaneous.** Ganser syndrome; Hysterical super-additions to

physical diseases, hysterical prolongation of illness and certain iatro-genic disorders.

It should be noted that all hysterical manifestations involve functions which are under the control or the influence of volition. This applies to the voluntary muscles concerned with vomiting, retention of urine and dyschezia. A great deal of confusion occurs because some authorities describe as hysteria, manifestations which are the bodily manifestations of emotional tension mediated by the autonomic nervous system.

(1) **Dysmnesic** forms of hysteria include amnesia, fugues, somnam-bulism, hysterical fits, multiple personality.

Hysterical amnesia may cover a short period of a person's life or may cover a large part of it or even the whole of it. Amnesia may or may not be associated with loss of personal identity. Amnesia usually occurs to escape from intolerable anxiety and distress about some problem or difficulty or situation in which the patient finds himself.

Amnesia is sometimes claimed as a defence when the patient has committed a criminal offence, but hysterical amnesia is not accepted in law as mental illness and therefore the patient is held to be responsible quite irrespective of the presence of amnesia.

As a deterrent during World War II and to avoid epidemics of amnesia, notices were sometimes put up that any soldier losing his memory would be dealt with disciplinarily in the same way as he would if he lost any other part of his equipment.

(2) **Fugues.** Fugue is a state of wandering, with amnesia for the period during which the wandering occurred. Again, the fugue is usually determined by a need to get away from some intolerable situation.

It should be noted that fugues may be of three kinds:

(a) Hysterical.

(b) As a manifestation of a depressive illness in which the patient is extremely distressed, wanders around, sometimes contemplating suicide and, because he does not register clearly what is happening to him, he is unable to remember the events which occurred during the period of wandering.

(c) Manifestations of organic mental states, for example post-epileptic phenomenon, or wandering in a state of confusion.

(3) **Hysterical Fits.** Hysterical fits may sometimes create confusion in diagnosis because of superficial similarities to grand mal epilepsy, but the following features will serve to distinguish between them:

Hysterical fits never occur when the person is alone and usually occur in reaction to a situation which is emotionally important.

Epileptic fits, on the other hand, can occur during sleep and come on out of the blue without being necessarily related to what has happened immediately before in the patient's experience; they may occur in dangerous situations such as in crossing a busy street, near the fire or when the person is in dangerous situations such as working at heights or whilst swimming in the sea. All these situations are dangers with epileptic fits.

There is no real loss of consciousness as in epilepsy, no sequence of tonic and clonic phases, no tongue-biting and no incontinence. Hysterical fits consist of purposive movements of both the limbs including struggling, fighting, scratching, clawing.

Thus, if during a fit the patient gives evidence of any purposeful movements, such as fighting or resisting or talking spontaneously, answering questions or deliberately attacking or biting, this indicates that the patient is not unconscious, that the cerebral cortex is acting and therefore it is not epileptic. Hysterical fits can go on for much longer than a single major epileptic fit.

HYSTERICAL CONVERSION SYMPTOMS

Hysterical Motor Conversion Symptoms

These may consist of paresis or paralysis of limbs or other parts of the body. They never involve single muscles but movements and conform to the patient's idea of the form of the symptoms.

Hysterical gaits tend to be bizarre and are not similar to any organic neurological gait; similarly, hysterical weakness when the patient is asked to contract the muscles of the limb, contraction of both agonist and antagonist will occur.

Sensory Conversion Symptoms

Special senses e.g. hysterical blindness, hysterical deafness, hysterical anosmia, hysterical loss of taste will occur for some special reason which determines the selection of the particular sense modality to be affected. Sometimes it may be the patient's weak point, for example myopia may be the determinant of the development of hysterical blindness in certain traumatic situations when the stress is sufficiently severe, or deafness may be determined by the occupation of the person, for example a telephonist, or it may be determined by a desire not to hear.

General Sensation

The most common hysterical symptom affecting general sensation is anaesthesia of the skin; this corresponds to the patient's idea of anaesthesia and is usually of a glove and stocking distribution and stops at one of the joints, wrist joint, elbow joint or shoulder joint and is quite different from the distribution or loss of sensation due to any affection of the sensory nerves.

Quasi-Psychotic States

This usually takes the form of hysterical pseudo-dementia or Ganser syndrome, which is characterised by tendency to give approximate answers. The answers are incorrect, but near enough to know that the patient has the mental capacity to work out an answer near the approximate answer and behaviour again corresponds to the patient's concept of what mental illness is. This condition most commonly occurs in prisoners.

Diagnosis

The diagnosis of hysteria must not be made on negative grounds, that is merely the absence of organic disease to account for the symptoms. It must be made on positive grounds in relationship to the patient's personality, to the situation in which it occurs and the gain which the patient derives from it. This gain need not be a real gain in the eyes of other people, but it may be a gain only from the patient's point of view. It should be noted that hysterical symptoms affect functions which come under conscious control and that they serve some personal gain to the patient. The reactions which are subserved by the autonomic nervous system and which may be biologically purposeful should not be confused with hysteria. Therefore one cannot get hysterical pylorospasm or hysterical mystagmus or tachycardia because these are outside the conscious control.

Hysterical symptoms may be super-added on organic conditions, for example disseminated sclerosis or physical injuries or any organic condition or neurological state.

Hysterical symptoms appearing for the first time in older people suggest the need to investigate carefully for an organic basis.

AETIOLOGY

At one time it was believed that genetic factors played an important role in the predisposition to hysteria, but twin studies have thrown considerable doubt on this and hysteria is nowadays regarded as a reaction to environmental problems in which the patient's personality plays an important part in determining the mode of reaction. Environmental circumstances determine the time of development of hysterical symptoms. A specific type of hysterical personality has been described which is characterised by the need to exaggerate, the need to be in the centre of attention and to give an impression to the outside world of being better than one is, of tending to manipulate people and situations for some personal need, to have shallow emotional reactions but which are often demonstrative and dramatic and histrionic, a tendency to be untruthful and to exaggerate statements and claims. Many patients feel they have been deprived of affection from an early age and have an intense need for affection and approval which it is very difficult to satisfy. When they do get the attention and approval which they need, they test the person who gives it to such an extent that very often this produces a withdrawal of affection. Hysteria may be regarded as a protective mechanism to safeguard the person from stresses and strains of life and anxiety which it finds difficult to tolerate.

TREATMENT OF HYSTERIA

It should be borne in mind that hysterics are suggestible and respond readily to harmful as well as beneficial suggestions. They usually crave attention but the more attention paid to their symptoms the more implicit will be the suggestion that these are serious and the longer will they tend to persist.

The hysterical symptom should as far as possible be ignored and no notice taken of any worsening of the symptom, but the slightest improvement should be encouraged. The patient must be persuaded by those with whom he is in contact to carry on living as normally as possible. Keeping a patient with hysterical symptoms in bed or helping a patient to walk with a hysterical gait only serves to impress the patient that he is ill and needs support. Every effort must be made to make the patient assume responsibility for his functional recovery, and the more active part he can be made to play in treatment the better.

The general rule in management is firmness and, what is even more important, it must be consistent firmness.

Sometimes symptoms will disappear if they are completely ignored, but it is sometimes necessary to tackle the symptom actively in order to prevent habituation and incapacity due to the symptom and early removal makes it possible to bring the patient to face his problems and be guided to a more salutary solution.

The best method undoubtedly is to produce full functional recovery in one session. It is, therefore, important for the physician to allow himself ample time for the therapeutic session and to be prepared to carry on with his treatment until full functional recovery is achieved.

The following procedures are useful tactical aids in some patients: (1) Hypnosis.   (2) Intravenous barbiturate narcosis.

Both of these will help to elicit further information about the psychopathology of the disorder, as well as increasing the patient's suggestibility to beneficial persuasion.

When the patient has recovered from his symptom he will often become more anxious because now he has to face his problems more directly. It is now necessary to discuss with the patient his reactions to life's difficulties. The hysteric tends to give in readily and retreat into illness in the face of difficulties, and the patient must be guided in dealing with the problems which precipitated his illness in a more satisfactory manner.

Hysterics tend to attempt things beyond their capabilities in order to impress people. They must be encouraged to accept their limitations and work within the limits of their abilities, and at the same time, to learn to gain satisfaction from whatever assets they possess.

FURTHER READING

Hysteria by D. W. Abse. J. Wright, Bristol (1966).

CHAPTER TWENTY-FOUR

OBSESSIONAL STATES

Obsessions can occur as symptoms in many psychiatric disorders or they may constitute the entire illness which are then referred to as Obsessional States.

DEFINITION

An obsession is a content of consciousness which, when it appears is accompanied by a subjective feeling of compulsion which the patient tries to resist but cannot get rid of, even though he may realise on reflection that it is irrational. The important features diagnostically are a feeling of subjective compulsion and the tendency to resist. The realisation that it is irrational is less helpful in diagnostis, as this may apply to a number of similar phenomena which are not truly obsessional.

CLINICAL FEATURES

The essential characteristic of an obsession is the fruitless struggle against a disturbance which is apparently isolated from the rest of mental activity and which the patient realises involves an act of will which he cannot help making and, although he tries to suppress or abolish the symptom, the effort is always in vain. The patient always realises that although it is an isolated disturbance, it is a part of himself.

Obsessional symptoms are distressing and repetitive. The following are examples of common obsessional symptoms: thoughts, doubts, compulsive actions, certain phobias, ruminations.

The majority of patients experience their first obsessional symptoms before the age of 25. The illness may come on in attacks or episodes. With regard to the age of onset, roughly half start their illness between 16 and 30 years and only 7·3 per cent after the age of 45 years. Sometimes environmental difficulties may precipitate or exacerbate obsessional states. The illness sometimes, however, shows spontaneous recovery; when it does take place, either spontaneously or associated with treatment, it is most common in the early years of the illness and much less likely after many years have passed since the onset of the illness.

Obsessions as Parts of Other Illnesses

Obsessional symptoms may occur in any psychiatric illnesses, e.g.:
(1) *Schizophrenia.* It is probable that the occurrence of obsessional

illness in schizophrenia represents the occurrence of two disorders rather than a single illness. There is some evidence that persistent obsessional symptoms may inhibit the development of schizophrenia. Sometimes obsessional symptoms may merge into those of schizophrenia. Ominous signs are the development of a loss of anxiety and concern about the illness and a decrease in tendency to resist.

(2) *Depressive States.* Sometimes obsessional symptoms in some patients occur in a setting of a depressive illness, sometimes in a depressive phase of a manic-depressive psychosis. The obsessional symptoms tend to improve with improvement in the depressive state.

(3) *Organic Brain Diseases.* The occurrence of obsessional symptoms in organic brain disorders has aroused a great deal of interest and speculation. In encephalitis lethargica, sometimes patients develop obsessional symptoms having previously been free from the disorder.

Sometimes obsessional symptoms occur only when the patient develops oculogyric crises. It is interesting that some metallic poisons, particularly those which produce extrapyramidal symptoms, may also produce obsessional symptoms—for instance, manganese poisons.

Differential Diagnosis

Obsessions need to be distinguished from the following, which may in some respects resemble superficially obsessions:

(1) Habit patterns in children which are not accompanied by a tendency to resist.

(2) Rituals which are intended to ward off fear. These may be secondary to some obsessions but, here again, the tendency to resist is not present.

(3) Over-valued ideas. Here, certain ideas dominate the patient's attention. Frequently the term obsessional is used when preoccupation is meant—for example, 'he is obsessed with motor cars'.

(4) Schizophrenic thought disorder particularly autochthonous ideas thought interpolation may superficially suggest obsessional symptoms but they lack a subjective feeling of compulsion and the tendency to resist. Similarly, stereotyped actions may suggest obsessive compulsions but have no tendency to resist.

Clinical Features of Obsessional States

Obsessional symptoms may vary in severity from mild and transient to totally incapacitating.

It is possible to describe primary obsessions and secondary obsessions, the latter arising from the former, e.g. an obsession of contamination may result in a compulsion to engage in repetitive hand-washing.

Obsessional thoughts consist of repetitive words or phases, sometimes of an obscene kind or of a religious or aggressive nature.

Obsessional ruminations are often about insoluble problems, e.g.

'why are we living', 'what is the purpose of life', 'is there a God', these questions being continually repeated to the great distress of the patient.

Obsessional doubts are exemplified by such actions as turning off the gas tap, posting a letter, switching off the electric light or when there is a choice of two alternatives as when walking along a country road and coming to a fork in the road, although it may be unimportant to take the right or the left fork, the obsessional patient may spend a great deal of time deciding first on this one and then on the other and vacillating from one decision to the other.

Obsessional phobias have the characteristics of obsessional symptoms, viz. a compulsion with a tendency to resist and inability to get rid of them. Fears of knives, fears of harming people, fears of objects and situations etc., when fulfilling these criteria, are obsessional phobias.

It must be noted that many phobias are not obsessional; they arise by a process of learning whereby a fear becomes attached to a thing, situation or person.

Motor acts of an obsessional kind are usually referred to as compulsions and are extremely varied. One of my soldier patients during the war had a compulsion to part his hair exactly in the middle. In the morning he spent half an hour in an attempt to get it right, first parting it to the left of the middle line and then to the right of the middle line until eventually it was more or less correct but never completely to his satisfaction. He had a compulsion to do things four times; on going to bed he would have to undress and dress four times and similarly on getting up. He had a compulsion to touch things four times. All this made his life very complicated and difficult; he was able to save himself a little time by touching things with his four fingers. He also always had to start doing things on the right, the right hand or the right foot, but the customary procedure in the Army is 'with the left quick march' and this used to put him off for the rest of the day.

Patients with obsessional states have varying degrees of anxiety, tension and distress and may have secondary depression.

Relationship to Obsessional Personality

The obsessional personality is described as being meticulous, conscientious, orderly and punctilious. They are clean, punctual, paying a great deal of attention to detail and being trustworthy, reliable and tending to take their work home in their minds at night.

They are precise, careful, cautious, pedantic and conservative. They dislike change and get very disturbed if their plans have to be altered. They become creatures of habit, rigid, unadaptable people. As employees they are appreciated, the salt of the earth, dependable and will work at their best without supervision. They set themselves very high standards and tend to be anxious.

Obsessional personalities are common in the community and are not necessarily related to obsessional illness. Some of them can develop obsessional states but there are many patients with obsessional states who do not have this type of personality before the illness.

Obsessional personalities are of importance in predisposition to the development of anxiety states and various psychosomatic disorders.

Psychopathology

A great deal of speculation exists on the origin of obsessional symptoms. The psychoanalytic school regard it as being related to fixation at the anal level and related to control of eliminative functions. The underlying mechanism of the obsessional state is conflict with repression, displacement and symbolisation (V Chap. 12).

Treatment

(1) *General Management.* It is important to give general support and help to the obsessional patient. Certain principles of management apply:

Treatment of Obsessional States

It is important for the patient not to try to fight his obsessional symptoms, that he should try to accept them as thoughts or impulses and let them come and pass off rather than to try to suppress or combat them.

The patient should be discouraged from testing himself to see whether he can overcome his obsessions by using willpower. In general, it is better if the patient remains in his normal occupation and carries out normal activities.

Medical Treatment

If anxiety and tension is marked the use of tranquilo-sedative drugs such as Librium or Valium can be quite helpful in making the patient's life more comfortable and making it easier for him to get to understand and live with his obsessional symptoms.

A proportion of patients with obsessional states will recover, with a simple regime of this kind.

If the obsessional state occurs as a part of a depressive illness the treatment is of the depressive illness itself.

Psychotherapy is of more value, in the understanding the psycho-pathology and genesis of the symptoms than in achieving therapeutic results. Obsessional states are notoriously resistant to psychotherapy because of the rigidity of the patient's personality and defences.

Hallucinogenic drugs have been utilised to facilitate psychotherapy. Lysergic acid has been used to make the patient more amenable to psychotherapeutic help. Similarly, phencyclidine (Sernyl) has also been used with similar success.

There will be a proportion of patients who will not respond to any of these measures and who continue to suffer from a very distressing and disabling obsessional state, and for some of these patients an operation of prefrontal leucotomy may be indicated and prove of great benefit.

The requirements for the operation are that there should be evidence of considerable anxiety, tension or emotional distress, that the previous personality should be reasonably stable and satisfactory from the point of view of general adjustment and not contain evidence of psychopathy or marked instability or antisocial behaviour, and that the social circumstances are adequate to help the patient in the important period of rehabilitation after the operation.

CHAPTER TWENTY-FIVE

PSYCHOPATHIC DISORDERS

The term psychopathic personality is emotionally charged and has been overworked, abused and ill-used. It is sometimes employed as a term of abuse for one's political or religious opponents and the term tends to engender hostile attitudes on the part of society.

Although many definitions have been given, the consensus of opinion is that the psychopath's behaviour shows a lack of social responsibility, consideration for others and of prudence and foresight.'

The psychopath's persistent antisocial mode of conduct ranges from inefficiency, lack of interest in any form of occupation to pathological lying, swindling, slandering, alcoholism, drug addiction, sexual offences and violent actions with little motivation and an entire absence of self-restraint.

If the term is to have any real value, it should be applied to antisocial or criminal behaviour, only after the strict exclusion of intellectual defect, psychosis, neurosis, cerebral injury or disease.

The characteristics of psychopathy are immaturity, self-centredness, little or no regard for the rights or convenience of others; the immediate satisfaction of desires is imperative, acting violently if frustrated, associated with lack of conscience or sense of guilt.

The Mental Health Act (1959) describes psychopathic disorder as persistent disorder of personality, whether or not accompanied by subnormality of intelligence, which results in abnormally aggressive or seriously irresponsible conduct on the part of the patient and requires, or is susceptible to, medical treatment.

A convenient definition is that a psychopath is a person who, from an early age, shows abnormality of character marked by episodes of antisocial behaviour and tendencies to act on impulse to satisfy the need of the moment, without giving due regard to the consequences of such action.

The various definitions applied to psychopathic personality have four common features:

(1) *Excluding cause*, viz. the condtion does not amount to mental defect, he is not insane or psychoneurotic; whether or not the person is of low intelligence it is independent of subnormality and mental illness.

(2) *Time factor*. The abnormality exists throughout life or from a comparatively early age and is usually recurrent, episodic or persistent.

(3) *Description of behaviour*, viz. antisocial, unable to accept social requirements on account of abnormal peculiarities of impulse, temperament or character; conduct is abnormally aggressive or irresponsible.

(4) *Personality characteristics* which have been described as part of psychopathy are marked egocentricity, lack of sincerity, lack of feeling and lack of guilt. In practice, one sees many psychopaths who possess these attributes quite clearly in certain circumstances.

The differentiation between aggressive and inadequate psychopaths is not satisfactory, as one form may turn into the other.

Scott classifies psychopaths as follows:

(1) *Persons trained to antisocial standards*. These are persons who are behaving as they were taught to behave and doing what is normal in their families or districts. The offender has learned this behaviour consistently and will not feel guilt about doing what he was taught to do. His family or circle will not be critical. The offence is strictly goal-motivated, intended as a means to material gain or the acquisition of prestige. The observer can easily find sympathy and find it possible to identify himself with the offender and his setting.

Treatment requirement is retraining.

(2) *Reparative behaviour*. Here the offence is part of an intelligently, laboriously and often unconsciously worked out policy, aimed at the adjustment of the individual to difficulties in his environment and to personal handicaps which that environment has produced in him, e.g. compensations for feelings of inadequacy, inferiority.

The offender is identified with his pattern of misbehaviour and is even proud of it. The offence is goal-motivated.

Treatment is retraining.

(3) *The untrained offender*. Here there are no steady standards of behaviour provided in early life. The adult is, therefore, without standards and weak in character. Conduct difficulties show themselves diffusely and from early childhood.

(4) *Rigid fixations*. Here learning has broken down and has been replaced by a fixed, maladaptive pattern of response. The crime is stereotyped, non-adaptive and non-goal-directed, which persists unaltered despite long periods in a controlled environment and is u tterly unimproved by severe punishment.

The offender dissociates himself from his behaviour but may be genuinely remorseful and anxious about it. He is bewildered about it.

The offence is stereotyped. It brings nothing but relief from immediate tension. The observer cannot feel sympathy with the offender.

Punishment is useless.

Aetiology

Studies of the degree of concordance of criminality in pairs of uniovular and biovular twins show that personality is dependent, to some extent, upon hereditary factors but that the environment may largely control the expression of the personality disposition.

Neuroses and psychopathic states are multifactorially determined.

Studies of the relationships between rates of juvenile crime and social disturbances conclude that there appears to be something particularly significant in social disturbances occurring in the fourth and fifth year of a child's life.

Constitutional attributes found in psychopaths also favour genetic factors, such as mesomorphic body build and abnormalities in the electroencephalogram which are correlated with aggressiveness.

The evidence regarding aetiology is conflicting and we are not yet in a position to make dogmatic statements as to the relative importance of inherited and environmental factors, except to say that it is the interaction of both rather than either one or the other which is important.

THE MANAGEMENT AND TREATMENT OF PSYCHOPATHY

Psychopaths notoriously lack persistence and determination and, even when they present themselves for treatment, they often want a magical cure and are prepared to do very little themselves to help. Very often they only seek treatment when they are in difficulties with the law or with their families.

Individual psychotherapy over a period of years, if the patient co-operates, may occasionally help to achieve a better adjustment.

Drug Treatment

In some aggressive psychopaths with marked aggressive outbursts, Amphetamines given with Epanutin have been found to be helpful, particularly if there is evidence of cerebral dysrhythmia.

Major tranquillisers and tranquilosedatives are of limited value in psychopathy itself, although one of the most recently introduced phenothiazines (Pericyazine) has been claimed to be helpful in the management of behaviour disturbances in psychopaths, but these claims have yet to be substantiated.

Group Therapy

Group therapy is often a preferable method of dealing with psychopaths and group therapy in a special hospital such as that at Belmont, Surrey, is particularly promising.

It is generally agreed that psychopaths admitted to psychiatric hospitals are probably better treated as a group in separate wards or units because of their tendency to act out their behaviour. It is interesting that patients with psychiatric illnesses such as depression or schizophrenia do not usually regard psychopaths as being ill. Psychopaths, in turn, very often manipulate people and situations and create a great deal of difficulties in the running of the ward or hospital.

In a proportion of psychopaths there is a tendency for greater maturity with greater normality and better adjustment to occur in middle life, but this is not invariably so.

CHAPTER TWENTY-SIX

SEXUAL DISORDERS

These disorders may be conveniently discussed as follows
(1) Disorders of Heterosexual functioning e.g. Impotence and Frigidity.
(2) Disorders in which the aim of sexual activity deviates from the normal, e.g. homosexuality; Exhibitionism, Tranvestism, etc.

HETEROSEXUAL DYSFUNCTIONS IN MEN

Sexual disability in men may take various forms such as:
(1) Absence of sexual desire for the sexual partner or absence of sexual desire in general.
(2) Inability to procure erection.
(3) Inability to sustain erection.
(4) Inability to ejaculate in spite of well sustained erection.
(5) Premature ejaculation.

The sexual act involves a chain of reflexes and anything which interferes with this chain can give rise to any of the above dysfunctions. The large majority of cases of the above forms of impotence are psychogenic. The most common cause of interference is anxiety.

One frequent situation which is associated with impotence is the honeymoon. Both partners are tired, excited, anxious and self-conscious and some ignorant and inexperienced. Not infrequently these factors combine to render a man impotent on this occasion.

On the next occasion, probably the second night of the honeymoon, he approaches the sexual situation with anxiety which, in itself, is sufficient to render him impotent or cause him to ejaculate prematurely. After this, secondary anxiety increases in snowball fashion until the man is convinced that he is abnormal or congenitally impotent.

Anxiety due to any cause, masturbation anxiety is possibly quite a common factor, but any form of anxiety or depression can produce impotence.

The following are other causes of impotence: Some men unconsciously identify their sexual partner with their mother or sister and the incest taboo asserts itself and they are impotent with their wives but may be potent with prostitutes or other women. Other men associate the sex act with aggression and violence; they have a very marked fear of violence and this may be another mechanism.

The above forms of impotence, particularly those due to general anxiety, are common.

Ejaculatory impotence, that is incapacity to ejaculate even when aroused and with erection, is much rarer. There are many reasons for this, some are very deep-seated such as fears of pregnancy, a deep-seated difficulty in giving is another cause. Another type is the professional man's impotence; the hard working professional man works all day and in the evening until the early hours of the morning and he virtually has no energy left over for love-making.

Any drugs which produce marked stimulation of the sympathetic nervous system can lead to impotence. This applies to the monoamine oxidase inhibiting drugs and amphetamines. In cases of impotence due to depression, mild doses of these drugs may, in fact, help by relieving the depression and therefore permitting libido to become enhanced, but large doses or prolonged medication will tend to have the opposite effect by stimulating sympathetic activity and thus interfering with sacral parasympathetic which subserves vasodilation.

HETEROSEXUAL DYSFUNCTIONS IN WOMEN

Disturbances in heterosexual activity in women may be classified as follows:

(1) Frigidity.
(2) Vaginismus.
(3) Dyspareunia.

Frigidity is lack of sexual feeling in women and may vary in degree from an intense feeling of revulsion to any sexual advance to varying sexual arousal without orgasm.

Frigidity may be primary or secondary.

Primary frigidity is when the woman has never experienced an orgasm and may be partial or complete.

Secondary frigidity is when a woman has experienced orgasm in the past but is unable to do so now. It may also be partial or complete.

Complete primary frigidity may be due to anatomical defects, aplasia; physiological deficiency in endocrine glands, viz. pituitary-ovarian functions or psychological, gives a total sexual anaesthesia.

Partial primary frigidity may be due to ignorance, fear or to feelings of hostility. These women have lacked sexual instruction from their parents and very often their husbands are ignorant of their needs and of sex techniques.

Secondary frigidity, physical causes may sometimes contribute by causing dyspareunia. Physiological factors are sometimes responsible during lactation.

Psychological factors include:
(1) Fears of pregnancy.

(2) Inadequate stimulation due to coitus interruptus or the husband being weakly potent or suffering from premature ejaculation.

(3) In professional women who are financially and socially emancipated, it becomes an emotional problem of dependency versus independency.

(4) Depression or anxiety symptoms may also be a contributory factor.

Vaginismus

Vaginismus is an involuntary spasm of the vaginal muscles, always psychogenic in origin. It is usually an automatic fear or anxiety reaction, sometimes coming on after painful experiences during intercourse.

In some women, it is a difficulty in accepting the full female role and is a manifestation of psychosexual immaturity.

HOMOSEXUALITY

Definition

The term homosexual is applied to sexual relationships whether overt or psychic between individuals of the same sex. It is derived from the Greek 'homo' meaning the same, rather than the Latin for man. It denotes the sameness of the two individuals involved in the sexual relationship and is the antithesis of the word heterosexual.

It has been shown that there is a continuous gradation among members of the general population between exclusively heterosexual and exclusively homosexual behaviour.

Kinsey (1948) proposed a very useful heterosexual-homosexual rating scale:

(0) Exclusively heterosexual with no homosexual tendencies.

(1) Predominantly heterosexual and only incidentally homosexual.

(2) Predominantly heterosexual but with more than incidental homosexuality.

(3) Equally heterosexual and homosexual.

(4) Predominantly homosexual but more than incidentally heterosexual.

(5) Predominantly homosexual but incidentally heterosexual.

(6) Exclusively homosexual.

It is difficult to estimate the prevalence of homosexuality for obvious reasons. Kinsey considered that 4 per cent of American men were exclusively homosexual.

It must be remembered that homosexuality can occur in apparently normal, stable persons free from psychiatric symptoms and who are otherwise socially well-adjusted. It can also occur in unstable personalities, persons with neurosis, psychopathy, mental subnormality, psychosis and organic mental states.

S.T.P.—8

Aetiology

Different authorities emphasise the importance of one or more of the following.

(1) Genetic factors.

(2) Constitutional predisposition.

(3) Conditioning factors.

(4) Psychodynamic mechanisms.

(5) The influence of psysiological and hormonal factors.

Twin studies provide some evidence that homosexuality may be genetically determined, but only in a proportion of patients. Studies of endocrine factors have been, on the whole, inconclusive.

With regard to personality, it must be remembered that masculinity and femininity is not an 'all or nothing' affair, because persons of each sex may show varying proportions of both. One may get extremely masculine females and extremely feminine males.

Surveys of homosexuals who have come to psychiatric care or who have come to the notice of Courts of Law tend to have a higher incidence of neurotic or schizoid types of personality but, on the whole, only showed minor differences from normals.

The following classes of homosexuals may be described:

(1) Adolescents and emotionally immature adults, who go through a phase in which they are uncomfortably aware of their attraction to both sexes and are in a quandry which they cannot solve. They usually respond well to supportive psychiatric treatment.

(2) Markedly abnormal personalities: (a) with marked effeminacy and often solicit and not infrequently become homosexual prostitutes, preferring the chase than the actual sexual contact.

(3) The inadequate, dull person who has never experienced loving relationships with anyone, and they are usually very socially isolated.

(4) The resentful, antisocial person who often has a long record of Court appearances.

(5) Homosexuality in relatively normal, intact personalities.

(6) Latent, well-compensated homosexuals. These may be intelligent, married and have children.

(7) Homosexuality occurring along with serious mental disability such as psychopathy, psychosis or organic brain damage. These patients are apt to injure victims in a way that none of the others would contemplate, nor do they take only predisposed victims.

Some authorities believe that parental influences may play an important role in the causation of homosexuality. Some implicate a maternal attitude of excessive strictness and perfectionism; others implicate father-deprivation at a time when awareness of homosexual attraction is not abnormal as a phase of development.

Treatment may be by psychotherapy or by aversion therapy.

Psychotherapy can help some homosexuals who are burdened by guilt, neurotic difficulties or intolerable sexual tension, and also those persons who request help in order to fortify them in restraining overt behaviour likely to involve them in trouble with the law.

It is the view of most practising psychiatrists that no cure can be offered to complete homosexuals with a Kinsey rating of 6. A great deal can be done to make the homosexual a more happy, well-adjusted and effective person.

Aversion therapy may be applied, either using apomorphine injections to produce vomiting or an electrical current to produce a painful stimulus. Whenever nausea, vomiting or pain are felt the patients are confronted with photographs of nude or near nude men whom they find attractive. This is repeated until a marked aversion develops. Sometimes substitution of photographs of sexually attractive women are presented, accompanied by injections of testosterone propionate.

It is difficult to evaluate the role of aversion therapy. It is important to realise that in many patients the goal of treatment has to be realistic and must be limited. Many patients cannot and have no wish to change their homosexuality. If they can be helped to be relieved of psychiatric symptoms and to adjust reasonably well in work and society a worthwhile result is achieved.

Exposure and Exhibitionism

Exhibitionism is one of the commonest sexual deviations.

There are two main groups:

(1) The simple or aggressive, where the deviant behaviour follows upon some rather obvious social or sexual trauma or as an accompaniment to a mental or physical illness.

(2) The phobic-impulsive group, with much more intense personality disturbance, often of immoral cast of mind and prone to other forms of character disorder and perversion, as well as to stealing. This group comprises phobic disorders, hysterical and obsessional reactions. The preconditioned liability for the exhibitionist to act existed in childhood where desires and exhibitionism were normal and later underwent repression. The age of onset of exposure is usually at puberty but very variable. Conditioning and habitual patterns become established. Stilboestrol might banish sexual fantasy but this would return immediately on discontinuing the drug.

Transvestism and Transsexualism

Transvestism is the impulse to wear the clothing of the opposite sex. Transexualism is the term given to describe the wish to change the anatomical sex.

Transvestites proper were defined as those men who obtained sexual gratification from dressing as women. In transvestism the clothes or the wearing of them may provide an end in itself, as they are usually endowed with sexual significance and the act of wearing them may provide the sole form of sexual expression. Many transvestites lack sexual drives and state that they feel mainly more contented and more comfortable while wearing female attire. The onset of transvestism and transexualism is usually before 12 years of age. It occurs in all social classes and in men and women.

Aversion therapy has proved effective in treating transvestism and may need to be supplemented by vocational, social and psychotherapeutic guidance to help readjustment.

Transexualism is more difficult to treat and the result of surgical treatment attempting to make the person appear more like the opposite sex has, on the whole, been disappointing. Its legality is doubtful in this country.

FURTHER READING

Textbook of Psychosexual Disorder by A. C. Allen (1962).
Sex in Society by A. Comfort. Duckworth, London (1963).
Sexual Behaviour in the Human Male by A. C. Kinsey, W. B. Pomeroy, C. Martin. Sanderson, Philadelphia (1948).

CHAPTER TWENTY-SEVEN

ALCOHOLISM AND DRUG ADDICTION

ALCOHOLISM

Alcoholism is a disease in an individual who has, over a long period of time, consumed large amounts of alcohol.

The disease is characterised by:

(1) A pathological desire for alcohol after ingestion of small quantities which act as a trigger dose.

(2) Black-outs during intoxication with alcohol.

(3) Physical dependence on alcohol after withdrawal following a drinking bout.

These are the cardinal symptoms of alcoholism. Heavy consumers who do not present these cardinal symptoms, or only exhibit one of them, are simply called alcohol abusers and this group cannot be clearly demarcated from the average normal consumer.

The prevalence of alcoholism is difficult to assess reliably for a variety of reasons.

Jellinek devised a formula which provides an estimate of the incidence of alcoholism with physical complications. According to this formula, there are 350,000 alcoholics in England and Wales, including 86,000 chronic alcoholics with mental and physical complications.

It has been estimated that 35,000 alcoholics were known as such to the general practitioners, although many did not seek treatment from their own doctor.

It should be noted that the term alcoholic is reserved for the individual in whom alcohol has induced mental and physical changes.

AETIOLOGY

Social Factors

Social pressures, economic trends and cultural attitudes all exert some influence on the pattern of drinking and, indirectly, the incidence of alcoholism.

Psychological Factors

There is no typical pre-alcoholic personality. What usually happens is that a proportion of all regular users of alcohol become occasional excessive drinkers during periods of stress or when depressed and, as a result of this, a smaller proportion become constant drinkers. Some of these, in turn, may eventually become alcoholics. Finally, a small group again, lose control and become addictive alcoholics.

In the pre-alcoholic phase, alcohol is taken to provide relief. This becomes more regular and tolerance is increased. The prodromal phase follows and is marked by black-outs in which the drinker, after a moderate intake of alcohol, may show no signs of intoxication and be able to carry out acts requiring skill and co-ordination, of which he subsequently has no recollection.

The prodromal phase advances with additional secret drinking, preparation for social gatherings with alcohol and periods of avid drinking followed by guilt feelings. At this point, the person avoids reference to alcohol in his talk and has more frequent black-outs.

The crucial phase is ushered in by a loss of control, in which the ingestion of even a small quantity of alcohol sets up a compulsive demand for more, which ceases only when his stomach or nervous system calls a halt.

In the subsequent chronic phase, prolonged periods of intoxication with abscence from work make their appearance and there is a deterioration in ethical attitudes.

Psychiatric Disorders Associated with Alcoholism

(1) *Delirium Tremens*

It is no longer held that delirium tremens is frequently due to sudden withdrawal of alcohol from heavy drinkers.

In the early stages, which may last some weeks, the patient is tense, anxious, jumpy and suffers from terrifying illusions and hallucinations at night. As a rule, the onset is sudden.

The features of delirium tremens are: disorientation, hallucinations of vision, equilibrium, sensation and hearing. The visual hallucinations are often quite frightening vestibular sensations of rocking and flying. Illusions are quite common, i.e. misinterpretation of cutaneous sensations, the patient believing that insects are crawling over him.

Clinical signs include ataxia, coarse tremor, jerkiness of speech and writing, active deep reflexes, sweating, rapid pulse, increased tension, albuminuria and pyrexia. Epileptic attacks occur in 10 per cent. Insomnia is highly characteristic.

The usual course is that, before the end of the first week, a crisis occurs during which the patient falls into a deep sleep to awaken clear in mind.

Fatal cases are usually those having pneumonia or when a delirium passes into a coma, the latter being due to polioencephalitis haemorrhagica superior.

Sometimes the delirium passes into a chronic Korsakow state.

(2) *Acute Alcoholic Hallucinosis*

In this condition, auditory hallucinations—the voices are often abusive, threatening—occur during relatively clear consciousness. At the onset there is increased acuity of hearing with noises in the head and poorly differentiated hallucinations such as banging, shouts, bells and screams. Many voices may be heard and identified and as a rule are not attributed to bystanders. The patient is frightened and is usually glad to seek refuge in a hospital or police station.

Sometimes delusions develop as a secondary development of the hallucinations.

Usually a full recovery in three or four weeks takes place but sometimes insight is never regained; delusions may persist and the condition can develop into a fairly typical paranoid schizophrenic illness.

Acute alcoholic hallucinosis may be a sequel to delirium tremens. A characteristic feature is the hearing of abusive voices which talk about the patient in the third person and experienced as occurring above the patient's head.

(3) *Chronic Alcoholic Delusional States*

Chronic alcoholics often become suspicious and paranoid in disposition but sometimes they may develop delusions of jealousy, which start when the patient is drunk but may continue when he is sober.

Most frequently the man accuses his wife of adultery with neighbours and he attempts to extort a confession from her. Undoubtedly his diminishing sexual potency, his sexual maladjustment, his bad conscience and his wife's inevitable aversion to him when drunk, play a part in the development of delusions of jealousy. However, delusions of jealousy may develop also in abstinent men in late middle life.

(4) *Korsakow's Syndrome*

Alcohol is only one of many causes of Korsakow's syndrome. It is most frequently seen in middle-aged alcoholics. The features are:

(1) Grossly disturbed memory.
(2) Fabrications to cover gaps in recollection.
(3) Disorientation in space and time.
(4) Clear consciousness.
(5) Poor judgment,
(6) Apathy, varying from empty euphoria to irritability.
(7) Polyneuritis is common but not invariable.

Pathologically, there are degenerative changes in the periventricular and periaqueductant grey matter and mammillary bodies on the dorsal medial nucleus of the thalamus.

The distribution of lesions is identical with Wernicke's encephalopathy and it has been suggested that both Korsakow's psychosis and

Wernicke's encephalopathy are due to thiamine deficiency, differences in symptomatology depending on the acuteness of the underlying disease process.

(5) *Wernicke's Encephalopathy*

Alcohol is one of the most common causes of this condition. Occular changes are constant; horizontal nystagmus is more common than vertical nystagmus. External rectus paralysis is an early sign. Ataxia with wide, reeling gait. There is lack of interest and lack of initiative but full consciousness in the early stages. There is difficulty in attention.

(6) *Marchiafava's Disease*

This is characterised by demyelination of the corpus callosum and optic tracts. The clinical picture is one of acute confusion with hallucinations and outbursts of excitement.

(7) *Pathological Intoxication*

Some people react severely to alcohol, even in small amounts. They may react with sudden violence which is similar to an epileptic automatism, ending in a deep sleep with complete amnesia.

E.E.G. studies show that the condition is correlated with psychomotor epilepsy. In these patients the alcohol acts as a stimulus in small doses, producing a thetor activity of 6 cycles per second in the temporal regions.

(8) *Chronic Dementia*

This may be the end result of prolonged alcoholism and may follow any of the above syndromes.

TREATMENT OF ALCOHOLISM

The first step in treatment is medical assessment of the patient's condition; whether he suffers from any known physical disorders which may complicate alcoholism, particularly cirrhosis of the liver and organic brain syndromes. The next step is psychiatric assessment, including the role played by his personality make-up; whether the patient drinks for pleasure mainly or as a defence mechanism to relieve emotional distress due to emotional problems; whether he is suffering from psychiatric disorders such as a depressive state or anxiety state or the syndromes specifically associated with alcoholism. It is then necessary to assess the patient's social relationships at work, with his family and friends. The patient's adjustment in these spheres will have an important bearing in his rehabilitation after treatment.

Acute alcoholic intoxication needs hospital treatment and skilled nursing.

Alcohol can be withdrawn abruptly. Adequate fluids and vitamin administration are important. Phenothiazines such as Prochloperazine and Promazine may be given to minimise the withdrawal effects and to cover up nausea and vomiting.

Long term treatment may involve specific therapeutic measures, such as aversion therapy with Apomorphine or treatment with Disulphuram.

Supportive psychotherapy is important and social therapy, particularly the help of Alcoholics Anonymous can make all the difference between success and failure in long term treatment.

Aversion Therapy

Apomorphine is the most commonly used agent for aversion treatment of alcoholism. It is a powerful emetic and each injection induces nausea and vomiting. The patient is allowed to drink his favourite drink and the injection is then given. This is repeated over a period of time until a marked aversion to alcohol develops. Sometimes the aversion gradually diminishes and a booster course may be necessary at intervals of 6 months or a year, depending on the patient.

Antabuse Treatment

Antabuse (Disulphuram) interferes with the metabolism of alcohol causing an increase in the level of blood acetaldehyde. This causes unpleasant reactions which make it difficult to continue drinking. The patient on Antabuse, on taking a small quantity of alcohol, has distressing symptoms including flushing, sweating, dyspnoea, headache, tachycardia, drowsiness, falling blood pressure, nausea and vomiting. If the fall in blood pressure is rapid, the patient may develop a peripheral circulatory collapse.

Antabuse is given 1·5 Gm. the first day, 1 Gm. the second day and 0·5 Gm. the third day. A test of the reaction of alcohol is carried out on the fourth day in order to demonstrate to the patient what will happen to him if he attempts to drink. The test dose of alcohol is the equivalent of 15 c.c. of alcohol as given in whisky, wine, beer or other drink to which the patient is addicted. After this, a maintenance dosage, usually 0·25 Gm. to 0·5 Gm. daily is given.

Antabuse is of value in the management of the alcoholic who generally wishes to overcome his addiction and who requires an additional prop to help him to overcome any craving that might develop particularly when confronted with difficult situations, disappointments or the temptation to be involved in various social events. If there is a relative who can supervise the administration of Antabuse, this greatly enhances the effectiveness of the treatment.

It is essential that the alcoholic must abstain from the use of alcohol absolutely and permanently and, as it usually takes a number of years for marked dependency on alcohol to develop, it may take some years before he is completely free from this dependency. The physician must bear this in mind and help the patient in shifting his dependency through better interpersonal relationships, new interests and satisfying achievements as a substitute for alcoholic indulgence.

If the patient joins Alcoholics Anonymous, this is extremely valuable in helping him to withstand the temptation to revert to alcohol.

DRUG ADDICTION

Drug addiction may be defined as a state of periodic or persistent intoxication, detrimental to the individual, to society or both and characterised by the following features:

(1) A strong drive, need or compulsion to continue taking the drug.

(2) The development of tolerance, with a tendency to increase the dose to produce desired effects.

(3) Physical and emotional dependence.

Physical dependence results from an altered physiological state, which necessitates continued administration of the drug in order to prevent the appearance of a characteristic series of symptoms referred to as the abstinence syndrome or withdrawal state.

The term drug habituation has been applied to the person who has a strong drive or need or compulsion to continue taking the drug on which he is emotionally dependent, but he does not develop the withdrawal state characteristic of addiction.

The World Health Organisation has suggested that the term drug dependence should be applied to both drug addiction, drug habituation and all types of drug abuse.

Drug dependence is defined as a state arising from repeated administration of a drug on a periodic or continuous basis. Its characteristics will vary with the agent involved.

Individuals may become dependent on a wide variety of chemical substances, with a diversity of pharmacodynamic effects ranging from stimulation to depression. All such drugs have at least one effect in common, in that they are capable of creating a state of mind in certain individuals which is termed psychic dependence. This is a psychic drive which requires periodic or chronic administration of the drug either for pleasure or to avoid discomfort.

True drug addiction is associated with physical dependence, which is an adaptive state characterised by intense physical disturbance when the administration of the drug is stopped or its action is counteracted by a specific antagonist.

Many of the drugs causing physical dependence also induce tolerance, which is an adaptive state characterised by diminished response to the same quantity of drug or requiring a larger dose to produce the same pharmacodynamic effect.

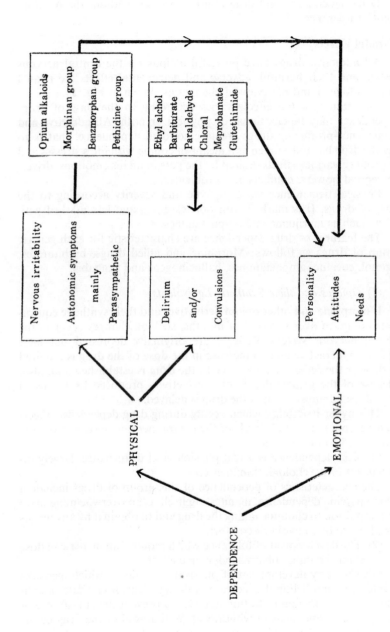

Fig. 13. Drug dependence.

Drug dependence and drug abuse can occur without the development of tolerance.

Harmful Effects

All addictive drugs have powerful actions on the central nervous system and their harmful, adverse and detrimental effects are related to neurological and behavioural changes as shown in Fig. 14.

The nature of the effects varies according to the class of drug; dependence may be emotional or physical or both. All addictive and dependence-producing drugs create emotional dependence, that is to say the drug has to be taken as a means of coping with life's stresses and to produce various effects desired by the person on his emotions, drives, perceptual powers, conflicts and problems.

Physical dependence varies in type and severity according to the class of drugs. It is marked with opiates drugs and less marked with drugs such as marijuana and amphetamines.

The features of drug dependence are characteristic for each generic group of drugs as follows: Morphine and allied drugs, barbiturates, alcohol, cocaine, amphetamines, hallucinogens and cannabis.

(1) *Opiates and their Synthetic Equivalents*

If morphine and other opium derivatives and their synthetic equivalents are given over a period of months, striking changes occur in the central nervous system. Reflexes are originally depressed but later become hyperactive and an increase in the dose of the drug is required to depress the reflexes as tolerance to the drug is established and, also, because of the greater degree of over-activity produced by the usual dose if the administration of the drug is delayed.

This hyper-irritability which occurs during drug dependence affects multineuronal arcs at all levels of the central nervous system, from the spinal cord to the cerebral cortex.

Physical dependence is a real physiological disturbance, largely independent of psychological influence.

The characteristics of dependence of this group of drugs include a strong psychic dependence, manifesting itself as an overwhelming drive or compulsion to continue taking the drug and to obtain it by any means for pleasure or to avoid discomfort.

(2) The development of tolerance which requires an increase in dose to maintain the initial pharmacodynamic effect.

(3) The early development of physical dependence which increases in intensity, paralleling the increase in dosage. This necessitates a continuation of drug administration in order to prevent the appearance of the symptoms and signs of withdrawal. Withdrawal of the drug or the administration of a specific antagonist precipitates a definite characteristic and self-limiting abstinence syndrome.

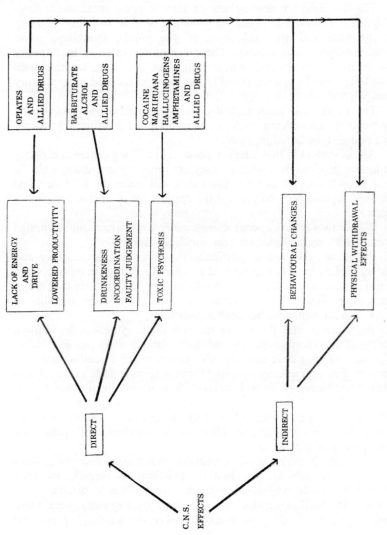

Fig. 14. Harmful effects of addictive drugs.

The abstinence syndrome with morphine appears within a few hours of the last dose, reaching its peak in 24 to 48 hours and subsides spontaneously most often within 10 days.

The first signs are development of anxiety, restlessness and feelings of tension, followed by frequent yawning, profuse sweating, running of the nose and eyes, dilatation of the pupils, trembling, goose flesh, diarrhoea and cramps. These symptoms increase in intensity for the first 24 hours and twitching of muscles occurs, together with vomiting, loss of appetite, inability to sleep and increase in respiratory rate.

The effects are predominantly parasympathetic but sympathetic over-activity also occurs, such as rise in body temperature, respiratory rate and systolic blood pressure.

All substances in this category possess, in varying degree, a capacity to induce physical dependence. They are mutually interchangeable, in that substitution of one for the other will maintain tolerance and physical dependence and prevent the appearance of abstinence phenomena.

Withdrawal effects appear more rapidly with heroin and, although present with methadone, are very much less severe.

Pethidine addiction is particularly associated with doctors and nurses. Tolerance is not as marked as with other drugs in this class and is not as complete. Large doses of pethidine produce muscle twitchings, tremors, confusion, hallucinations and even convulsions. Inability to work is greater than with morphia addiction.

Barbiturates and drugs like meprobamate, glutethimide, chloral, paraldehyde, chlordiazepoxide and other tranquilosedatives give rise to a pattern of subjective and objective effects which resemble that with alcohol. For example, symptoms of intoxication include ataxia, dysarthria, impairment of mental function, loss of emotional control, confusion, poor judgment and, occasionally, a toxic psychosis. Withdrawal of the drug is characterised by an abstinence syndrome, which is entirely different from that following the withdrawal of opiates and the opiate group of drugs.

The signs occurring most consistently in the usual order of appearance include anxiety, involuntary twitching of muscle, intention tremor of hands and fingers, progressive weakness, dizziness, distortions in visual perception, nausea, vomiting, insomnia, weight loss and a precipitous drop in blood pressure on standing or even on sitting.

Other effects which may be hazardous to life may occur including hyperpyrexia, grand mal convulsions and/or delirium resembling alcoholic delirium tremens.

Abrupt withdrawal is hazardous because of the serious effects and the difficulty in controlling them.

Amphetamines

Chronic intoxication with amphetamines shows the following features: Anorexia, nervousness, insomnia, tremor, irritability, loss of weight and, in sufficiently high doses, a schizophrenic-like psychosis with hallucinations.

Abrupt suspension of administration produces marked somnolence, apathy and inertia.

If the dose is not sufficient to cause anorexia, nervousness and insomnia, the abstinence syndrome may be minimal or absent and a return to normal behaviour occurs.

Cocaine

Cocaine is a powerful cortical stimulant producing euphoria and excitement, with feelings of increased muscular and mental strength. Its pleasurable effect is of short duration and the addict has to take doses at frequent intervals in order to produce sustained effect.

Following the feeling of euphoria, there usually occur marked feelings of anxiety and fear, sometimes with hallucinations and paranoid delusions. To counteract this associated fear and anxiety, cocaine is frequently taken in combination with the opiate drugs, particularly heroin.

The unpleasant effects produced by cocaine are more marked when it is taken intravenously and include mainly sympathomimetic effects such as nervousness, hyper-reactive reflexes, sweating, hoarsness, increase in pulse rate and blood pressure and, with high doses, a psychosis.

Paranoid delusions may constitute a real danger, as the intoxicated person might mistake the identity of individuals, even of friends around him, and interpret their behaviour to mean that they were going to harm him.

Tolerance develops but physical dependence is not marked. Psychic dependence is sufficient in some patients to rate cocaine only second in order of preference to heroin.

Cannabis Sativa (Marihuana)

Marihuana is an intoxicant and its characteristic effects occur within a few minutes when it is smoked but, after ingestion by mouth, half an hour to an hour may elapse before the appearance of symptoms. The effect of an oral dose may last from five to twelve hours.

The effects are a feeling of power with distortions of time, space, kinaesthetic and body image perceptions which are usually regarded as pleasurable. Mild inebriation takes place immediately following smoking, a voracious appetite for food occurs which is just the reverse of the effects induced by opiate drugs.

Marihuana diminishes inhibitions, increases suggestibility and increases auditory sensitivity.

The drug is misleading and particularly dangerous because it does not appear on the surface to be addictive, as its withdrawal produces no clear abstinence syndrome in the majority of people.

Psychic dependence can be marked and addicts, when deprived of the drug, have a strong desire to consume it whenever it is available but those who are mildly addicted can take it or reject it at will; but in many parts of the world it is often the first step to heroin addiction, particularly among teenagers and young people, who first of all become habituated to marihuana and then pass to heroin or cocaine mixed with heroin.

The Prevalence of Drug Dependence and Drug Addiction

It is notoriously difficult to obtain accurate figures of the prevalence of drug addiction and there are many obvious reasons for this. A further complicating factor is the relationship between the prevalence of drug usage and the actual incidence of drug addiction and drug dependence.

The number of known addicts to narcotics in Great Britain has increased from 199 in 1947 to 554 in 1960.

The pattern of addiction is changing; for example, the number of known heroin addicts has increased from 68 in 1959 to 237 in 1963 and, for the first time, there are now more addicts to heroin than any other narcotic drug. Twenty-eight new cases of heroin addiction are known to have occurred during the first quarter of 1964.

Whereas in the past about a third of the known heroin addicts started their addiction in the course of medical treatment, about 94 per cent of the present known addicts started their addiction in other ways.

The age distribution has also changed, with an increasing number below the age of 20 years and the great majority of new addicts belonging to this younger age group.

The number of cocaine addicts has also increased, from 30 in 1959 to 171 in 1963 of whom 168 also take heroin.

It has been estimated that the number of patients dependent on barbiturates to an unacceptable extent was at least 23,000 in 1959 and those dependent on amphetamine may have been four times as numerous.

The total number of amphetamine addicts is probably greater than realised and there appears to be a high prevalence of amphetamine usage by teenagers and young adults, including the notorious 'purple hearts'.

Marihuana smoking appears also to have become more prevalent in recent years among teenagers and young adults.

Factors Concerned in Addiction

There are three main factors operating in the occurrence of addiction:
(1) The pharmacological and physiological properties of the drug.

(2) The personality, degree of stability and attitudes of the individual.

(3) Environmental, social and cultural influences.

Pharmacological and Physiological Factors

Addictive drugs are usually those which produce some noticeable subjective effect within a short time of their administration. The effects are desired by the individual either to escape from problems or to be relieved of anxiety or to gain pleasurable or new experiences.

With regard to the drugs which produce physical dependence, it has been shown that there are minimum requirements regarding daily dosage, interval of administration and total duration for the establishment of physical dependence. For example, with barbiturates the daily intake needs to be 0·5 g. at six to eight hourly intervals for four to six months.

Personality

Addicts show the whole range of personality characteristics from the normal to the neurotic, psychotic, psychopathic and sexually deviant.

Although many addicts show marked personality disorders with emotional instability, immaturity and impulsiveness and, although these undoubtedly increase vulnerability to addiction, these traits are also quite common in non-addicts. It is also clear that a number of addicts were previously normal, stable, well-adjusted persons.

It is also important to bear in mind the harmful effects of drug dependence and addiction on the person's behaviour and interpersonal relationships. The behaviour changes, the falling off of reliability and efficiency, the need for deception and the measures needed to obtain drugs to counteract abstinence syndromes can all exert adverse effects on the person's disposition and personality, but these are not necessarily permanent, as follow-up studies of addicts have shown.

The drug addict is a person with certain personality characteristics, who happens to have selected this way of coping with his problems for a variety of reasons of which he is usually unaware. *Not the least of these reasons is his access to a social group in which drug use is both practised and valued.*

Social-cultural Aspects

Addicts can come from all social classes and from all races and countries but there tends to be a difference in prevalence which is related to cost, availability, degree of social acceptability, religion, economics, class consciousness, ethics, group mores and many other factors which influence the acceptance of certain drugs.

Moslems, in general, reject alcohol but accept the consumption of hashish, although both are officially banned by the Moslem religion.

Oriental opium-producing countries show a much higher rate of addiction than do others, such as Scandinavia. Many observers have noted that Orientals keep their opium habits under much closer control than do non-Orientals. In the United States three of the States, New York, California and Illinois account for approximately 77 per cent of the known addicts, most coming from the large cities. Of these, 25 per cent of known addicts are native-born whites. Negroes, Puerto Ricans, Cubans and Mexicans make up the rest.

In the post war period, in New York in particular, there has been a marked increase in the use of narcotics by teenagers and young adults and one of the few intensive epidemiological studies on narcotic addiction has been carried out by *Chein* (1956) in New York. His group consisted of boys aged 16 to 21 years who, during a four-year period, had come to the attention of some official agency connected with narcotics. It was found that the districts in which teenage drug usage flourished were usually the most overcrowded, underprivileged areas, with the lowest income, lowest level of education and highest incidence of breakdown of family life. Round about the age of 16 was found to be a particularly susceptible time and it was thought that at this age there was no major institution playing a controlling role or strongly involved with their lives. The control group who had had opportunities but had not become drug addicts differed from the addicted group, in that there was a greater availability of information on the dangers and effects of drug usage and also that the attitudes of significant adults were such as to disapprove and lessen the tendency to drug addiction.

It may also be said that the use of drugs creates a fraternal spirit which may lead to social organisation which, in turn, is reinforced by the rejection of the addict by society. Further strengthening occurs by economic and psychological factors. The prohibitions placed on the use of drugs may, to some extent, make the consumption more attractive to youngsters.

Preventive Aspects

Measures which could help in the prevention of drug addiction are the following:

(a) *Research* is urgently needed into the personality attributes and environmental factors conducive to addiction.

(b) *Legal measures* such as making the unauthorised possession of drugs illegal would help to control traffic in drugs.

(c) *Medical measures* would include care in prescribing; when drugs such as morphia have to be prescribed the addition of amiphenazole or tetrahydroaminacin are reported to eliminate the addiction hazard.

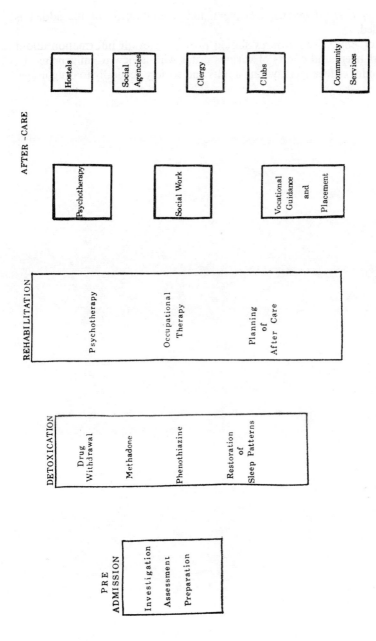

FIG. 15. Stages in treatments of drug addiction.

(d) *Early diagnosis*, treatment and rehabilitation of the addict is needed.

(e) *Educative measures* should provide relevant information about the dangers and effects of various drugs with a view to influencing the attitudes of teenagers, young adults and society generally to drug usage.

CHAPTER TWENTY-EIGHT

MENTAL RETARDATION

Mental retardation (synonyms—Mental deficiency, subnormality, amentia) is a state of arrested development of the mind existing from birth or from an early age.

Mental retardation varies in severity and can result from a variety of causes.

It has been estimated that about 5 per cent of all babies born are retarded to some degree. Some of these suffer from physical malformations and have a high mortality rate. It has been estimated that, in the school age period, between 1 and 4 per cent of all children are retarded.

It is useful to grade mental retardation according to severity:

(1) *Slightly retarded* patients with I.Q.s between 50 and 70. These, under the Mental Health Act, would be referred to as Subnormal, and previously as high grade defectives or Feebleminded.

(2) *Moderately retarded* with I.Q.s in the 30 to 50 range. These would now be regarded, together with (3) below, as severely subnormal and previously as medium grade imbeciles.

(3) *Severely retarded* with an intelligence quotient below 30, also regarded as severely subnormal and previously as low grade defectives or Idiots.

1. Slightly Retarded Patients (Synonyms—Subnormal, High Grade Defectives, Feebleminded, Moron)

This group comprises by far the largest proportion of mentally retarded patients. The intelligence quotient range is between 50 and 70 and the upper level merges into the lower range of the normal frequency distribution of intelligence.

The intelligence quotient is not the best guide to mental subnormality because psychological, educational and social factors operate in a fairly direct manner in producing the important problems associated with slight retardation.

This group is mostly derived from the lower end of the normal frequency distribution curve of intelligence and is multifactorially determined, as is normal intelligence.

Whilst saying this, it is also important to remember that all diseases and factors which cause gross mental deficiency may operate in attenuated form to produce mild degrees of mental defect.

Clinical Features

As children, mentally retarded persons tend to be slower, to lack in alertness, curiosity and spontaneity compared with the normal child. They are inert and passive, easily fooled, credulous and easily led into delinquent, criminal or other forms of undesirable behaviour. They are easy dupes for the schemes of others.

Thinking tends to be concrete, as the ability to handle concepts and abstract nodes of thinking is limited.

Patients at the upper intelligence ranges of subnormality may show no obvious signs of mental retardation but are usually late in passing the milestones of development. If they attend an ordinary school, they fail to make progress and often need to be transferred to special classes or to special schools.

In the case of well-to-do families, mentally subnormal children are often looked after in private schools.

After leaving school, they may settle down to a job of a simple, routine nature, providing it is within the limits of their mental capacity and providing they are relatively stable.

It must be emphasised that level of intelligence, *per se*, is not the most important criterion in mental subnormality. Intelligence quotient gives a guide as to the upper limits that the person can achieve, but it does not provide an index of the person's capacity to adjust to society.

In the high grade mental defective, aspects other than intelligence need to be assessed, such as emotional stability, impulsiveness and social behaviour, which are far more important deciding factors as to whether action for care, supervision and control is needed.

At school, subnormal patients are often a disturbing element; their behaviour tending to be antisocial, impulsive, unreliable and unpredictable.

After leaving school, they often have poor work records and change jobs unduly frequently. They may become delinquent and, as a result, be sent to Approved Schools, Borstal or Prison.

2. Moderately Retarded

These are patients who are at the upper part of the severely subnormal range. Their intelligence quotient ranges from 30 to 50. They are incapable of earning their living and fending for themselves in society but they can be taught to look after themselves, to wash, dress and feed themselves. They are incapable of learning in ordinary schools and are appropriately dealt with at occupation centres and, later, may be found work in a sheltered workshop.

3. Severely Retarded (Severely Subnormal)

These are patients with an intelligence quotient below 30. The lower in the scale the patient is placed with regard to intellectual endowment, the greater the frequency for anatomical and physiological abnormalities to be found; e.g. disporportionate and stunted growth of the head, limbs and body are frequent. Neurological phenomena, e.g. hemiplegia and diplegia frequently occur and epileptic fits occur in about half the patients. Expectation of life is limited; some die in the first two years of life and a large number die before reaching adult life. The most common causes of death are intercurrent infections (e.g. pneumonia), the development of circulatory failure or death due to epilepsy, usually in status epilepticus.

Recognition of Mental Retardation in Infancy and Childhood

The following are some useful landmarks of development in the normal child for comparison with suspected mentally subnormal children:
(1) Smiling in response to the mother's overtures at 6 weeks.
(2) Grasping at an object when placed in the hand at 3 months.
(3) Ability to go for an object and get it at 5 months.
(4) Ability to lift head from the supine when lying on a firm surface at 6 months.
(5) Walking when held with hands at 9 or 10 months.
(6) Walking without support at 13 to 15 months.

Speech

(1) 6 months able to say 'mum, mum'.
(2) 8 to 9 months, 'Da, da, da', 'Ma, ma, ma'.
(3) 10 to 11 months able to say one or two words with meaning.

Other Useful Pointers

(1) Turning head to a sound at 3 months.
(2) Playing games, such as peep-bo at 6 months.
(3) Wave hand good-bye at 10 months.
(4) Imitate parents coughing, putting tongue out, knocking on the table at 6 to 9 months.
(5) Chewing at 6 months.
(6) Feeding self with a cup and placing it back on the table without help at 15 months.

In taking the history, questions about the delivery of the baby and the condition of the baby immediately after birth and during the first two or three weeks are important; e.g. whether delivery was difficult and whether birth asphyxia, twitching, convulsions, drowsiness, sucking difficulties, birth injuries, etc., were present.

CAUSATION OF MENTAL RETARDATION

Mental retardation may be largely genetically determined or may be due to factors operating during pregnancy, at birth or during infancy and childhood.

An aetiological classification of different forms of mental subnormality is shown in Table 5.

1. Genetic Factors

Genetic and environmental factors interact in the production of mental subnormality.

The following genetic mechanisms play a role in the pathogenesis of some forms of mental subnormality:

(1) Major single gene mutation.
(2) Cytogenetic aberration.
(3) Multifactorial (polygenic) inheritance.

2. Pregnancy

Certain infections of the mother may damage the foetus, e.g. German measles, syphilis, toxoplasmosis. Certain drugs can act as teratogenic agents when given during pregnancy.

3. Birth

Prolonged or difficult birth, instrumental delivery, etc., giving rise to anoxia in the baby, excessive oxygen to premature babies.

4. Infancy and Childhood

Any disease, trauma or metabolic disturbance which interferes with growth or damages the central nervous system can cause mental retardation.

Mental Retardation due to the Action of a Single Mutant Gene

The forms of mental subnormality due to the action of a single gene are seen in Table 5.

It has been estimated that single gene inheritance accounts for one-sixtieth of all cases of mental retardation.

Patients afflicted with phenylketonuria, Hurler's disease and tuberose sclerosis are usually severely mentally subnormal.

Mental Retardation due to Cytogenetic Aberration

Chromosomal aberrations may occur during meiosis as well as during mitosis. The most frequent anomaly is non-dysjunction. This results in an abnormal number of chromosomes in both daughter cells, one having one chromosome too many and the other having one too few. The Denver classification, now widely accepted, numbers the human autosomes from 1–22, the sex chromosomes being classified separately. The individual chromosomes are distinguished from each other by the total length, the length of the long arm and the site of its centromere.

TABLE 5

AETIOLOGICAL CLASSIFICATION OF MENTAL SUBNORMALITY

Polygenic or Multifactorial	Single Recessive	Single Dominant	Chromosome anomaly Cytogenetic aberration	Embryopathy	Birth	Infancy and Childhood
High grade defective	Phenylketonuria	Tuberose sclerosis	Down's syndrome (Mongolism)	Rubella	Cerebral haemorrhage and other damage.	Cretinism
'Subnormality' Mental Health Act	Galactosaemia	Some late infantile varieties of Tay-Sach's	Trisomy XXX syndrome	Syphilis		Kernicterus
	Hurler's disease		Klinefelter's syndrome (XXY)	Toxoplasmosis	Excessive oxygen to premature babies	Cerebral palsy
I.Q. 50–70	Tay-Sach's disease (infantile type)		Turner's syndrome (XO)	Kernicterus		Encephalitis
Social and psychological factors also important	Craniostenosis			Teratogenic agents		Trauma
	Microcephaly					Schizophrenia
	Laurence-Moon-Biedl syndrome					Nephrogenic diabetes insipidus

The following are some forms of mental subnormality due to cyto-genetic aberration:

(1) Klinefelter's syndrome.

(2) Trisomy X syndrome.

(3) Mongolism (Down's syndrome).

Klinefelter's syndrome and Trisomy X syndrome are due to a non-dysjunction of at least one of the sex chromosomes. Mongolism is usually due to non-dysjunction of a small autosome. In rare instances the condition is caused by the transmission of a supernumerary auto-some which is fused with another autosome by translocation. There appears to be a relationship between older maternal age and the tendency to develop these chromosomal aberrations.

Biochemical Aspects of Genetical Transmission of Mental Subnormality

The genes produce their effects by controlling enzyme systems and by chemical functions in the body. It has been estimated that a bio-chemical factor plays a role in the aetiology of between 2 and 4 per cent of cases of severe mental subnormality.

Normal metabolism occurs through sequential steps, each step being regulated by a specific enzyme. The situation is a steady state, each intermediate product being metabolised as it is formed by the succeeding enzyme in the sequence. It is now known that each enzyme in turn is controlled by one specific gene within the chromosome.

In the case of human inborn errors of metabolism, it appears that clinical manifestations of enzyme defects are most frequently due to toxic effects of excessive accumulation of normal metabolites above the metabolic block, as has been observed in phenylketonuria and galacto-saemia.

The following are types of inborn errors of metabolism associated with specific forms of mental subnormality:

(1) Protein metabolism—Phenylketonuria, Maple syrup disease, Hartnupp disease.

(2) Lipide metabolism—Amaurotic familial idiocy, Gaucher's dis-ease, Neumann-Pick's disease.

(3) Carbohydrate metabolism—Galactosaemia, Gargoylism.

(4) Miscellaneous—Wilson's disease (copper), Toni-Fanconi syn-dromes (cysteine).

Multifactorial Inheritance

Intelligence is polyfactorially determined and the distribution of intelligence in the normal population is in the form of a normal frequency curve. The lowest ranges of this frequency distribution constitute men-tally subnormal patients and it deals with the majority of patients with an I.Q. above 50. Below this one finds a variety of causes—genetic, environmental, traumatic, inflammatory, etc.—which have caused the arrest of the development of the mind.

Three-quarters of all cases of mental subnormality represent the lower extreme of the lower range of intelligence frequency distribution.

CLINICAL TYPES OF MENTAL SUBNORMALITY

Recessive Transmission

Phenylketonuria

Phenylketonuria is an inborn error of metabolism occurring at the rate of one per 20,000 of the British population and transmitted in the recessive manner.

It is an enzyme defect like the majority of hereditary metabolic errors. The enzyme defect is due to a failure of the enzyme system in the liver to convert phenylalanine into tyrosine, with the result that phenylalanine and its products accumulate in the blood and damage various organs, particularly the C.N.S.

The biochemical disorder in phenylketonuria affects the entire metabolism of the body. For example, patients tend to be fairer than their siblings and are liable to dermatitis. The main effect, however, is on the brain. The level of phenylalanine in the blood becomes high and secondary disturbances of various metabolic processes essential to normal function in the brain occur.

Patients with phenylketonuria may, however, appear normal and the diagnosis is made on examination of the urine. The metabolites are not usually detectable in urine until the second or third week and sometimes not until the sixth week. The fourth week of life is probably the optimum time for routine testing and the sixth week probably detects more cases. The test is simple and is a modification of the ferric-chloride test in which a paper strip (phenistix) is impregnated with ferric-chloride and applied to the wet napkin.

In recent years there has been considerable interest in the treatment of phenylketonuria by diet in which the quantity of phenylalanine is restricted to the minimum compatible with well-being. Follow-up studies of children who from an early age received this diet correctly revealed that the majority were of normal intelligence.

In addition, it was clear that the diet produced definite changes in the patient in the direction of normal, e.g. the hair became darker during treatment and fairer when the treatment was relaxed. The level of 5-hydroxytryptamine, which is depressed in the blood if the patient is untreated, also moved towards the normal level. Although isolated cases of untreated phenylketonuria are of normal intelligence, they are rare. The overwhelming number of patients are severely or moderately subnormal in intelligence.

Galactosaemia

Here, the genetically determined enzyme defect is a failure in break-down of galactose with the result that phosphate accumulates in the body.

Children are normal at birth but later develop feeding difficulties, enlargement of the liver, jaundice, enlargement of the spleen, hepatic failure, sub-cutaneous haemorrhages, oedema, wasting. Eventually death occurs from hepatic failure or infection.

Severe mental retardation is common.

Treatment is by giving a lactose-free diet, if possible from early infancy. This can lead to considerable improvement in physical and mental state.

Hurler's Disease

This is a genetically determined metabolic disorder autosomally sex linked.

The biochemical abnormality results in over-production of certain mucopolysacharides which can be detected in the urine.

Growth is stunted and disproportionate, the skull is malformed, the bridge of the nose is depressed, the tongue protrudes and the neck is short. Liver and spleen is enlarged and corneal clouding and abnormalities of the cardiovascular system sometimes occur.

These patients show behavioural difficulties.

Death usually occurs in childhood from circulatory failure or pneumonia.

Amaurotic Family Idiocy (Taysach's Disease, Cerebral Macular Degeneration)

This is a genetically determined disorder of metabolism in which anglioside is stored in excessive amounts in the brain cells. There are three forms, the infantile, the early childhood variety and the juvenile form.

The early infantile form is confined more or less to Jewish people. The child is born normal and remains normal up until about six months. Then it becomes listless, apathetic, showing no interest in its surroundings and losing the ground it has gained. It begins to show signs of visual failure which ends in blindness. Later it develops widespread paralysis. It gradually wastes away and usually dies within two years of the onset. Diagnosis of the disease is revealed by the optic atrophy which causes the blindness and the appearance of a cherry-like spot at the macula.

The early childhood form begins at three years of age after a period of normal development. It is characterised by progressive deterioration in mental growth, spasticity and blindness. The blindness is due to optic atrophy, a reddish brown macula spot being present. The disease is usually fatal within a few years.

The juvenile form starts between 6 and 12 years of age. Visual failure progresses to blindness, optic atrophy is present and a deposit on the retina of a scattered pepper and salt pigment, ataxia, paresis, terminating hopeless dementia, complete paralysis and death. Some late juvenile varieties are dominantly transmitted.

Microcephaly

A small size of head is the distinctive feature. In the adult a small skull is associated with a face of normal size giving a bird-like shape, characteristic of microcephaly.

There are two groups of microcephaly. One is genetically determined, due to a single recessive gene. The other microcephalic disorder shows a variety of types of mental subnormality.

The majority of patients are severely subnormal and about half suffer from epilepsy.

Laurence Moon Biedl Syndrome

This is characterised by retardation from infancy which does not usually amount to very severe subnormality, with retinitive pigmentosa, defective vision, polydactyly of hands and feet, obesity and hypogenitalism. Among relatives, incomplete forms of extra digits occur, obesity and hypogenitalism, etc.

Single Dominant

Tuberous Sclerosis (Epiloia)

This is due to a single dominant gene and it usually causes severe subnormality. It has been estimated that up to 50 per cent of cases are due to new mutations.

Tuberous Sclerosis is characterised by the following features:

(1) Severe mental retardation.

(2) Adenoma sebaceum of the face which begin during the second to forth year of life and have a butterfly distribution on the face.

(3) Cutaneous Naevi, cafe au lait pigmentation, white patches due to absence of pigment.

(4) Epileptic fits.

(5) Changes in the bones, osteosclerosis, periosteal thickening.

(6) Glial nodules appear in the brain causing epilepsy, paralysis, premature puberty and calcification of the overlying skull.

(7) Rabdomyomata of the heart which cause heart block and cardiac failure exist.

(8) Fibrosis of the lungs.

(9) Mixed tumours of the kidneys.

The majority of patients die young from intercurrent infections such as pneumonia or from status epilepticus, cardiac or renal failure.

Cytogenetic Aberrations
Mongolism (Down's Syndrome)

Mongolism was first described by Langdon Down and he so named it because of a superficial resemblance to Oriental people. Nowadays the term Down's Syndrome is becoming much more widely used.

About one in every 600 live births is mongoloid but the high infancy mortality of mongolism reduces its incidence in the general population to one in 1,000. Mongolism accounts for one-thirtieth of all cases of mental retardation. Most mongoloids fall into the category of severely subnormal but usually in the upper range of this group however. Few of them have an intelligent quotient above 60.

In 1959 it was found that mongolism was associated with an extra chromosome.

In the normal somatic cell there are 22 pairs of non-sex chromosomes (autosomes) and a pair of sex chromosomes, the latter being XX in the female and XY in the male.

The incidence of mongolism in cousins and the occurrence of trisomy in more than one mongol sibling when the chromosomes of the parents are normal suggests an underlying genetic mechanism as a cause of non-dysjunction.

If an additional chromosome is present resulting in three matched chromosomes instead of the usual pair, the individual is said to be trisomic for this chromosome. The majority of cases of mongolism are trisomic for one of the two smaller pairs of autosomes.

It is usually considered that trisomy of chromosome 21 is the most common anomaly associated with mongolism.

Other chromosomal abnormalities occur less frequently, e.g. translocation and chromosome mosaicism.

The translocation chromosome is frequently found in mongols of phenotypically normal parents. The occurrence of chromosome mosaicism in mongolism may be associated with incomplete manifestation of the syndrome and the ultimate mental development of such patients has varied from normal to severe retardation.

One important advance arising from chromosome studies is that it helps to explain differences in the probability of producing further mongols by young mothers who have given birth to mongols as compared with those of later age at birth. The incidence of mongolism in relationship to maternal age shows two peaks, one being at an earlier age, and this suggests that two mechanisms are involved. In the case of young parents, if the mongol child has trisomy 21 and the parents have normal chromosomes, the chances of a second child being born a mongol are of 1 or 2 per cent, irrespective of maternal age. However, if one of the parents is a carrier of a translocation chromosome, the chances of a second mongol child being born are greatly increased, as high as one in three.

The risk of a woman below 25 years of age giving birth to a mongoloid child is 1 in 2,300 and is 1 in 100 for women between 40 and 45 years and 1 in 46 for women older than 45.

The Trisomy XXX Syndrome

This comprises less than 1 per cent of mentally retarded women. They have three female sex chromosomes instead of the normal two. They are often retarded but they can produce normal children.

The Trisomy XXY (Klinefelter's) Syndrome

This occurs in only 1 per cent of male defectives. Men with this abnormality may be mentally normal mental retardation occurs in $\frac{1}{6}-\frac{1}{2}$. These patients have two X chromosomes instead of the usual one, as well as a Y chromosome. Half of the affected men are chromatin positive, i.e. they are genetically female.

They show under-development of genitals with small testicles, scanty pubic of female distribution and scanty facial hair, sometimes gynaecomastia and are infertile.

Turner's Syndrome (Monosomy X)

Here the patient has one X chromosome instead of two. It is characterised by ovarian agenesis, absence of secondary sex characteristics at puberty in girls, small stature, digital anomalies, webbed neck, congenital heart disease, renal anomalies, intellectual subnormality and other developmental errors occur.

Some of these patients may be of normal intelligence.

Embryopathy

Embryopathy is a term given to damage to the foetus by a variety of agents operating before birth. Examples are:

(1) *Rubella*. Infection of the mother within the first three months of pregnancy with German Measles causes some two-thirds of the children to suffer from congenital defects such as congenital cataract, congenital heart defects. Microcephaly, deafness and deaf mutism may all result.

(2) *Syphilis*. Syphilis, like rubella, is one of the few diseases in which there is good evidence that maternal infection during pregnancy may damage the infant. The risk is high and it has been estimated that a woman with latent syphilis has only one chance in six of bearing a normal child if she is untreated. Transmission of infection probably does not occur until the fifth month of pregnancy which gives a period of grace during which infections discovered by routine ante-natal seriological investigations can be treated.

The effects on the infant are such as to produce well-recognised syndromes such as general paralysis, meningo-vascular syphilis.

Syphilitic mental deficiency is eminently preventable and should disappear. The incidence of this type of mental deficiency has declined with the decrease in the incidence of syphilis, but with the recent increase, it again becomes a danger.

(3) *Toxoplasmosis.* This is the result of human infection with toxoplasma gondi. When a pregnant mother suffers from this, the child can be affected and the condition is characterised by encephalomyelitis, cerebral calcification, hydrocephalis and chlorio-retinitis, the symptoms being apparent at birth or soon after. The prognosis is very poor and those patients who survive are usually mentally retarded and epileptic.

(4) *Kernicterus.* This is due to rhesus incompatibility which results in over-production of bilirubin, which causes brain damage. The striate body hipocampus, subthalamic nuclei, cerebellate nuclei and cranial nerve nuclei are particularly prone to become damaged.

Affected infants show clinical features from the second to the sixth day after birth. They are severely jaundiced, have a temperature, vomit, cannot be wakened, show respiratory distress, have twitching limbs and face, rigidity, opisthotonos and convulsions.

Those who survive show permanent sequelae such as mental retardation.

(5) *Teratogenic Agents.* A number of agents have been recognised as being potentially harmful to the foetus if administered to the mother during pregnancy. These include X-radiation, drugs such as colchicine, physostigmine, quinine, thalidomide and heavy metals such as lead and cobalt. Sex hormones and cortisone may also produce inter-sex abnormalities in children. Hypovitaminosis with A and D may also produce maldevelopment.

Causes Operating at Birth

Prematurity is a possible cause of mental retardation and is sometimes associated with blindness. The administration of oxygen has been considered to be a factor in these patients. Oxygen poisoning is considered to be a cause of retrolental fibroplasia. Birth trauma can occur with prolonged and difficult labour, high forceps delivery and anything that causes anoxia, such as anaesthesia, protracted labour, twisting of the umbilical cord.

Causes Operating in Infancy and Early Childhood

Head injuries after birth, due to accidents, can cause retarded development depending on the site and severity of the injury. Poisons, particularly lead poisoning from lead paint scraped off cots, doors, etc., infections, meningitis, including tuberculous meningitis and meningococcal meningitis, if they are not treated with antibiotics or do not respond satisfactorily, can lead to severe mental retardation, encephalitis to virus infection.

This was common in the epidemic of influenza in 1917; it is associated with mental retardation, extra-pyramidal symptoms, hyperkinseis, personality difficulties, vicious propensities and impulsive behaviour.

ENDOCRINE FACTORS

Cretinism

This is due to hyperthyroidism beginning in foetal life and, if failure of thyroid function occurs after a normal infancy, it is then referred to as myxoedema. Cretinism is endemic in goitrous areas, the mother usually having a goitre. If untreated, there is marked retardation, physically and mentally.

The child is apathetic and somnolent, quiet, cries little, has difficulty in feeding due to his torpor and difficulty in sucking due to enlarged tongue. Constipation is characteristic. The skin is dry and thick lips, hands and external genitalia are often eczematous; temperature is subnormal, pulse is slow, the tongue is large and protruding, features are coarse, neck is thick with superclavicular pads of fat and the abdomen is large with an umbilical hernia.

Fusion of the epiphysis is delayed, so is dentition. Anaemia and hypertonia of the muscles occur.

Diagnosis:

Cretinism can usually be diagnosed within the first few months of life. The cretinous child has to be distinguished from mongolism and Hurler's Disease and from various other causes of mental retardation.

Mongolism is diagnosable at birth. The mongol is active, the features are course, the skin is fissured and the head small and rounded. The child is not usually constipated and will show chromosomal abnormalities, which are not shown in the cretin.

Hurler's Disease is distinguishable from cretinism by enlargement of the liver and spleen, cornea paucities, X-ray appearance of bones and failure to respond to thyroid treatment.

It is important that cretinism be diagnosed as early as possible because, if thyroid treatment is delayed, mental and physical retardation can be permanent.

A dry thyroid extract in doses of 6 mgms. until two months of age, 12 mgms. at six months, rising to 200 mgms. at twelve years is usually adequate to produce normal growth and

If signs of hyperthyroidism occur, the dose should be reduced.

Treatment must be continued throughout life.

Cretinism is of particular interest as it is the first form of mental deficiency to respond to treatment.

S.T.P.—9

Cerebral Diplegia ('Cerebral Palsy)

This may result from any process which damages the brain before birth, during birth, within the first few years of life and this includes a number of conditions already considered under group determination, genetic factors, embryopathy, birth injuries, anoxia at birth, infections, trauma and vascular accidents after birth. Spasticity of the limbs and myotonic twitches often occur.

The term diplegia is not satisfactory as it refers to a paralysis affecting both arms or legs, whereas all varieties of paralysis of the limbs can occur from monoplegia, haemiplegia, paraplegia, triplegia and quadraplegia.

Tendon reflexes are exaggerated and plantar reflexes are usually extensor.

Athetosis occurs in many patients and tremors and choreic movements less frequently.

Epilepsy is common and speech and hearing defects may also be associated with the condition. About three-quarters of the patients show mental retardation. A proportion of patients may have normal or even above normal levels of intelligence.

TREATMENT AND TRAINING OF THE MENTALLY SUBNORMAL

It has been estimated that 8 per 1,000 of the population are mentally subnormal but that, at most, only 2 of these will need admission to hospital.

The majority of mentally retarded patients, both children and adults, are looked after at their homes most of their lives.

Admission to hospital is determined mainly by behavioural difficulties in the patient or by social factors. For example, the child's behaviour may be so difficult, so destructive and noisy that the family, although they would like to keep him at home, are unable to do so. Social factors such as overcrowding, incompetent parents or complaints by neighbours are also factors that may influence the need for admission.

In the case of adults, admission may become necessary when parents die or become unable to look after them.

In recent years there has been an even greater tendency for maintaining mentally subnormal individuals outside hospitals as useful members of the community. Research studies have shown that young medium grade subnormal children, who were cared for in small groups which tried to provide a substitute family environment, developed social and verbal abilities more rapidly than a comparable group of children who remained in a large ward of a mental deficiency hospital. Recent studies of the learning abilities of adult imbeciles have shown that some of them attained the standards necessary for employment in open industry and others became self-supporting in sheltered workshops. Many such patients can live at home or in hostels and travel to work each day.

Patients in the community can attend Occupation Centres and Training Centres. Children of school age can receive special education in special schools or special classes.

Nowadays, patients can enter a hospital for the subnormal informally but some have to be admitted compulsorily from home as a result of a Court Order.

In hospital, children are given education and training suitable to their ability and adult patients are given instruction in adult social behaviour and training in various forms of employment. Industrial workshops are utilised by some hospitals, in which patients are employed in repetitive work for outside firms. Physical training, recreations and social activities also form part of the regime of treatment.

Phenothiazine derivatives have greatly improved the behaviour of disturbed and destructive mentally subnormal patients.

FURTHER READING

The Social Problem of Mental Deficiency, by O'Connor and Tizard J., London (1956).

Tredgold's Textbook of Mental Deficiency, 10th Edition by R. F. Tredgold and K. Soddy (1963).

CHAPTER TWENTY-NINE

CHILD PSYCHIATRY

Child psychiatry is of comparatively recent origin. The first Child Guidance Clinic was established in the United States in 1921 and the first Child Guidance Clinic in Great Britain was opened in 1926.

Child Guidance Clinics are run by a team consisting of psychiatrists, psychologists and psychiatric social workers.

The Psychiatrist is the head of the team and he investigates the medical and clinical aspects. The Psychologist measures intelligence, aptitudes, personality and deals with educational problems. The Psychiatric Social Worker investigates the social aspects and serves as a liaison with the parents.

Psychiatric disorders of children may be arbitrarily classified as follows:

(1) Disturbances of eliminative functions.

(2) Disturbances of eating.

(3) Disturbances of sleep.

(4) Unhealthy behavioural and emotional responses, e.g. aggression, jealousy, lying, stealing, fears, phobias.

(5) Gratification habits, e.g. thumb-sucking, masturbation, daydreaming, tension habits such as nail-biting and tics.

(6) Educational backwardness.

(7) Speech difficulties.

(8) Psychosomatic disorders.

(9) Severe psychiatric disorders, e.g. childhood schizophrenia and manic-depressive illness.

I DISTURBANCES IN ELIMINATIVE FUNCTIONS

Enuresis

Involuntary micturition is normal in infancy both by night and by day. Daytime control should be acquired in the second year and in the third year a dry bed should be achieved.

In the absence of disease, repeated involuntary micturition occurring after the third year is termed Enuresis. If due to organic disease, the description urinary incontinence is applied.

Four stages in the progress of normal control of micturition may be described:

(1) The automatic bladder of infancy.

(2) The small bladder of increasing capacity in which the impulse to void is still uninhibited.

(3) The bladder which will hold three ounces or more but in which the impulse is still succeeded by micturition.

(4) The adult functioning bladder in which the contractions are inhibited by cortical activity.

The incidence of enuresis is variously estimated as between 5 and 15 per cent. The high figure includes children who are occasional and intermittent bed-wetters and the low figure includes only those whose enuresis is unremitting for long periods. In adults the incidence is probably less than 1 per cent.

Enuresis may be

(1) The primary type.

(2) The acquired type.

The primary type is characterised by a failure to develop control by the usual age and the acquired type denotes enuresis developed after the child has acquired normal control.

The child has to pass through the stage of automatic emptying of the bladder as a young infant to the stage of awareness of the full bladder, usually at 12 to 18 months, when he tells the mother that he is passing urine or just about to do so. Then there is the stage of learning to inhibit the contraction of the detrusor muscle and to hold the urine through the use of the external sphincter and perineal muscles. The next stage is the control of intra-abdominal pressure through the use of the diaphragm and abdominal muscles, to the final stage when the person is able to start and stop the flow of urine at any degree of bladder filling.

Many bed-wetters have urgency and frequency of micturition by day, suggesting that bladder emptying is necessary at an earlier stage of bladder distention than usual. A factor which may be responsible is a delayed maturation of the nervous system in these patients.

There is a well-known genetic factor in enuresis.

Many observers have stressed the importance of environmental factors, including the influence of family relationships and attitudes. There is a relationship between the incidence of enuresis and insecurity in relationship to unhappiness in the home, broken homes and loss of parents. There is a higher incidence in the lower social classes.

True anatomical factors occur extremely rarely. Spina bifida occulta is not a factor. Spina bifida is closely related to enuresis only when there is a meningocele or other obvious neurological signs.

Acquired enuresis is nearly always psychological in origin, related to psychogenic factors such as disturbance and insecurity.

Acquired enuresis occurs most commonly in children from the age of 5 to 8 years and the onset is usually related to normal stresses of childhood, e.g. after an illness, an operation, the birth of a sibling, temporary or permanent loss of a loved person, etc.

Children who suffer from nocturnal enuresis not infrequently are deep sleepers.

TREATMENT

Methods of treatment include:
(1) Psychotherapy.
(2) Bladder training.
(3) Drugs.

Psychotherapy

This consists in parental guidance; anxiety must give place to confidence and hope. The child should be encouraged to make his own record of dry nights, such as putting a star in his diary for dry nights and no record being made for wet nights. A system of rewards of dry nights is also a useful measure.

Bladder Training

Restriction of fluid intake has no therapeutic value. The child should be thoroughly wakened at the parents' bedtime and made to pass water and he should be fully conscious of the act. Older children may be given an alarm clock to waken them at some time between 10.30 p.m. and rising.

Daytime training should be instituted in the holidays. The child should be sent to the lavatory at fixed but gradually increasing intervals, beginning at one hour and increasing the interval by a quarter of an hour every second day. If the child can hold its water for three-hour periods in the day, dryness at night is facilitated. This method is most successful in children with irritable bladders and daytime frequency.

Drug Treatment

Anticholinergic drugs such as Belladonna, if given in adequate doses—10 minims of the tincture twice a day and 20 minims at night, increasing until signs of intolerance appear.

Probanthine bromide is slightly more successful than Belladonna.

In children who sleep very deeply, amphetamine may be given; this serves the purpose of lightening sleep and also acts as a sympathomimetic agent which is similar in action of the bladder to the anticholinergic drugs.

When enuresis occurs early in the morning, the slow-acting preparations such as dexamphetamine spansules are indicated.

Treatment of Nocturnal Enuresis by the Electric Alarm

This apparatus consists of a pad which lies on the mattress under a draw sheet and is connected by a flex to a bedside bell activated by a $4\frac{1}{2}$ volt dry battery. Contact of the urine with the pad closes the electric circuit and rings the bell. In this method response is almost instantaneous; inhibition occurs before the patient is fully awake.

Constipation

Toilet training establishes control of bowel activity and this is one of the earliest experiences where the person has to conform to the needs of the outside world.

Constipation in children is usually due to faulty parental attitudes to bowel evacuation. Excessive concern may be a factor; at other times evacuation of the bowel may be the scene of a battle between the mother and the child and it may be only one manifestation of a general attitude of resistance. Other factors are fears of being alone or the utilisation of bowel activity to get attention.

The less fuss and anxiety paid to bowel evacuation the better.
Encopresis is the passage of stools at inappropriate times and places after the age of 2. It is more common in boys and its maximum occurrence is between the ages of 6 and 12. The following are the usual reasons:

(1) An effort to withhold bowel action in school and then soiling occurs on the way home from school, due to anxiety and the inability to hang on any longer. This explains the isolated case.

(2) Continuous soiling from infancy is found sometimes with low social standards in the family.

(3) Soiling after improvement may occur with emotional upsets.

(4) Encopresis may occur after constipation at any time with emotional upsets.

II BEHAVIOUR PROBLEMS CONCERNING EATING

Loss of Appetite

Loss of appetite not due to physical illness is usually due to psychological causes and is usually attributable to the attitude and management of meals by the parents. Loss of appetite or refusal of food may be the result of:

(a) *An effort on the part of the child to get attention.* In other words, he may use this as a means of controlling other people.

(b) *Negativism.* Refusal of food may be a manifestation of negativistic behaviour. This is a common cause between the ages of 2 and 3 years. This age period is often called the period of resistance.

(c) *Daydreaming.* The child may be engaged in phantasy and too preoccupied to eat.

(d) *Anxiety or unhappiness in the child.* These emotional states can impair appetite.

(e) *Parental influences,* such as (1) nagging (2) over-solicitude (3) threat or coercion. The child reacts to these influences by refusing food or by a loss of appetite and frequently minor battles occur between the

254 A SHORT TEXTBOOK OF PSYCHIATRY

child and the parent over the meal table. Usually the more tense and emotional the adult, the more resistant becomes the child's refusal of food.

In advising the parents on the management of these common forms of behaviour difficulty, it is important to emphasise to them that the child's health is not likely to be endangered in any way if he misses some meals. The child should come to the table at the proper times and be given the first course without fuss and no attention or threat. If the child does not want the food it should be taken away without scolding or blame. It is equally undesirable to praise children for eating, as this gives them the wrong impression and attitude with regard to taking food.

It is better to put too little food on the plate and let the child ask for more than to overload the plate to such an extent as would destroy anyone's appetite. In negativistic children, again, small quantities will result in demands for more food.

The remedy is to avoid undue tension and fuss of any kind. If this approach is consistently applied, feeding difficulties usually disappear. The child may continue to refuse food for the first few days and the parents must be prepared to persist in the new method and natural hunger usually wins in the end.

Over-eating

Over-eating may occasionally be due to psychological causes and children who for some reason or other lack adequate affection may resort to over-eating as a compensation. Food is connected with love and the taking of food in some people has potent effects in relieving emotional tension. A number of cases of obesity due to psychogenically determined over-eating have been described.

III SLEEP DISTURBANCES

Sleep is an essential biological need. The young infant will spend most of its time sleeping between feeds. During childhood the amount of sleep required is less but, in children, the amount of sleep required is greater than in adults.

The common problems of sleeping are:
(1) Insomnia.
(2) Night terrors.
(3) Sleep-walking.

Insomnia

Insomnia is frequently due to anxiety or emotional tension. The child may feel insecure, may be afraid to be on its own, or may have fears of the dark, fears of ghosts or other terrifying objects.

The process of going to sleep should be made as happy as possible and should be accompanied by giving of affection and attention to the children. The form of punishment of sending children to bed after some misdemeanour has certain specific disadvantages in so far that, if it is repeated frequently the going to bed may become associated with punishment and this, again, may go to form an unfavourable attitude to sleeping on the part of the child.

The child should be encouraged to sleep on its own as young as possible. It should be soothed and comforted by the mother before going to sleep and night lights should be avoided as far as possible. It has the effect, if anything, of confirming their fears that the darkness is something to be afraid of and postpones the successful overcoming of this fear by children.

Sleep-walking (Somnambulism)

This is a state of dissociated sleep in which the child walks about in a state of bodily activity with consciousness considerably dimmed.

Sleep-walking may be due to a number of causes. The most common causes are an over-anxious and highly strung child; occasionally the individual sleep-walking may be reliving some past experience or acting out some hidden wish.

Night Terrors

These are to be distinguished from nightmares, in so far that in night terrors the child wakes up in a state of great fear and is still, at the same time, asleep. This, again, may be regarded as a dissociated sleep.

A nightmare, on the other hand, is a terrifying dream which may wake the patient. Although distinct phenomenologically, it is doubtful whether the distinction has any practical significance, although in night terror they usually regard it as being a more severe symptom than nightmare.

IV UNHEALTHY BEHAVIOURAL AND EMOTIONAL RESPONSES

Aggressive Behaviour Problems

Anger is an emotion we all experience when frustrated. In children it shows itself in temper tantrums such as screaming, kicking, throwing themselves about on the floor. This type of reaction most commonly occurs in the second year. Temper tantrums do not do any harm but, if they persist, they indicate that there is something wrong with the child's emotional adjustment, that the child cannot stand postponement of his demands.

The cause of temper tantrums lies often in the family's background. Parents, sometimes, may be anxious and highly strung and the family atmosphere is one of continual tension; the temper tantrum, in this instance, serving as a release mechanism for pent up emotional tensions.

Other tantrums may be a manifestation jealousy. The best way to deal with these tantrums is to try to soothe the child; do not increase its frustration but restore a state of security.

Jealousy

Jealousy is a condition which frequently occurs in children and is a condition which is brought out when there is an element of competition. Jealousy seems to be more common in girls than in boys. The most common cause is a rivalry between brother and sister and rivalry which develops with the arrival of the new baby.

Jealousy on the arrival of a new baby may show itself in various ways, depending on the child. He may react by bed-wetting, by having temper tantrums, by being anxious and depressed or by becoming more simple and childish in his behaviour. Rivalry is a common cause of many types of maladjustment in children.

It is important for parents to tell children in the family of the expected new arrival and that it will be necessary for mother to devote a certain amount of time to the new baby. The parent must be tolerant of these jealousies and attempts to revert to infantile behaviour to secure similar affection. The mother must continue to give adequate affection to the other children and let them realise that they have greater enjoyment in life than a young baby.

Lying

In the first two years many mis-statements are due to inability or lack of perfection in speech. They are due to the fact that words are improperly understood and the child is not sufficiently developed intellectually to be precise in its expression or in its description of events.

Up to the age of 4, phantasy lying tends to become more frequent; children at this age tend to live in a world of make believe. Very often children will describe the products of their phantasy as if they existed in reality. Phantasy lying is not always an attempt to deceive but is very often just an expression of a very vivid imagination. Very often the child will tell you, when asked, whether the things he described were real or whether they were 'pretending' and, if they were a product of phantasy, he will usually admit that they were pretending.

Defensive lying is carried out in order to avoid punishment or in order to get out of a difficult situation. The incidence of this type of lying increases with probability of getting punishment. Sometimes children tell lies in order to get approval or admiration; when children are talking together there is a temptation for a child to invent stories to make himself the centre of attention; this tendency will be marked in children who feel inadequate or inferior.

Pathological lying is not a common condition; it shows itself more in late adolescence. These people are usually unstable, have a great verbal facility and very often are charming in personality; they make up stories as they go along and elaborate to a fantastic degree.

A great deal can be done in the management of children to help them to avoid lying, such as if one knows that a child has done something wrong, he will not be asked if he has done it, but why. Children have to be trained to speak the truth and to regard it as a virtue.

Stealing

The word stealing is not applicable in the first two years of life because it implies that the child knows he is doing wrong. He needs to be taught the law of property and what is mine and what is thine.

Stealing may be due to a variety of factors; it may be a result of severe temptation, taking something which the child wants. The feeling will be a part of an ordinary impulse.

In individual types of stealing, a variety of motives such as an unhappy home, lack of affection or insufficient material things may be present. A child with low intelligence and with difficulty in controlling his impulses may steal indiscriminately, or stealing may serve as a release of emotional tension. This is present in emotionally unstable children.

School Phobia (School Refusal)

School phobia refers to a persistent refusal to attend school, the child remaining at home with the full knowledge of his parents. School refusal would be a more appropriate term.

Truants behave differently, usually absenting themselves both from school and home.

School refusers are more intelligent, of a higher social class and behave better at school. They are more timid and have been less frequently separated from their mothers in early childhood than the truant. The school refusers often have over-protective mothers and there is more neurosis in the family. School phobics are afraid of separation from their mothers and homes and this separation anxiety, rather than fear of school, is probably the underlying problem.

The treatment of early cases, consists in firm support and encouragement to the mother and child towards a return to school. Attempts to force the child will only create greater panic.

If this fails, psychotherapy usually for both mother and child may be required. A compromise solution such as allowing the mother to remain with the child at school may bring about an early return.

Change of school, in itself, is useless but a change sometimes provides a fresh start and can help if combined with other methods.

Gratification Habits

Habitual manipulation of the body for pleasure in children ranges from thumb sucking to picking the nose, ears, plucking eye lashes and hairs, fondling of genitalia and masturbation, head banging and grinding of teeth. The most common are nail biting and thumb sucking. All these habits were once accorded more importance than they deserved. When marked they may indicate an underlying anxiety or insecurity and the important thing is to deal with this by parental guidance.

V EDUCATIONAL BACKWARDNESS

When a child is educationally backward the causes are often multiple.

The following sets of causes are the most common:
(1) Intellectual problems.
(2) Emotional problems.
(3) Emotional immaturity and over-dependence on the family.

Intellectual Problems

The usual problem is that a child of limited intelligence or poor intelligence is pushed beyond his capacity. This leads to anxiety which further increases his difficulties.

In assessing his problem, it is not only important to assess his mental age in relationship to his chronological age in giving his intelligence quotient but, also, his attainment as measured by his educational age.

Occasionally a very intelligent child may not be doing as well as he might, because he may be bullied by other children or he may be bored and therefore has not sufficient incentive to work.

Emotional Problems

These may be due to faulty parental attitudes—over-protection, rejection and perfectionism. School refusal and school phobia is one outcome of this.

Problems of Maturation

Some children mature late, both in co-ordination and concentration.

WORD BLINDNESS (SPECIFIC DEVELOPMENTAL DYSLEXIA)

Word blindness describes patients who, despite adequate vision and intelligence, are unable to read words.

Early investigators considered dyslexia to be the result of a specific lesion in or near the angular gyrus of the parietal lobe. More recently, it has been regarded as a delayed or incomplete maturation in the parieto-occipital areas. It is a difficulty in Gestalt functioning, Gestalt seeing, Gestalt recognition, object comprehension and visual association.

There may be a category of persons in whom the language processes are imperfectly lateralised in either hemisphere and who therefore lack determinate cerebral dominance.

Genetic factors are important. Halgren confirmed that, in 88 per cent of his cases, one or more other members of the family also had a reading problem. Another study found concordance in all 9 dyslexic monozygotic twins and discordance in 20 of 30 pairs of dizygotic twins.

Backwardness in reading may be due to a number of causes in addition to congenital dyslexia. It may be due to low intelligence, emotional difficulties with regard to reading, negativism or other emotional difficulties. Patients with congenital dyslexia are often average, superior or very bright in intelligence.

Thirdly, the child may have a severe hearing handicap. This is another cause of poor reading.

In word blindness patients, reading and spelling are not only poor but bizarre; handwriting is cramped, uneven, variable in slant and spacing. There is no demonstrable evidence of brain damage and no primary emotional disorder. They are better than average, often of high intelligence and have relatively good ability to learn mathematics. They persist in reversing and inverting letters far beyond the age at which it is usual for children to do so. They do not express themselves fluently in writing or in speech. They often give a history of being late in learning to talk, of confusing right and left, of being ambidextrous and of having others in their families who have a similar problem in learning to read and spell.

Treatment

Prevention is always better than cure. Before entry to school, enquiries should be directed into the possibility of word blindness. This is indicated by a history of being late in talking, right-left confusion, ambidexterity, difficulty in reading or spelling in other members of the family. It is then advisable to carry out simple tests of visual and auditory recall and to recommend that an alphabetic phonetic method of teaching reading spelling should be the one chosen for this child.

Children so taught are not rendered slower or less understanding readers. Instead, because they have become thoroughly familiar with the component parts of words, they approach them with less anxiety, more confidence and greater pleasure.

VI SPEECH DIFFICULTIES

In fully developed speech there are three phases:
(1) The reception of sounds by the ear and brain.

(2) The interpretation and regrouping of these sounds and their associated ideas

(3) The final expression of these symbolic sounds in speech.

In other words, there are receptive, formative and expressive aspects of speech.

Receptive Difficulties

Delayed development of speech can arise from failure to understand speech owing to complete or partial deafness. Children with useful hearing in the lower frequencies of sound but with deafness in the higher frequencies are sometimes difficult to detect.

Expressive Difficulties

This refers to children in whom the main difficulty is with articulation, which can occur with general spasticity of the muscles in spastic children.

Formative Difficulties

One of the simplest to understand but one of the rarest of these disorders is the aphasia which may accompany severe hemiplegia, whether congenital, from birth injury or acquired in the early years of life through encephalitis or vascular accident. In some of these children the defective interpretation and regrouping of sounds and their associated ideas is further complicated by clumsy articulation. In these cases it is important to rule out mental subnormality.

Dyslalia

This is a common disorder in which there is defective articulation of one consonant to multiple substitutions and omissions with varying degrees of intelligibility. It is probable that in these cases during the early development of speech the rapid development of language is associated with a partial failure of both perception and imitation of speech sounds, leading to faulty habits of articulation which persist even when the underlying dysfunction has passed.

This type of speech difficulty improves quickly and spontaneously. Treatment between the ages of 4 and 5, however, is useful in allaying the mother's anxiety and rescuing the child from nagging correction too.

VII PSYCHOSOMATIC DISORDERS IN CHILDREN

We have already discussed certain psychosomatic disorders such as asthma, peptic ulcer, ulcerative colitis, migraine, etc., which can occur in children and our attention will now be confined to disorders which are particularly related to childhood.

Recurrent pain is probably the commonest psychosomatic disorder after infancy. Recurrent abdominal pain with no organic cause is usually psychogenically determined. Children tend to be over-conscientious.

Recurrent abdominal pains, recurrent febrile attacks and recurrent headaches can be a mode of stress reaction in children as well as in adults.

The Periodic Syndrome

Some authors regard recurrent abdominal, head or limb pains as part of a wide spectrum of disorder, the periodic syndrome, of which other components are vomiting and fever. The different components may occur singly, as in cyclical vomiting or recurrent pyrexia, or together in various combinations. Vomiting of infancy tends to be superseded by abdominal pain in childhood and eventually recurrent headache or migraine in adult life.

VIII SEVERE MENTAL DISORDERS IN CHILDHOOD

The term childhood psychosis has created a great deal of confusion because it contains a number of different diagnostic groups in addition to schizophrenia.

We will confine our attention to childhood schizophrenia and manic-depressive illness.

It should be borne in mind that severely disturbed behaviour can occur in children suffering from epilepsy, Hurler's disease, tuberous sclerosis or as a result of toxic infective conditions, phenylketonuria, cerebral lipoidoses, congenital syphilis and encephalitis lethargica and, sometimes, with sensory deprivations such as auditory imperception and blindness.

Childhood Schizophrenia

The following criteria are helpful in diagnosing schizophrenia in childhood:

(1) Impairment of emotional relationships with others.

(2) Apparent unawareness of personal identity to a degree appropriate to his age.

(3) Pathological preoccupation with particular objects or certain characteristics of them without regard to their accepted functions.

(4) Sustained resistance to change in the environment and a striving to maintain or restore sameness.

(5) Abnormal perceptual disturbances in the absence of discernible organic abnormality.

(6) Acute, excessive and seemingly illogical anxiety as a frequent phenomenon.

(7) Speech either lost or never acquired, showing failure to develop beyond a level appropriate to an earlier age.

(8) Distortion in motility patterns.

(9) A background of serious retardation in which islets of normality or near normality, or even exceptional intellectual function or skill may appear.

Autism

Kanner introduced infantile autism as a separate clinical entity, although later he agreed that it was probably the earliest form of schizophrenia.

Infantile autism was described as lack of affective rapport, the child appearing to be detached, lacking emotional contact and with overt failure to develop speech—either complete lack of speech or pedantic, bizarre type of speech with features suggestive of obsessionalism.

Manic Depressive Illness can occur in childhood but is extremely rare and for practical purposes hardly enters into the differential diagnosis of psychiatric illness in children.

FURTHER READING

Child Psychiatry by Leo Kanner. Thomas. Springfield (1957).

CHAPTER THIRTY

PSYCHOTHERAPY

Psychotherapy may be defined as treatment involving communication between the patient and the therapist, with the aim of modifying and alleviating illness. Many authorities would add that this form of treatment deliberately establishes a professional relationship with the patient with the object of removing, modifying or retarding existing symptoms, of mediating disturbed patterns of behaviour or the promotion of positive personality growth and development. There are various forms and different degrees of complexity, duration and expense of psychotherapy; e.g. the psychotherapy can be:

(1) *Supportive,* dealing with current problems and helping the patient to overcome his symptoms and cope more satisfactorily with them in the future and with life generally. This can be very active and skilled treatment and for many it is the treatment that they need.

(2) *Suggestion and Persuasion.*

(3) *Hypnosis.*

(4) *Abreactive Techniques.*

(5) *Intensive prolonged psychotherapy,* e.g. Freudian or Jungian analysis.

(6) *Group therapy,* based on psycho-analytic principles or sometimes on other guiding rules, depending on the interest of the therapist and the type of patient he has to treat.

The psychiatric conditions which, as a rule, are suitable for psychotherapy are as follows:

(1) Acute reactions to stress, panic, terror, escape reactions.

(2) Hysteria of recent origin with no previous history of severe neurosis.

(3) Acute tension.

(4) Aggressive, protesting behaviour in childhood and adolescence.

(5) Reactive depression.

(6) Modification of attitudes to distress of physical illnesses.

(7) Psychosomatic disorders.

(8) Failure of adaptation to cerebral deterioration and senile decline.

(9) Disorder of habit, including addictions.

(10) Obsessional states occurring in early life in sound personalities.

In most forms of psychotherapy the interview is the main vehicle of treatment. Psychotherapeutic methods have in common the fact that they depend almost entirely on communication between patient and doctor, which may be spoken or implied by expression and gesture. Before embarking on treatment, it is important to decide the objective for each case. The therapist may ascertain the factors causing the patient's symptoms quite clearly after one interview, but it is usually unwise to tell the patient all you know. Premature interpretation will be rejected. Unpleasant truths may take time to be accepted. It is important for the psychotherapist to keep quiet and not to be afraid of pauses and silences. More than half the battle in psychotherapy is to be a good listener.

DOCTOR-PATIENT RELATIONSHIP

Patients may exhibit positive or negative feelings of great intensity towards the doctor. The reaction depends more on the patient's personality and experience than the doctor's. The doctor must learn to tolerate his patient's emotions. If he is hostile and annoyed with his patients, he cannot get their confidence and co-operation. Doctors who regard neurotic patients as weak and spineless are not likely to help them. The doctor should be sympathetically warm and accepting at the outset, which will enable him to build up a good relationship with the patient. If later the patient has to be dealt with in a more firm and positive manner, it can be done on the basis of the patient's confidence in the doctor and in a way that he can more readily accept.

Suggestion

Suggestion is probably the oldest form of psychotherapy and one used in everyday life. Whenever one person tries to influence another, suggestion usually plays a part. It is extensively employed in advertising, propaganda, religious and political activities. It plays a part in every psychotherapeutic relationship and indeed plays a prominent part in any successful doctor-patient relationship. The bedside manner of the successful physician is compounded of a large variety of different features—his general appearance, speech, the interest he shows in the patient, his general behaviour, demeanour, his impressiveness and, in general, his 'presence'. Any treatment, whether it is in the form of a tablet, a bottle of medicine or other form of therapeutic procedure, always has an element of suggestion. The colour and the taste of a medicinal mixture sometimes have more potent effects by suggestion than the active pharmacological ingredients.

Suggestion is defined as a process of communication resulting in the acceptance with conviction, of the communicated proposition in the absence of logically adequate grounds for its acceptance. It therefore involves the active influence of one mind upon another without any necessary logical basis. Treatment by suggestion can be traced as far back as the methods of healing used by the ancient Greeks. The therapeutic methods used in those days involved the invocation of miracles, of which there were two kinds, religious and magical. Interesting examples of religious miracles took place at the Temple of Aescalapius at Epidaurus. Patients came long distances and laid valuable gifts so as to influence the gods favourably. They spent some nights in public prayers and exhortations. Then, in front of the statue of a god, they were given advice in the form of oracles and prophetic dreams.

During the Middle Ages, churches and saints were invoked to cure particular diseases, e.g. St. Clare for eye disease, St. Ralph for plague, St. Fiacre for haemorrhoids. By the simple authority of the name and the mere influence of the words, pious personages would sometimes produce remarkable cures, which were regarded as the outcome of divine intervention. Kings used to cure scrofula. Magical remedies in which were all kinds of curious concoctions were used for treating diseases throughout the Middle Ages. Red coral, viper broth, crab's eye and powdered stag's horn were favourite medieval remedies.

Unobtrusive suggestion, of course, takes place in all successful methods of treatment, not only in psychiatry but in medicine and surgery. The benevolent attitude of the long-experienced general practitioner, the smile of the pleasant nurse, the clean smell of antiseptics in hospital, the colour and taste of the medicine can all play an important part by suggestion in promoting the patient's recovery. Suggestion is superficial, symptomatic treatment and alone it is not enough. It should be combined with a further attempt to deal with the causative factors and the patient should be given some insight into his condition.

Treatment such as massage, radiant heat, sun-ray treatment, mud baths and colonic lavage owe a large part of their success to suggestion. Some physicians obtain excellent results merely by their personalities and by the suggestions they unconsciously or otherwise give. Suggestion, therefore, probably has the widest use of all methods of psychiatry. It is not only used deliberately by psychiatrists but unconsciously by good nurses, physicians and surgeons all the time. It plays a great part in our ordinary lives in many processes which we tend to think are due to the activity of the intellect but which, on closer examination, are found to operate by the subtle means of suggestion, disguised as intellectual explanation. The hoardings in the street, the reiterated policies of our newspapers, the doctrines promulgated from the pulpit are all suffused with suggestion, although disguised under the category of economical, ethical and political values. Propoganda, in all its forms, relies mainly on the power of suggestion.

The history of the treatment of many disorders shows that any spontaneous improvement occurring during the administration of treatment was put down and attributed to the treatment. Another common factor in all the treatments is that they all had an influence by suggestion. Recent work on the effect of placebo tablets, to which patients developed marked reactions, indicates that inert preparations may exert marked therapeutic effects by suggestion and may also produce marked autonomic and other bodily changes by psychogenic influences.

Reassurance

Reassurance is involved in many forms of treatment and in doctor-patient relationships generally. Patients, whatever they are suffering from, often have anxieties regarding the possibility of more serious diseases or regarding their mental stability. Many patients with mild neurotic symptoms have a severe dread of becoming insane. Patients with various bodily manifestations of emotional tension often harbour fears of cancer, or other serious diseases.

All too frequently, patients with psychiatric symptoms are told by their physicians that there is nothing wrong with them. This very often only tends to make the patient more frightened because they know there is something wrong and they are suffering symptoms and varying degrees of unhappiness and disability. They feel bewildered and more anxious because they feel that their condition has not been properly diagnosed and that there is still something wrong which has not been found. It is important to realise that negative reassurances of this type are not by any means as effective as positive reassurances.

In patients suffering from psychiatric disorders, the physician should make the patient understand that he realises that there is something wrong but that the trouble is not due to a physical disease and that his symptoms are manifestations of an emotional illness. A description of the nature and the origin of the symptoms should always be given in terms suitable to his intelligence and personality. Such positive reassurance with explanation is much more effective than a mere negative reassurance.

Although many general physicians and general practitioners think that psychotherapy begins and ends with reassurance, this is by no means so and very rarely does it prove to be adequate treatment in itself.

The relationship with the therapist gives the patient a feeling of acceptance and security, even though such feelings may not be expressed verbally. Reassurance is mainly effective for recent or superficial disturbances and is usually ineffective in deep-seated problems and personality difficulties.

Supportive therapy is the most commonly used method of dealing with problems of an emotional nature. The object is to bring the patient to an improved state as rapidly as possible with symptomatic improvement or recovery, so that he is able to resume normal life and activities. Supportive therapy includes guidance in such matters as education, employment, health and social relationships, always letting the patient make the final decision himself.

Environmental manipulation attempts to remove or modify disorganising elements in his environment. Social work is the best example of trained, skilful, environmental manipulation.

Persuasion is a therapeutic method based on the belief that the patient has the ability to modify his abnormal emotional processes by will power or by application of common sense. Appeals are made to the patient's reason and intelligence, in order to help him to abandon neurotic aims and symptoms and to regain self-respect. Persuasion, in order to be effective, must be based on a good doctor-patient relationship. The patient must feel that the doctor is intensely interested in him and wants to help him. Persuasion involves explanation of the origin of the symptoms and encouragement to adopt more salutary reactions to his problems. It is probably fallacious to assume that the effectiveness of persuasion therapy depends on the operation of the intellect and it is probable that suggestion also plays an important role. Persuasion as a variety of psychotherapy in asthma can be helpful if it is effective in helping the patient's understanding of himself, helping him to relinquish neurotic reactions, tendencies and aims and if it achieves a better general readjustment. This will minimise the tendency for the patient to develop neurotic reactions or emotional tensions which, in turn, can precipitate attacks of asthma.

Supportive therapy is indicated for individuals with a reasonably stable personality who, up to the present illness, have made satisfactory adjustment but who have broken down under the impact of severe stress in the environment. Supportive therapy can also be helpful for less stable or more neurotic individuals.

Distributive Analysis and Synthesis

This type of treatment is a derivative of the psycho-biological school founded by Adolf Meyer. Psycho-biological therapy involves the systematic examination of all the factors that contribute to the individual—heredity, constitution, early childhood conditioning, later personal experiences, various fears of the person's life, educational, economic, work, marital, inter-personal, social, religious. The therapeutic objective is the retraining of unhealthy or unsatisfactory attitudes. During interviews positive elements are stressed, success is emphasised and hopeful elements brought to the foreground. The patient's assets are utilised to facilitate his adjustment.

GROUP PSYCHOTHERAPY

The treatment of patients by psychotherapy in groups was first introduced as a time-saving measure but subsequent experience demonstrated that the method had special therapeutic possibilities, which did not occur in individual psychotherapy.

The number of patients is usually 6–8. Some patients do poorly with group therapy; these include psychopathic personalities, acute severe psychotic conditions, patients who act out too readily and patients with low intelligence. The length of the group therapy session is customarily 1-1½ hours and usually held once or twice weekly. Patients are seated around in a circle. In the first session the participants are introduced by their christian names and the purpose of group discussions is explained.

Group therapy may be conducted:

(1) For purposes of re-education with a view to alteration of attitudes and behaviour patterns.

(2) For purposes of psycho-analytic therapy.

The possible therapeutic aims and goals of group therapy are:

(1) Guidance and practical advice.

(2) Education or orientation.

(3) Spiritual strength and fellowship

(4) Socialisation.

(5) Abreaction.

(6) Facilitation of associations and the production of deeper material for analysis.

(7) Symptomatic relief.

(8) Improved adjustment and adaptation to reality.

(9) Increased understanding and insight into emotional problems and conflicts.

(10) Modification of personality and character.

Group Analytic Psychotherapy

This method has been well developed by Foulks who states that its most significant features are:

(1) Seven or eight members meet for 1½ hours, sitting in a circle together with the analyst.

(2) No programme or directions are given, so that all contributions arise spontaneously from the patients.

(3) All communications are treated as the equivalent on the part of the group of the free association of the individual under psycho-analytic conditions. There is also a corresponding relaxation of censorship.

(4) The therapist retains an attitude corresponding to that of the psycho-analyst during individual treatment.

(5) All communications and relationships are seen as a part of the total field of interaction, namely the group matrix.

(6) All group members taken an active part in the total therapeutic process.

The natural history of the therapeutic group is as follows. In its early stages, there may be much anxiety and guilt in individual members over their consumption. Conflicts are invariably present; these are related to conflicts of a conformity, authority, dependency and change. It is the primary conflict of man as a group animal. The first conflict, therefore, is one of conformity to the group. The second is conflict to authority and authority figures. The third conflict evolves around the problem of dependency. The fourth, conflict of a change.

The natural history of the group usually goes through an initial phase which is termed the 'therapeutic honeymoon', in which great hopes are placed on the therapist; the patient has to orientate himself away from the doctor-patient axis towards the patient-to-patient axis of the group. Patients then usually get down to discussing individual symptoms. The intermediate phase is when the group truly becomes a group. The centre of reference is no longer the therapist alone. They address each other and respond directly to each other with general support and then analyse and interpret their own interactions and feelings. The terminal phase should always be gradual to allow the patient an opportunity to work through the many anxieties and depressions that in therapy, as in life, associate themselves with endings.

Group Psychotherapy for Children

This is classified according to the ages—namely, nursery, early childhood, late childhood, adolescence; also early adolescence and late adolescence.

The nursery group is about 4–5 children in a small room, with a flat tray divided into two compartments containing sand and water and some toy materials. In the early stages, areas are respected and each child cultivates his own plot. Later, they become interested in other people's work and begin working and playing with each other.

Early childhood, 5–9 years of age. Groups are strung here, according to Foulks and Anthony, in conjunction with a sedentary occupation such as drawing, painting or modelling. The period is usually divided into a discussion phase followed by an activity phase. At the end of the discussion period, the group choose their activity for the day.

Adolescent groups. These are usually kept to one sex, optimal number about 6.

HYPNOSIS

Hypnosis is a state of artificially induced increased suggestibility.

The technique of hypnosis usually aims at narrowing the patient's attention and awareness to the hypnotist alone and, although the condition may have the appearance of sleep, it is physiologically quite different from sleep. Electroencephalographic recordings, for example, are similar to those of the waking state.

A part of the patient's mind is 'en rapport' with the hypnotist and hypnosis is regarded by some authorities to be a state of induced dissociation.

There are different levels of hypnosis, ranging from a light hypnotic state to a deep trance.

Deep Hypnosis

Deep hypnosis, or a deep trance, is qualitatively different from the lighter stages of hypnosis. The patient is extremely relaxed, breathing becomes slower, post-hypnotic suggestions will be executed with amnesia. Suggestions are extremely effective; it is possible to make the subject hallucinate, e.g. to visualise scenes or to experience smells.

In a deep hypnotic trance the patient can open his eyes and remain in a trance; it was for this reason that the terms deep trance and somnambulism were applied to this state.

About 5 per cent of the population can be hypnotised into a deep trance without difficulty; some others can be trained to develop a deep trance with intensive efforts over a period of time.

There are, however, many people who are not suitable subjects for hypnosis and can never be deeply hypnotisable.

Hypnotic Techniques

A variety of techniques are available for inducing hypnosis.

It is necessary to prepare the patient and to explain what hypnosis means. It is important to explain that it is not a state of sleep and, secondly, that it is not essential for amnesia to occur to obtain beneficial therapeutic results.

It can be explained to the patient as a state of relaxation in which his field of awareness becomes narrowed and that, in this state, the suggestions will be much more effective.

The hypnotist's rate of inducing hypnosis must be governed by the rate at which a patient responds to hypnotic suggestions.

The following are some examples of techniques used:

First of all the patient should be seated comfortably in a chair or lying down on a couch and should be encouraged to let all muscles go loose and relax; to let the body sink down in the couch; to let all the muscles be as loose and relaxed as possible. They are then asked to pay attention to what the hypnotist is saying; they are then asked to try to pay attention to the right hand or the left hand and to try to feel the sensations of touch coming from the hand; they are asked that, as soon as they feel any movement in the thumb or fingers, to lift it up to indicate which one it is. Slight movements invariably take place and the patients lift up the appropriate finger. This is then followed by suggestions that the hand and the arm is getting lighter and will rise upwards steadily to touch the forehead and, as it rises, the patients get sleepier. When the hand touches the forehead they go off into a deep sleep. The depth of hypnosis can then be increased by further suggestions, by counting ten and, by the time one has finished counting ten, they will be in a deep state of hypnosis.

The advantage of this technique is that one is unlikely to make mistakes and the rate of hypnotic suggestions for induction are governed by the response of the patient.

Other techniques are to get the patient to fixate his vision on a key or a finger or a light and to give suggestions that the eyelids are getting more and more tired and will close, and that the tiredness is passing over the head and down various parts of the body.

Sometimes one can induce a hypnotic state rapidly by getting the patients to hyperventilate and, in some patients, this with suitable suggestions puts them into a deep hypnotic state.

If the patient is a suitable subject, hypnosis can be one of the quickest ways of carrying out psychotherapy.

(1) For psychological investigation, i.e. to elicit the nature of underlying conflicts and problems and to facilitate the recall of forgotten experiences which may be emotionally important.

(2) To abreact past experiences.

(3) To modify symptoms and attitudes.

(4) In the treatment of psychosomatic manifestations such as asthma. A word of warning here; it is unwise to use hypnosis in a patient suffering from status asthmaticus, particularly if they are suffering from the effects of anoxia, because any further slowing down of the respiratory rate may further endanger the patient. However, in other forms of asthmatic attacks where anoxia has not become a problem, hypnosis in certain subjects can produce dramatic results.

In the treatment of psychosomatic disorders, it is usually necessary to induce deep hypnosis to achieve the best results.

Abreactive and Other Techniques Used as Adjuncts in Psychotherapy

The term abreaction was introduced by Freud to denote the release of emotion when buried material was brought to the surface and described.

A number of aids to psychotherapy have been introduced in order to facilitate release of buried material, to help the patient to talk if he is embarrassed and to facilitate the free expression of emotion.

(1) *Intravenous barbiturates.* Ten per cent sodium amytal injected intravenously at the rate of 1 cc. per minute, whilst the patient counts backwards and until he repeats a number or starts counting a normal progression. This indicates the stage of optimum narcosis; he feels relaxed, is suggestible and is able to talk more freely. Sometimes the release of emotion is hindered by the relaxing effect of the intravenous sodium amytal despite facilitating verbal expression and communication.

Intravenous sodium amytal is also useful in the diagnosis of patients with muscular pains which might be due to emotional causes or due to physical causes. The injection of a small amount of sodium amytal, insufficient to cause analgesia, will produce relief if the symptom is due to emotional tension.

Intravenous sodium amytal is also useful in resistive, mute or catatonic schizophrenics, to make them more amenable, communicative and easier to feed. It is also useful in doubtful cases of schizophrenia to obtain information from the patient to establish the diagnosis.

Intravenous Thiopentone has a shorter duration of action and is preferred by some people for facilitating psychotherapy and abreaction.

(2) *Intravenous methedrine.* 15–30 mgms. methedrine injected intravenously often has powerful stimulating effects in the verbal production by the patient and the abreaction of emotions relating to past experiences.

Whereas one might analogically describe the action of intravenous barbiturates as taking the brake off a car when the engine is running, thus enabling it to run more quickly, the action of methedrine would be compared to pressing the accelerator with the brake off.

The most dramatic effects with intravenous methedrine usually occur on the first occasion. Patients will often keep on talking with great productivity eight hours or more later.

Intravenous methedrine is contra-indicated in schizophrenia and border-line schizophrenic patients and must be used with care in severely anxious patients because of its sympatheticomimetic effects.

(3) *Hallucinogenic drugs*, like lysergic acid and sernil, can also be used in hospital conditions for purposes of abreaction.

(4) *Inhalation anaesthesia* has also been used for abreactive purposes —chloroform, nitrous oxide, trilene and ether.

Ether has been used to facilitate an excitatory type of abreaction. It is given on an open mask and, during the phase of excitement, the patient is encouraged to remember and re-enact, with full emotional intensity, past experiences.

Muscular Relaxation

Increased muscle tension is a common manifestation of all forms of emotional tension and is responsible for a number of the patient's symptoms, e.g. certain types of headache are due to increased muscular tension of the scalp muscles; pains in the back of the neck, the back and the limbs may be due to increased muscular tension. Tremors are also manifestations of increased muscular tension.

The symptoms arising from increased muscular tension often give rise to additional anxiety, because the patient may believe that they indicate some serious disease and thereby tend to set up a vicious circle. Treatment consisting in training the patient for muscular relaxation is a valuable therapeutic adjunct. It not only can provide symptomatic relief but, in so far as states of anxiety and tension, have both emotional and somatic aspects. Relief of muscular tension often provides a general alleviation of the degree of anxiety felt.

Muscular relaxation may be helpful in asthmatic subjects suffering from anxiety tension symptoms, particularly when they have neuro-muscular symptoms. Also, relaxation may be helpful when combined with breathing exercises, as the latter can be more effectively intro-duced when combined with training in muscular relaxation.

FURTHER READING

Psychotherapeutic Techniques in Medicine by M. Balint and E. Balint. Tavistock Publications, London (1961).

CHAPTER THIRTY-ONE

BEHAVIOUR THERAPY

Behaviour therapy may be defined as the attempt to alter beneficially, human behaviour and emotions by the application of the laws of modern learning theory.

Behaviour therapy is used for the treatment of neurotic symptoms which in this context are defined as any persistent habit of unadaptive behaviour acquired by learning.

Neurotic symptoms are unadaptive conditioned autonomic responses together with associated muscular and skeletal activities.

Some symptoms are a failure to learn an adaptive response, e.g. nocturnal enuresis.

Behaviour therapy uses the following techniques of relearning and unlearning in the treatment of symptoms:

(1) Aversion conditioning.
(2) Negative learning or extinction based on negative practice.
(3) Reciprocal inhibition based on relaxation.
(4) Operant conditioning.

1. Aversion Therapy

Aversion conditioning is achieved by associating stimuli relating to the symptom to be treated with unpleasant effects following the administration of apomorphine, emetine or by the administration of a painful electric shock. The latter enables a more precise timing in the occurrence of the effect of the noxious stimulus and the stimuli related to the symptom to be treated.

Aversion therapy is used when the symptom or pattern of behaviour is pleasurable to the person, e.g. alcoholism, transvestism, homosexual inclinations, etc.

2. Negative Learning

This has been used in the treatment of involuntary movements such as tics. It consists in getting the patient to adhere to a rigid schedule of massed practice of voluntarily carrying out the movements of the tic at intervals throughout the day. This sets up a state of inhibition which impairs or prevents the appearance of the tic movement.

3. Reciprocal Inhibition

Many forms of neurotic behaviour are acquired in an anxiety-generating situation.

Treatment can be used on the suppression of anxiety responses by responses which are physiologically antagonistic to anxiety.

Wolpe of South Africa developed the technique of systematic desensitisation, which consists of enquiring first of all into the stimulus situations which provoke anxiety in the patient and to rank these stimuli in order from the most to the least disturbing, i.e. a hierarchy of stimulus situations.

Then the patient is asked to visualise the least disturbing stimulus when he is in a state of relaxation produced by hypnosis or intravenous anaesthetic.

Whenever marked disturbance occurs the therapist withdraws the stimulus and calms the patient.

Each stimulus is visualised for 5–10 seconds and 2–4 items presented in each session, each item usually being presented twice.

As soon as the patient is able to visualise the items without disturbance, the therapist moves on to the next item in the next session.

Eventually the patient is able to visualise all the former noxious stimuli without anxiety and this ability to imagine the noxious stimuli with tranquility is transferred to the real life situation.

4. Operant Conditioning

Operant behaviour usually affects the environment and generates stimuli which 'feed back' to the organism. Any response or behaviour which is rewarding and therefore reinforcing increases the likelihood of further similar responses.

This method has been used with varying degrees of success in the treatment of behaviour disorders in children, in multiple tics, hysterical symptoms, stammering, etc.

It may be said that Behaviour therapy achieves the best results in persons who previously were reasonably well adjusted and who have a limited number of symptoms. In many patients symptoms and unadaptive behavioural responses continue autonomously, even when the original psychodynamic factors cease to be important or active.

Further research is urgently needed to assess the place of behaviour therapy in relation to other available methods of treatment.

FURTHER READING

Behaviour Therapy and the Neuroses by H. J. Eysench (Ed.). Pergamon Press, London (1960).

CHAPTER THIRTY-TWO

PSYCHOPHARMACOLOGY

In just over a decade the introduction of new psychotropic drugs has transformed psychiatric treatment and provided a potent stimulus for research into mental illness.

Psychotropic drugs are pharmacological agents which exert powerful effects on the higher functions of the central nervous system. Psychopharmacology is the study of the pharmacological, biochemical, physiological, neurophysiological, psychological, clinical, therapeutic, social and epidemiological aspects of psychotropic drugs.

Psychotropic drugs can be classified according to their pharmacological and clinical effects into:

(1) Hypnosedatives.

(2) Tranquillosedatives.

(3) Tranquillisers, subdivided into (a) major tranquillisers or neuroleptics and (b) minor tranquillisers.

(4) Central nervous system stimulants and antidepression drugs.

(5) Psychotomimetic or hallucinogenic drugs.

They may also be classified as follows:

(1) Anti-anxiety drugs; these include some of the hypnosedatives, tranquillosedatives and minor tranquillisers.

(2) Antidepression drugs.

(3) Antipsychotic drugs—the major tranquillisers or neuroleptics.

MAJOR TRANQUILLISERS OR NEUROLEPTIC DRUGS

Neuroleptic drugs fall chemically into the following groups:

(a) Phenothiazine derivatives.

(b) Alkaloids from Rauwolfia Serpentina.

(c) Butyrophenone derivatives.

Neuroleptic drugs are used in the treatment of severe psychiatric disorders such as schizophrenia and for controlling disturbed behaviour in patients with organic mental disorders and in mental subnormality.

Neuroleptics have a general depressant action on the central nervous system but their main action is on subcortical structures, in contrast to barbiturates which predominantly affect the cerebral cortex.

Neuroleptics exert their main actions on (1) the limbic system which is intimately concerned with emotional reactions, (2) the hypothalamus, particularly autonomic centres and (3) the reticular system which is intimately concerned in producing and maintaining a state of awareness. These phylogenetically older parts of the brain have a series of feedback mechanisms with the cerebral cortex which subserve the integration of visceral, emotional and somatic components of motivated behaviour.

The predominant action of neuroleptics on subcortical structures explains their capacity for controlling abnormal behaviour and various manifestations in severe psychiatric disorders, such as delusions and hallucinations in schizophrenia, without significantly affecting clarity of consciousness.

It is interesting that these areas contain large amounts of neurohormones including noradrenaline and serotonin and are remarkably sensitive to psychotropic drugs.

The phenothiazines block the action of these neurohormones, whereas the Rauwolfia alkaloids deplete the neuronormonal depots.

Phenothiazine Derivatives

Chlorpromazine was the first phenothiazine tranquilliser and has stood the test of time and extensive trial in all parts of the world.

The phenothiazine nucleus consists of two benzene rings joined by a sulphur atom and a nitrogen atom as follows:

A large number of new phenothiazine transquillisers have been derived by chemical substitution at R_1 and R_2. Differences in chemical structure are associated with differences in potency, clinical and pharmacological effects and also the production of toxic and side-effects.

Potency varies according to the type of radical at R_1; for example, fluorine substituted for chlorine increases potency, whereas removal of chlorine gives rise to Promazine which is one-third as potent as Chlorpromazine but free from the risk of producing jaundice.

The new phenothiazine drugs can be classified according to the side-chain at R_2 into (1) those with aliphatic side-chains, (2) those with piperidine side-chains and (3) those with piperazine side-chains, as will be seen in the Table.

In general, the aliphatic derivatives are the phenothiazine drugs of choice for controlling disturbed, over-active behaviour. Piperazine derivatives are more potent, have a longer duration of action and have greater anti-emetic properties, but a greater tendency to produce extrapyramidal side-effects.

Chlorpromazine

Indications: (a) Psychiatry.

(1) The treatment of schizophrenia.

(2) Controlling over-active disturbed behaviour, agitation and tension in other psychiatric disorders including (a) organic dementia (b) mental subnormality and (c) hyperkinetic states in children.

(b) In general medicine Chlorpromazine is used:

(1) For relieving tension and emotional distress in physical illness.

(2) For relief of pain and distress in inoperable cases of secondary carcinoma.

(3) For relief of vomiting.

(4) To help patients to regain lost weight.

(5) Management of withdrawal states in alcoholism and drug addiction.

Laevopromazine is particularly effective for relieving anxiety and agitation associated with depression but does not relieve the depression itself.

Thioridazine is an almost pure psychosedative, has little anti-emetic action and less potentiating effect on alcohol, barbiturates and anaesthetics.

Piperazine Derivatives

These drugs are more potent and have a longer duration of action, increase alertness, drive and initiative and are to be preferred to Chlorpromazine for schizophrenic patients who are inert, apathetic and show loss of initiative.

Trifluorperazine appears to be more effective in paranoid schizophrenia than Chlorpromazine.

Piperazine drugs have a marked tendency to produce extrapyramidal side-effects which include dystonic reactions of the head, neck and body, spasms and myoclonic twitches; also rigidity. These side-effects are readily abolished by terminating the drug, reduction of dosage or by the administration of anti-parkinsonian agents concurrently.

Alkaloids Derived from Rauwolfia Serpentina

The main alkaloid derivatives are Reserpine, Deserpedine and Resinamine, all of which produce tranquillisation and reduction of activity. In contrast to Chlorpromazine, their autonomic effects are stimulation of the parasympathetic nervous system producing such side-effects as slowing of the heart rate, nasal congestion, dyspepsia and diarrhoea. They also differ from the phenothiazine derivatives in taking much longer to produce their beneficial therapeutic effects; sometimes as long as six weeks administration may be necessary.

After a preliminary sedative phase lasting ten days or so, there is a stage of turbulence lasting some weeks and this is then succeeded by an integrative phase when the patient becomes more co-operative, interested, friendly and with a resolution of symptoms.

Reserpine and related alkaloids have now been superseded in the treatment of schizophrenia by the phenothiazine drugs.

A serious complication of Rauwolfia alkaloid therapy is the occurrence of a severe depressive state, which may be of suicidal intensity and may need electroconvulsive therapy.

Butyrophenone Derivatives

The best-known member of the butyrophenone derivatives is Haloperidol, which is similar in action to the piperazine phenothiazine drugs.

It is highly potent and is one of the best drugs for controlling Hypomania and Mania.

Side-effects and Toxic Effects

It is necessary to distinguish between side-effects on the one hand and toxic or hypersensitivity of reactions on the other.

Side-effects depend entirely on dosage and may occur in any patient if the dose is high enough. Toxic and hypersensitivity of reactions occur only in some patients and are not closely correlated with dosage.

(a) *Side-effects*

The following are common side-effects: Drowsiness, apathy, hypotension, dryness in mucous membranes and extrapyramidal manifestations.

Toxic and hypersensitivity reactions include blood dyscrasias, dermatitis, which is usually light-sensitive and appearing on the exposed areas, jaundice and increased tendency to epilepsy.

The various phenothiazine derivatives differ in potency and clinical application, which are presented in summarised form in the Table.

ANTIDEPRESSION DRUGS

There are three main groups of drugs used for elevation of mood:

(1) Central nervous system stimulants including the Amphetamines, Pipradol and Methylphenidate.

(2) Monoamine oxidase inhibitor drugs.

(3) Tricyclic antidepressants (Thymoleptics) including Imipramine, Amitriptyline and Nortriptyline.

Prior to 1957, the only agents available were central nervous system stimulants which had a limited application and serious disadvantages.

The disadvantages of amphetamines include tolerance, dependency and addiction. A short-lasting elevation of mood is followed by post-medication increase of fatigue, irritability and depression. They have little effect in moderately severe or severe depressions and the main indication for the amphetamine drugs is in patients with a short-lasting, early-morning depression of moderate or mild degree of severity.

Monoamine Oxidase Inhibitors

The finding that Reserpine, which sometimes causes severe depression and produces a fall in the level of noradrenaline and serotonin in the central nervous system and that Iproniazid raises the level with concurrent increased psychomotor activity, provided a stimulating hypothesis for research on the biochemical and pharmacotherapeutic aspects of depression.

Reports of serious liver damage with Iproniazid led to its discontinuation in many parts of the world but stimulated a great deal of research into newer monoamine oxidase inhibiting drugs, with the aim of discovering more effective and safer drugs in this class.

A large number of compounds have been discovered, which are shown in Table 6.

The majority of monoamine oxidase inhibitors are hydrazine derivatives and the risk of liver damage seems to be associated with some members of this group but other members, such as Isocarboxazide (Marplan), have not been reported to cause liver damage.

One of the most potent monoamine oxidase inhibitors is Tranylcypromine, which is not a hydrazine derivative and has a quicker mode of action in producing elevation of mood because it has a direct stimulating action on the central nervous system, as well as its monoamine oxidase inhibiting action on which its long-term action depends.

This drug, although therapeutically efficacious in treating many cases of depression, sometimes produces marked side-effects such as extremely severe headache, which may come on spontaneously but is often precipitated by eating cheese and yeast extracts which contain substances such as Tyramine, which interact with the physiological and pharmacological effects of Tranylcypromine to produce marked fluctuations in blood pressure which are the basis of the severe headache.

The monoamine oxidase inhibiting group of drugs are an important advance in the treatment of depressive states and, in some patients, they are the only measures which are effective. They must be used with caution, and care must be taken in administering other drugs with them, because of the potentiating actions with sympathetic drugs and the very severe reactions produced by Pethidine and some of the tricyclic antidepressants.

Patients must always be warned not to eat cheese or marmite and to avoid taking alcohol because of its potentiating effect.

The Tricyclic Antidepressant Drugs

Imipramine, similar chemically to Chlorpromazine, was first investigated for its efficacy as a tranquilliser and, as these properties were not marked, the drug was overlooked for a number of years until *Kuhn* (1958) tried it for the treatment of depression with good results. It has now been used for many years in all parts of the world and there is general agreement that it is an effective drug in the treatment of some forms of depression.

Experimental work has shown that it influences many brain mechanisms, stimulating some and depressing others. It is characteristic of the action of Imipramine that it takes one to three weeks to produce beneficial effects, despite rapid absorption.

This led to the belief that one of the breakdown products of Imipramine was responsible for its therapeutic action. One of these—a demethylated derivative, Desipramine—is the one believed to be particularly effective.

Desipramine, which is a secondary amine in contrast to Imipramine which is a tertiary amine, is alleged to have a more rapid onset, starting usually within three days with a peak activity on the fourteenth day.

Amitriptyline is a tertiary amine with marked sedative actions. Nortriptyline is a secondary amine which is more rapid in action, probably more effective and has a greater energising and alerting effect than Amitriptyline.

The tricyclic (thymoleptic) group of antidepressants are quite dissimilar in chemical structure to the monoamine oxidase inhibitors and resemble more closely the major tranquillisers.

Whereas the monoamine oxidase inhibitor drugs inhibit the breakdown of monoamines, producing an increase of noradrenaline and serotonin in the brain and peripheral organs, the thymoleptic drugs potentiate the effects of these amines by inhibiting the rebinding of noradrenaline, which increases the availability of the free amine at the level of the receptor organs.

HALLUCINOGENIC DRUGS

Hallucinogenic drugs have been used by man from time immemorial for religious rituals, festivals and orgies, and to facilitate communications with the spirit world. Ancient Aztecs used ololiqui the active principle of which was only isolated a few years ago.

Mescaline derived from the peyotl cactus was used hundreds of years ago by Mexican Indians. Aztecs also used sacred mushrooms from which two active hallucinogens have been recently isolated, viz. Psilocybin and Psylacin.

The most powerful hallucinogen lysergic acid diethylamide is derived from ergot alkaloids. Hallucinogenic drugs produce dissociation of higher neurological and mental functions and have marked effects on perception, thinking and feeling.

The above hallucinogens are chemically similar in that all contain the indole nucleus. It is an interesting fact that recent research has demonstrated that the basic chemical structure of the most powerful hallucinogen (L.S.D.), which itself is not of natural origin, has been found in the oldest naturally occurring drugs used in ancient times for hallucinogenic purposes.

The above hallucinogenic drugs stimulate the sympathetic nervous system and induce a general state of arousal. The latter effect has been shown to be due to stimulation of the reticular system by stepping up sensory input rather than by direct pharmacological action.

Hallucinogenic drugs vary widely in potency. For an adult male weighing 151 pounds the average dose to produce clinical effects is 500 mg. of mescaline, 20 mg. of psilocybin and 0·1 mg. of lysergic acid. Lysergic acid is the most powerful drug known. It acts more quickly than other hallucinogens and some of its effects last for eight or nine hours.

One important hallucinogen in clinical use is chemically distinct from the ones already discussed in that it is not an indole derivative, and is chemically more related to pethidine. This is Phencyclidene (Sernyl) which was first used as in anaesthesia because of its marked analgesic properties due to its action in blocking sensory impulses at the level of the thalamus.

When used in general surgery, patients were post-operatively disturbed, agitated and hallucinated. Phencyclidene given intravenously in a dose of 0·1 mg./kg. body weight produces immediate effects. Feelings of numbness of face and lips and marked changes in body image occur with feelings of euphoria. Thought processes are disturbed. Following a line of thought is difficult. Interpretation of proverbs becomes difficult and tends to be concrete as in schizophrenia. With higher doses hallucinations occur in a setting of clear consciousness. The acute symptoms subside after 45–50 minutes.

It is believed that phencyclidene acts selectively on the sensory cortex, thalamus and midbrain producing a syndrome of sensory deprivation which causes symptoms similar to those of schizophrenia.

The main medical uses of hallucinogenic drugs are

(1) To produce models of psychoses for research by clinical, neurophysiological, biochemical and psychological methods.

(2) To facilitate psychotherapy in patients resistant to normal methods, e.g. obsessional studies, personality disorders, psychosexual problems, alcoholism, etc.

The use of hallucinogens in psychotherapy is thought to decrease inhibitions and to facilitate abreaction of emotions relating to traumatic past experiences. The way they are used and their therapeutic value lies mainly in the use made by the psychotherapist of the drug-induced state.

TABLE 6

Generic Name	Trade Name	Usual Daily Dosage Range (mg.)	Autonomic Reactions	Hyperflexion	Hypertension	Hepatic Pathology	Blood Dyscrasia	Peripheral Oedema	Other Effects
Iproniazid	Marsilid	5–75	+	+	+	+	+	+	
Phenelzine	Nardil	15–75	+	+	+	+	+	+	
Nialamide	Niamid	35–300	+	+	+	+	+	+	
Isocarboxazid	Marplan	10–30	+	+	+	o	o	o	
Tranylcypromine	Parnate / Actomol	10–30	+	+	–	–	–	+	Severe headaches occasionally occur
Amphetamines	Benzedrine Dexedrine Methedrine	5–20		+	+	o	o	o	Sympathetomimetic side-effects. Addictive Psychotic episodes
Phenmetrazine	Preludin	12·5–75	+	+	+	o	o	o	Sympathetomimetic side-effects. Addictive Psychotic episodes. Increased anxiety
Pipradol	Merat …	5–25							Anxiety symptoms, schizophrenic manifestations made worse
Methylphenidate	Ritalin	5–20							

TRICYCLIC ANTIDEPRESSANTS

Generic Name	Trade Name	Usual Daily Dose (mg.)	Anti-Cholinergic side-effects	Hypotension	Extra-pyramidal	Confusional state	Rash
Imipramine	Tofranil	50–150	++	++	+	+++	++++
Desipramine	Pertofran	50–150	++	++	o	+++	++++
Amitriptyline	Tryptizol	50–250	++	++	o	+	+++
Nortriptyline	Aventyl	30–150	+	+			

Generic Name	Trade Name[s]	Daily Dosage [mg.] Low	High	Autonomic	Behavioural Effects	Extrapyramidal	Hypotensive	Seizures	Liver Pathology	Blood Dyscrasia	Oedema	Skin Rashes	Principal Indications	Limitations and Disadvantages
Dimethylamine series														
Chlorpromazine	Largactil Thorazine	75	1,000	+	+	+	+	+	+	+		+	Overactivity, disturbed behaviour in schizophrenia. Acute and chronic organic mental state (mental defectives and disturbed children)	Little use for anxiety states. Limited value for inert and apathetic schizophrenia
Trifluopromazine	Vespral	20	150	+	+	+	+	+	+	+	+	+	As above	As above
Laevopromazine	Verachi	25	700	+	+	+	+	+	±	±	+	+	As above—greater sedative action	Markedly hypotensive
Piperazine series														
Prochlorperazine	Stemetil Compazine	15	100	+	+	+	+	+	±		o	+	Vomiting, tinnitus, prevention of migraine. Schizophrenia, including inert and apathetic patients	Dystonic reaction in higher doses

Drug	Trade name									Uses	Notes
Perphen-azine	Fentazin	6	64	+	+	+	+	±	+	+	Schizophrenia. Disturbed behaviour in psychiatric and physical disease	Dystonic reaction in higher doses
Thio-propazate	Dartalan	15	150	+	+	±	o	±	+	o	+	Schizophrenia acute and chronic. Overactive disturbed behaviour in all psychiatric disorders. Management of Huntingdon's chorea. Little or no danger of liver damage	More effective and safer than chlorpromazine
Flu-phenazine	Moditen Permtil Prolixin	0.5	10	+	+	+	±	+	+	+	Mainly for preventing anxiety and tension	
Trifluo-perazine	Stelazine	3	30	+	+	±	+	±	+	o	+	All types of schizophrenia. Low doses for anxiety symptoms	Extrapyramidal side-effects frequent
Piperidine series												
Thiorid-azine	Melleril	30	600	+	+	+	+	+	+	+	As tranquillosedative in neuroses and psychoses	Side-effects frequent

CHAPTER THIRTY-THREE

PHYSICAL METHODS

CONVULSIVE THERAPY

The application of therapeutic convulsions in the treatment of mental illness was introduced in 1935 by *Meduna*. He induced major epileptic fits by means of intravenous cardiazol for the treatment of schizophrenic patients because of the belief held at the time that epilepsy and schizophrenia were biologically antagonistic.

Although this theory has been disproved it has continued to a restricted degree in schizophrenia but its main field of application is in severe depressive states.

Cerletti and *Bini*, just before World War II, introduced the electrical method of inducing therapeutic convulsions as it was less distressing to the patient, technically easier and the effects more certain. Nowadays the treatment is given under general anaesthesia with thiopentone or methohexitone. These anaesthetics are given intravenously and then a muscle relaxant such as succinylcholine is given to modify the muscular contractions.

Therapeutic convulsions unmodified by muscular relaxants carry the risk of producing bony injury or dislocation which are a definite but rare risks.

The treatment is usually given twice weekly until improvement occurs. Sometimes improvement in depression occurs after one or two treatments but, usually, after three or four or even later. The improvement, once it develops after a particular treatment, will tend to build up until complete recovery takes place. The number of treatments required varies with the individual case; some patients recover with six or seven but many require twelve or more.

When full recovery is achieved, it is wise to keep in mind that it may be necessary to give one or two more treatments after a week or longer in the event of recurrence of depression. Failure to do this has resulted in many cases not deriving as much benefit from the treatment as they otherwise could.

The electrodes are placed on each side of the frontal part of the head and the current can be administered in various ways, e.g. in Joules or Volts and using different wave forms. It is necessary to obtain a full convulsion in order to achieve therapeutic benefit; subconvulsive shocks are not helpful.

Electronarcosis is a more intensive and prolonged form of E.C.T. treatment, in which there is a continued passage of the current over a period of up to seven minutes.

Electroconvulsive therapy is sometimes followed by difficulty in remembering events, but this usually passes off after varying periods of time. It is important to warn patients about this beforehand.

Indications for Electroconvulsive Therapy

(1) Severe depressive states.

(2) Schizophrenia with an admixture of depression or, in failure to respond to phenothiazine drugs, E.C.T. can be given concurrently.

THE SURGICAL TREATMENT OF MENTAL ILLNESS (PSYCHOSURGERY)

Moniz introduced the operation of prefrontal leucotomy and for intractable psychiatric disorders.

A variety of operative procedures have been devised since this time and are collectively referred to as psychosurgery.

Originally the standard prefrontal leucotomy operation consisted in severing the white matter of each frontal lobe as widely as possible. This operation had many undesirable side-effects such as apathy, lethargy, inability to control aggressive impulses, high incidence of epilepsy, and the efficacy of the treatment was due to the introduction of the thalmo-frontal connections, notably between the dorsal/medial thalamic nuclei and the frontal cortex. In order to achieve the maximum therapeutic effect with the minimum undesirable effects, modified leucotomy operations have been devised since. These include bimedial leucotomy, blind rostral leucotomy, orbital undercutting, frontal undercutting.

Bimedial leucotomy involves a cut in the white matter, made under direct vision and to sever the thalmo-frontal bundle, which is known to be the main pathway from the thalamus to the frontal pole and orbital frontal surface.

The variations known as bimedial leucotomy, orbital undercutting and blind rostral leucotomy are of comparable therapeutic value. Bimedial leucotomy and orbital undercutting have the advantage of being open operations and the extent of the lesion which they produce can be controlled with greater accuracy.

In deciding on whether a leucotomy is indicated, it is usual to try all available therapeutic measures first as the operation involves causing permanent damage to the brain, but failure of therapeutic methods is not in itself an indication for leucotomy. This must be done as a result of a careful assessment of all aspects of the case, including the patient's personality, the form of his mental illness and his social circumstances. Firstly, the main indication for leucotomy is for the relief of emotional tension and distress, whether this is in the form of an anxiety state, an agitated depression or any other form of distress, if of sufficient severity to interfere with the patient's life and well-being. Clear evidence of emotional and/or its bodily manifestations must be present before an operation is carried out. An assessment of the patient's personality is of the utmost importance because the leucotomy operation will not improve the patient's personality and, as control may be somewhat diminished, it is undesirable to carry out operation on patients who are of ill-adjusted, unstable, anti-social, psychopathic or markedly hysterical personality. People who are in any event impulsive have difficulty in self-control; these are states of personality which are in danger of being made worse by leucotomy. The patient's personality should be reasonably well-adjusted as shown by the patient's adjustment at school, work, marriage and social relationships generally. The main point when assessing personality is that the contra-indicative attributes must not be present.

The third aspect which merits careful assessment are the social circumstances of the patient. The operation of leucotomy is one stage of treatment and in order to achieve the best results, prolonged rehabilitation is usually necessary. Although immediate symptomatic improvement usually takes place, in many patients it requires careful nursing, active occupational and recreational programmes and eventually returning to suitable work with the aim of making the person an effective member of society. It is for these reasons that it is important that the patient should have relatives, friends or family who will be supporting, understanding and helpful during the process of rehabilitation. With the careful selection of patients results of modified leucotomy are very encouraging, particularly as the operation is carried out on those patients who are of long standing and have failed to respond to the ordinary therapeutic measures.

FURTHER READING

An Introduction to Physical Methods of Treatment in Psychiatry (4th Edition) by W. Sargant and Slater. E. and S. Livingstone, Edinburgh (1963).

CHAPTER THIRTY-FOUR

OCCUPATIONAL THERAPY

Thomas Carlyle once wrote 'Blessed is he who has found his work, let him ask no other blessedness'. This is true for all people and is particularly true for patients who have recovered from a prolonged illness or have to spend long periods in hospital.

Rehabilitation is the process of getting a person who has been ill or has a disability back into as full working capacity as possible, commensurate with his ability to perform the tasks required.

Occupational therapy is activity and work prescribed as treatment.

Occupational therapy may be the initial and a very important first step in rehabilitation.

When patients enter hospital they enter into a new life and interests, emotions and energies taken up in the normal activities 'hang fire' as it were. Emotions do not hang fire for long and soon become attached to symptoms and magnify them.

The patient has plenty of time to think about himself and his symptoms and may become introspective. When a patient has to stay in hospital for long periods, normal habits of work tend to be lost. The ordinary motives, rewards, punishments and incentives of everyday life are missing. It is not surprising, therefore, that patients who have to stay in hospital for long periods without having any work to do may become inert, apathetic and useless, in other words 'hospitalised'.

This was found during the First World War, when large numbers of patients treated in hospitals over long periods tended to deteriorate and morale weakened. When occupational therapy was provided, this tendency to deterioration was prevented.

Occupational Therapy has the following advantages:

(1) It diverts the patient's attention from himself on to other things.

(2) His interest and energies are directed to work.

(3) It maintains normal habits of work.

(4) It provides an incentive and a goal.

(5) It enables the patient to have a feeling of achievement when he completes the task.

(6) It stimulates interest and attention.

(7) It may teach the patient a new skill or hobby.

(8) The feeling of doing something useful and pride in achievement will help his self-esteem.

(9) It helps to make the patient more accessible and more co-operative with other forms of therapy.

(10) Aids production of positive attitudes and helps decision.

(11) Aids focussing of attention and aids integration.

Occupational therapy must arouse and sustain the patient's interest. In order to do this, the following considerations have to be borne in mind:

(1) Adults must not be given childish activities.

(2) The initial act and the goal must not be too far removed from each other. In other words, the patient should be able to complete the work within a reasonable time so that the goal is always in sight and acting as an incentive.

(3) The work should be progressive in skill, difficulty and complexity so that the patient can obtain a feeling of success and continued progress.

(4) The standard of the expected performance must be based on the capacity of the patient and not on other people's standards.

(5) The work must be within the capacity of the patient but not so easy that interest is not evoked.

(6) Encouragement and not criticism should be used.

The aims of occupational therapy are:

(1) To promote recovery.

(2) Mobilisation of the total assets of the patient.

(3) Prevention of hospitalisation.

(4) Creation of good habits of work and leisure.

(5) Rehabilitation with return of self-confidence.

Rehabilitation

This is the act of making a disabled person fit to engage in a full-time job, commensurate with his or her ability to perform the duties required. The individual with his needs, interests and capacities is the foundation on which to build the edifice of rehabilitation.

Many patients who felt themselves unloved or rejected before the illness, develop psychologically protracted convalescence.

Interest is the primary motivating force in effective rehabilitation and progression should be made from interest to effort.

Rehabilitation is now recognised as a form of therapy applicable to nearly every form of illness or infirmity, in greater or lesser degree, and affecting the whole period of hospitalisation and convalescence.

Rehabilitation will not be appropriate for persons suffering from painful, incurable diseases or for the aged chronic sick or in the early stages of treatment of certain diseases calling for absolute rest for a period.

Subject to such exceptions, rehabilitation is appropriate for general medicine and surgical conditions, ante-natal treatment and post-natal convalescence and for psychiatric disorders.

Rehabilitation in its modern concept involves:

(1) Introduction of methods of physical rehabilitation into every ward adapted to individual disabilities and stages of recovery, commencing as early as possible after admission.

(2) Planning of convalescence with a view to speeding up the recovery of physical and psychological functions.

(3) Out-patient rehabilitation would greatly benefit such conditions as sprained joints, septic hands.

(4) Expert supervision and planning of patient's daily activities to ensure proper balance of work and rest.

The patient's daily programme should be carefully prescribed so as to fill his day with reasonable balance of work, rest and recreation.

Passive Physiotherapy

This includes heat massage and electro-therapy relaxation. This is only required in a minority of patients, as the main emphasis of rehabilitation is on active movements which the patients themselves carry out.

This stimulates active interest and participation, inducing a feeling of responsibility for his part in the treatment.

Remedial Exercises

Two distinct but complementary aims are:

(a) General bodily toning up.

(b) Restoration of functions to the disabled part.

The exercises may be started in bed and continued, when the patient is able, in the gymnasium or out of doors.

The movements may be:

(1) Assisted by the Therapist.

(2) Free.

(3) Resisted by pulleys and weights or springs.

Organised Games such as medicine ball, volley ball, badminton etc.

These stimulate spontaneity and freedom of movement. The competitive spirit and excitement tends to take away the patient's anxious preoccupation with the diseased part.

Occupation Therapy

(a) Diversional.

(b) Remedial—for particular muscle groups.

Basket-work, carpentry, embroidery, gardening.

Lectures, Discussion Groups and Entertainments

These promote intellectual stimulation, interest and relaxation.

Social Worker may be required to help in home problems, so that the patient can continue with rehabilitation as free as possible from worries.

Re-employment

The Disablement Rehabilitation Officer (DRO) of the Ministry of Labour is specially trained to place disabled persons in suitable work.

Arrangements can be made for the DRO to see the patient in hospital before discharge, furnished with information and recommendation by the doctor in charge.

CHAPTER THIRTY-FIVE

LEGAL ASPECTS

The Mental Health Act 1959 repealed all previous legislation on mental disorder.

The Act removed rigid distinctions between mental illness and mental deficiency from legal and administrative viewpoints.

The term mental disorder covers all forms of mental ill health. Mentally disordered patients therefore, include both mentally ill and subnormal patients.

The Act abolished the terms mental deficiency, mental defective, idiot, imbecile, feeble-minded and moral defective.

The term psychiatric hospital includes mental hospitals and hospitals for the mentally subnormal.

Four categories of mentally disordered patients are recognised:
(1) Mental illness.
(2) Severe Subnormality.
(3) Subnormality.
(4) Psychopathic disorder.

The Act distinguishes these groups only in connection with powers of compulsory detention in hopsital or regarding a guardianship in the community.

MENTAL ILLNESS

Severe subnormality means a state of arrested development of mind, so severe that the patient is incapable of leading an independent life or of guarding himself against serious exploitation or, in the case of a child, that he will be incapable to the degree when adult.

Subnormality refers to a state of arrested or incomplete development of mind which includes subnormality of intelligence. Such a patient requires special care or training but arrested development of mind does not amount to severe subnormality.

Psychopathic disorder means a persistent disorder or disability of mind whether or not including subnormality of intelligence, which results in abnormally aggressive irresponsible conduct on the part of the patient and requires or is susceptible to medical treatment or to care or training under medical supervision.

The aim of the Act is to separate the subnormal from the severely subnormal patients and to treat the former either in separate units or in association with patients suffering from certain types of mental illness.

The severely subnormal need special hospital care to meet their particular needs.

Psychopathic patients may be treated in separate units or in hospital in association with the subnormal or with the mentally ill.

The centres provided by local health authorities for the occupation or training of mentally subnormal patients are now referred to as Training Centres, in the case of children, and in the case of adults, Training Centres or Occupational Centres, depending on what they do.

COMPULSORY ADMISSION

The new Act abolished the procedure of Certification and Detention by judicial authority. Under the 1959 Act, patients are admitted to psychiatric hospitals either informally, which is the most common method, or compulsory admission under the following arrangements:

(1) Section 25—Admission for Observation.
(2) Section 29—Emergency Admission for Observation.
(3) Section 26—Admission for Treatment.
(4) Section 60, 61, 67—Admission on Court Order.

When compulsory detention, either for observation or for treatment, becomes necessary in the patient's or other people's interests, an application, based on the written recommendation by two medical practitioners, must be made by the nearest relative or the Mental Welfare Officer to the managers of the hospital to which admission is sought. This applies to Section 25 and 26 of the Act. A similar procedure is necessary to place a patient under guardianship under Section 33.

The medical recommendations have to be signed within a specified period prior to the date of application. One of the physician's must have special psychiatric knowledge and be approved for the purpose by the local health authority. The other physician should be the patient's general practitioner.

In the case of urgent necessity, application may be made by any relative or Mental Welfare Officer, supported by one medical recommendation. This expires in 72 hours unless a second medical recommendation is received by the managers of the hospital.

Appeal

In the case of a patient admitted compulsorily and detained, the nearest relative or the patient may apply, within six months of his admission, to a Mental Health Review Tribunal for his discharge.

A similar procedure applies to guardianship.

Duration of Authority

Patients are detained in hospital or detained under guardianship up to one year, which is renewable in the first instance for a period of one year and thereafter for successive periods of two years.

A psychopathic or subnormal patient subject to guardianship shall cease to be so subject on reaching the age of 25 years.

Discharge

This is relatively easy and may be made by the responsible medical officer or the managers, in the case of hospital patients, and by the medical officer or the nearest relative in the case of guardianship.

If the responsible medical officer advises the managers against discharge, the patient or nearest relative can apply to a Mental Health Review Tribunal to consider the case.

THE LAW DEALING WITH THE CARE OF PROPERTY OF MENTALLY ILL PATIENTS

It is sometimes necessary for special arrangements to be made to manage the property and affairs of persons who, by reason of mental disorder, are unable to do so themselves.

This is carried out by the Court of Protection. The Court is only directly concerned with mental patients' property and not with the persons. The provision exists to protect the property of patients but not to exercise control over the patients themselves.

The normal procedure is to appoint a Receiver, who is vested by the Court of Protection with various powers of acting on behalf of the patient and may be regarded as the statutory agent of the patient. Medical evidence is required for the Court to establish its jurisdiction. The medical evidence must satisfy the Court that the patient is incapable, by reason of mental disorder, of managing and administering his property and affairs.

Any mental illness or disorder or disability of the mind suffices to give the Court jurisdiction if, by reason thereof, the person is incapable of managing his property and affairs. The degree of mental disorder required to give the Court jurisdiction is quite distinct from and less severe than that required for compulsory detention.

The most common group of patients for whom these provisions are needed are mental disorders in elderly patients.

Testamentary Capacity

For a person to have testamentary capacity he must understand the nature of a Will, must be able to grasp the extent of his property and to form a proper judgment as to the nature of the claims to his bounty.

The doctor, when asked to advise as to testamentary capacity, should show by his report that he has considered each of these three essentials, and if he is not provided with the necessary particulars, he should refuse to advise until he is properly instructed.

CRIMINAL RESPONSIBILITY

From the legal point of view, responsibility means liability for punishment.

Defence may plead unsoundness of mind for any criminal charge but, in fact, this is usually only done in charges of murder.

In 1843 McNaughton shot and killed Sir Robert Peel's secretary. It was shown that McNaughton suffered from a number of delusions of persecution and that killing had been inspired by these delusions and the Judge directed the jury to find him not guilty. Public reaction was very great and culminated in a debate in the House of Lords when the now famous McNaughton Rules were formulated.

The Rules state that, in order to establish a defence on grounds of insanity, it must be proved:

(1) That, at the time of committing the act, the accused was labouring under such a defect of reason from disease of the mind as not to know the nature and quality of the act he was doing or, if he knew what he was doing, he did not know that it was wrong.

(2) If the accused commits an act by reason of delusion, the degree of responsibility is based on the justification which the delusion would provide if it were true.

Medical men have objected to these rules ever since they were introduced, as the only thing that matters legally is whether the accused passes the McNaughton test and important clinical aspects of his case get passed over.

From the outset, it was realised that the rule dealing with partial insanity was absurd. Attempting to evaluate insane delusions as if they were true, whilst ignoring the underlying mental illness of which the delusions were themselves evidence, was recognised to be ridiculous 80 years ago.

The diagnosis of insanity is left in the hands of jurymen. The rules make no provision for the effect upon conduct of pathological emotional disturbances as opposed to disturbances of reason or knowledge.

The administration of the McNaughton Rules can also be criticised on the following grounds:

(1) They are inequitable as between case and case.

(2) They are inequitable as between judge and witness. The judge is free to ignore the rules if he so wishes and, if he so wishes, he can always tie the medical witness down to them as strictly as he likes.

(3) By applying or not applying the rules in his direction to the jury, the judge can exercise a large measure of control on the jury's decision. The judge and not the jury becomes the arbiter in what is supposedly a matter of fact. The rules are not applied candidly; if they were to be so, the judge would point to the jury that nobody is hardly ever mad enough to be covered by the rules.

In 1957 the Homicide Act introduced the doctrine of diminished responsibility into English criminal law. The Act states that when a person kills or is a party to a killing of another, he should not be convicted of murder if he was suffering from such an abnormality of mind (whether arising from a condition of arrested or retarded development of mind or any inherent causes or induced by disease or injury) as substantially impaired his mental responsibility for his acts and admissions in doing or being a party to the killing. If these circumstances apply, the verdict is manslaughter and not murder.

THE CRIMINAL JUSTICE ACT OF 1948

This deals with offences other than homicide and applies to a person charged before a court of summary jurisdiction with an act punishable by imprisonment and, when the court is satisfied (a) that the person did the act (b) on the evidence of at least two doctors that he is suffering from a mental disorder (c) that he is a proper person to be detained, the court may order him to be detained in a mental hospital.

The Act also empowers a court, if satisfied by expert medical evidence that an offender shows mental abnormality not severe enough to justify compulsory detention, to place the offender on probation and to require him, for a period not exceeding twelve months, to undergo psychiatric treatment in an appropriate hospital or elsewhere as an Informal resident or non-resident patient, if this is considered likely to be beneficial to the offender and providing the arrangements can be made.

Fitness to Plead

An accused person should be mentally capable of instructing counsel, appreciating the significance of pleading guilt or not guilty, challenging a juror, examining witnesses and understanding and following the evidence and court procedure.

If the prisoner is found to be insane, an order is made for his detention during Her Majesty's pleasure and admission to Broadmoor is the usual procedure.

A Mentally Ill Person Serving as a Witness

It is admissible for a psychiatric patient to serve as a witness, but his mental state must always be taken into account in assessing his reliability. He is also able to make an Affidavit if his evidence is likely to be reliable.

CIVIL LAW
Contract

A contract made by a person before the onset of mental disorder is binding. A person suffering from a mental disorder may make contracts for the necessities of life and such contracts are binding. He may also make contracts for articles other than necessities, but such contracts are not binding if it is clear that they would not have been made but for the mental disorder at the time of making the contract.

Marriage and Divorce

A marriage is not valid if, at the time of the marriage, either party was so mentally disordered as not to appreciate the nature of the contract.

Nullification of the marriage may also take place if the petitioner did not know at the time of the marriage that the other party was suffering from a mental illness or subnormality or was subject to recurrent bouts of mental illness or epilepsy. The petition has to be filed within a year of the date of marriage.

A petition for divorce may be presented on the grounds that the respondent is 'incurably of unsound mind' and has been continuously under care and treatment for a period of at least five years immediately preceding the presentation of the petition.

DIFFERENCES IN THE LAW IN SCOTLAND

The Mental Health Act 1959 and the Mental Health (Scotland) Act of 1960 are based on the same principles but there are certain differences in the provisions of the Acts.

In Scotland the authority for the detention of a patient still requires legal authority, viz. the Sheriff who may, if he thinks necessary, interview the patient, the petitioner and doctors and there is a Right of Appeal by the patient to the Sheriff against his detention. There is no Mental Health Review Tribunal in Scotland.

There is also a central authority called the Mental Welfare Commission consisting of 7–9 commissioners, whose functions are to exercise general protective functions on behalf of patients.

There is no Court of Protection for patients in Scotland. Sums over £100 are dealt with by a curator bonis by the Courts with similar functions as a Receiver in England.

The Scottish Act does not define categories and the term Mental Disorder means Mental Illness or Mental Defect. It has proved possible for the psychopath and the high grade mentally subnormal patient to be dealt with in very much the same way as under the Mental Health Act of 1959 but without using these designations.

Emergency admission is for seven days instead of three days.

Doctors approved for the purposes of recommendations of the Act are approved by the Regional Hospital Board in Scotland and not by the Local Authority as they are in England.

AUTHOR INDEX

SUBJECT INDEX